The Gun Digest

SPORTING RIFLE TAKE DOWN & REASSEMBLY GUIDE

By J. B. Wood

DBI Books, Inc., Northfield, Ill.

About Our Cover

A sectionalized view of one of America's most popular centerfire rifles graces our cover—Ruger's Model 77. Detailed disassembly information can be found on page 158.

ISBN 0-910676-36-4

CONTENTS

INTRODUCTION

During the years I have been a professional gunsmith and gun writer, one of the most frequently asked questions by readers has been, ''How do I take it apart?'' When the limited space of a column answer permitted, I gave the routine takedown steps.

In many cases, I had to tell the reader that nothing had been published on his particular piece. Occasionally, I recommended that the reader try to obtain an instruction booklet from the manufacturer or importer, but this was not always the best answer. In the case of some imported guns, the direct-translation was somewhat humorous to read, or was of little help in actual disassembly and reassembly. In the case of guns no longer made, the instruction sheets are often valuable collector items and are not readily obtainable.

Obviously, something was needed in this area—a book that would cover takedown and reassembly of most of the modern guns, a number of older ones, and some of the tricky aspects of the more well-known pieces. This is the idea behind the book you have in your hands.

In the area of reassembly, many of the published instructions end with the words, ''Reassemble in reverse order.'' In most cases, this may be the only instruction needed and nothing more will be said here. In others, though, this procedure is insufficient. In this book, reassembly directions will seldom be reduced to a single line in order to avoid an embarrassing trip to the gunsmith carrying a box full of parts. I am confident that the reassembly tips given are clear enough to permit the easy reassembly of all the guns covered. The tips do not include each and every step along the way—only the more complicated ones. You shouldn't have any trouble.

There are elements in total takedown that require, in many cases, the special tools and skills of the gunsmith. The very knowledgeable amateur may be able to detail strip certain guns to the last pin, spring and screw, but some mechanical aptitude is necessary. This book is designed for both the average gun person and the professional. While it covers routine field-stripping, it also covers complete takedown and reassembly.

For simple takedown, the tools needed will seldom be more than screwdrivers of the proper size. Complete takedown will often require several other tools, some of which are not available at the corner hardware store. For this reason, I am including a section on tools, as well as a list of sources for some of the specialized items.

There are a few general rules to be observed in the takedown of any gun. An occasional rap with a plastic mallet may be necessary to free a tight assembly, but for the most part, no force should be used. Never pry; always wear safety glasses as compressed springs can be dangerous. Never take a gun down outdoors, over tall grass, or indoors over a shag carpet. Read the instructions through, at least once, before you begin.

I assume a certain basic intelligence in the reader, and will not start each set of takedown directions with the repeated advice that the gun must be entirely unloaded. *Before you start the takedown of any gun, make a thorough visual check to be sure it's empty.* Check the chamber and magazine *and* be sure they are *empty*. In this area, any mistakes could be very hazardous to your health, so be certain.

An exploded drawing accompanies each gun to aid you in assembly/ disassembly. Those drawings also serve to orient parts and their relationship to the firearm's actual function.

J. B. Wood
Raintree House
Corydon, Kentucky

A Note On Reassembly

Most of the firearms covered in this book can be reassembled by simply reversing the order of disassembly, carefully replacing the parts in the same manner they were removed. In a few instances, special instructions are required, and these are listed with each gun under ''Reassembly Tips.'' In certain cases, reassembly photos are also provided.

If there are no special instructions or photos with a particular gun, you may assume that it can just be reassembled in reverse order. During disassembly, note the relationship of all parts and springs, and lay them out on the workbench in the order they were removed. By following this procedure you should have no difficulty in reassembly.

TOOLS

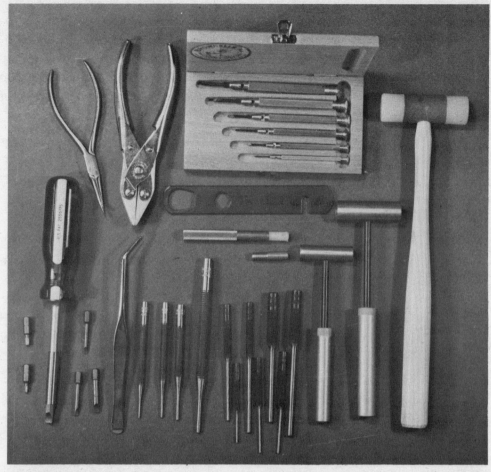

Countless firearms, old and new, bear the marks, burrs, and gouges that are the result of using the wrong tools for taking them apart. In the interest of preventing this sort of thing, I am including here a group of tools that are the best types for the disassembly of shotguns. Except for the few shop-made tools for special purposes, all of those shown here are available from one of these three sources.

Brownells, Inc.
Route 2, Box 1
Montezuma, Iowa 50171

B-Square Company
P.O. Box 11281
Forth Worth, Texas 76109

Williams Gun Sight Company
7389 Lapeer Road
Davison, Michigan 48423

General Instructions:

Screwdrivers: Always be sure the blade of the screwdriver **exactly** fits the slot in the screw head, both in thickness and in width. If you don't have one that fits, grind or file the tip until it does. You may ruin a few screwdrivers, but better them than the screws on a fine shotguns.

Slave pins: There are several references in this book to slave pins, and some non-gunsmith readers may not be familiar with the term. A slave pin is simply a short length of rod stock (in some cases, a section of a nail will do) which is used to keep two parts, or a part and a spring,

together during reassembly. The slave pin must be very slightly smaller in diameter than the hole in the part, so it will push out easily as the original pin is driven in to retain the part. When making a slave pin, its length should be slightly less than the width of the part in which it is being used, and the ends of the pin should be rounded or beveled.

Sights: Nearly all dovetail-mounted sights are drifted out toward the right, using a nylon, aluminum, or brass drift punch.

1. The tiniest of these fine German instrument screwdrivers from Brownells is too small for most gun work, but you'll see the rest of them used frequently throughout the book. There are many tight places where these will come in handy. Cost is about $17 for the set.

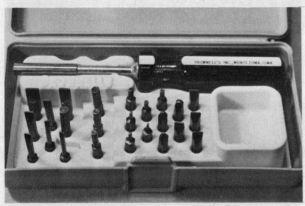

2. When a larger screwdriver is needed, this set from Brownells covers a wide range of blade sizes and also has Phillips- and Allen-type inserts. The tips are held in place by a strong magnet, yet are easily changed. These tips are very hard. With enough force you might manage to break one, but they'll never bend. Price of the complete set is about $21.

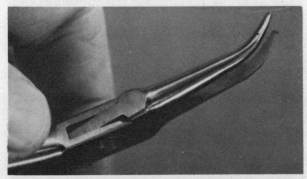

3. You should have at least one good pair of bent sharp-nosed pliers. These, from Brownells, have a box joint and smooth inner faces to help prevent marring. Price is about $8.

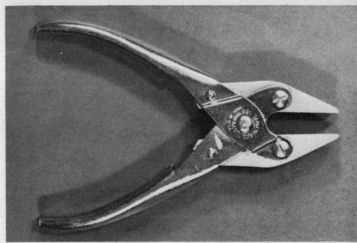

4. For heavier gripping, these Bernard parallel-jaw pliers from Brownells have smooth-faced jaw-pieces of unhardened steel to prevent marring of parts. Price is about $8.

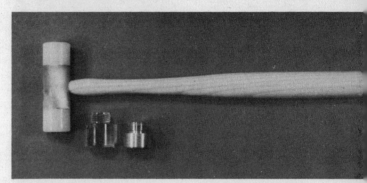

5. For situations where a non-marring rap is needed, this hammer from Brownells is ideal. It is shown with nylon faces on the head, but other faces of plastic and brass are also available. All are easily replaceable. Cost is about $8 with three faces.

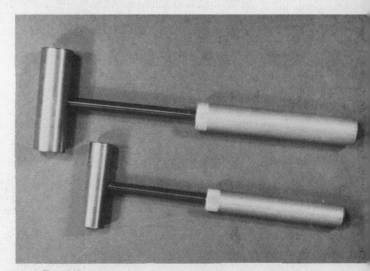

6. For drifting out pins, these small all-metal hammers from B-Square are the best I've seen. Two sizes (weights) are available and they're well worth the modest cost. About $15 for both.

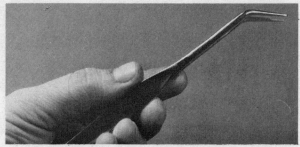

7. For situations where reach and accessability are beyond the capabilities of sharp-nosed pliers, a pair of large sharp-nosed forceps (tweezers) will be invaluable. From Brownells, about $2.

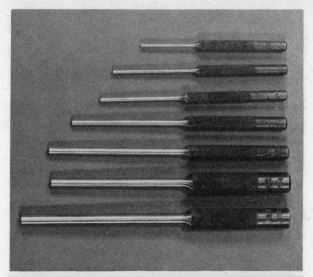

8. One of the most-used tools in my shop is this nylon-tipped drift punch, shown with an optional brass tip in place on the handle. It has a steel pin inside the nylon tip for strength. From Brownells, and absolutely essential. Price is about $2 for the set.

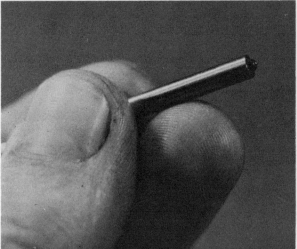

10. These punches by Mayhew are designed specifically for roll pins and have a projection at the center of the tip to fit the hollow center of a roll pin, driving it out without deformation of the ends. From Brownells, about $12 for the set.

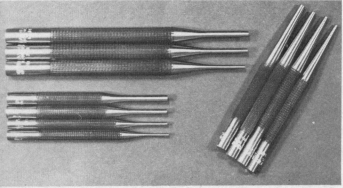

9. A good set of drift punches will prevent a lot of marred pins. These, from Brownells, are made by Mayhew. The tapered punches at the right are for starting pins, the others for pushing them through. Two sizes are available—4 inches (about 98¢ each) or 6 inches (about $1.25).

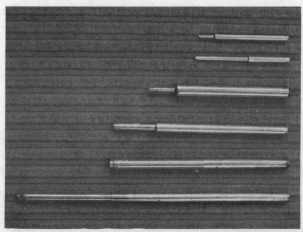

11. Some of the necessary tools are easily made in the shop. These non-marring drift punches were made from three sizes of welder's brazing rod.

REMINGTON MODEL 600

Data:	Remington Model 600
Origin:	United States
Manufacturer:	Remington Arms Company Bridgeport, Connecticut
Cartridges:	222, 243, 6mm, 308, 35, 6.5mm Remington Magnum and 350 Remington Magnum
Magazine capacity:	4, 5 or 6 rounds, depending on caliber
Over-all length:	37¼ inches
Barrel length:	18½ inches
Weight:	5½ pounds

This handy little carbine, and its counterpart, the Model 660, did not stay long on the scene. The Model 600, with its distinctive ventilated barrel rib, was made from 1964 to 1967. The successor, the Model 660, was made from 1968 to 1971. During this time, a version called the "Mohawk 600" was produced, a gun very similar to the Model 660, but without the barrel rib. Mechanically, these three are virtually identical, and the same instructions will apply.

Disassembly:

1. Open the bolt and move it part-way to the rear. Use a small tool to depress the bolt stop, located at the left rear of the receiver on the inside, next to the bolt. Hold the stop down, and remove the bolt toward the rear. As the bolt emerges from the receiver, it must be lifted to clear its right lug over the safety.

2. Grip the underlug of the cocking piece firmly in a vise, and pull the bolt forward until a gap appears between the front of the cocking piece and the rear of the bolt endpiece. Insert a thin piece of steel plate between the cocking piece and the bolt endpiece. Note that on some models, such as the one shown, a slot is provided on the side of the cocking piece for the insertion of the plate. Release the spring tension, and the plate will trap the striker at the rear.

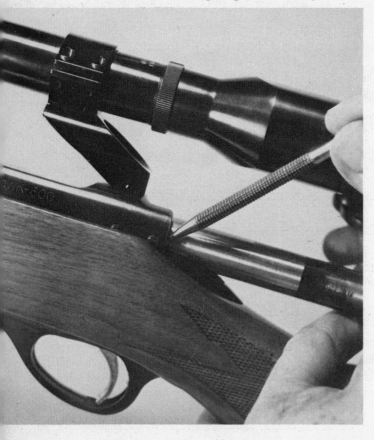

3. Taking care not to dislodge the plate, unscrew the bolt endpiece from the rear of the bolt. The factory advises against further disassembly of the striker system, since reassembly can be difficult without special tools. I will note here that the cocking piece is retained on the rear of the striker shaft by a cross-pin.

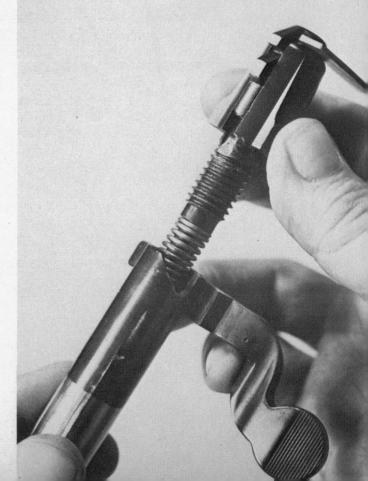

4. The ejector is retained in the front of the bolt by a cross-pin. Restrain the ejector when drifting out the pin, and remove the ejector and spring toward the front.

5. The extractor is retained inside the bolt face recess by a small rivet, and if unbroken it should not be removed. If removal is necessary, the rivet is driven inward. The ejector must first be removed.

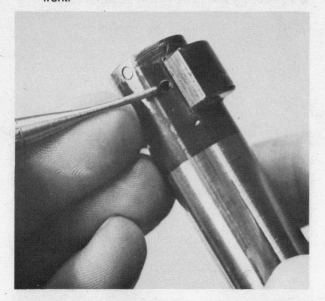

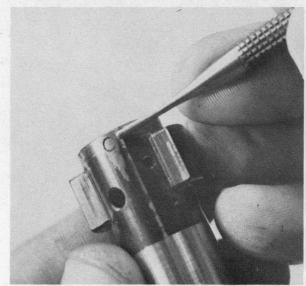

6. Remove the large screw on the underside at the front of the trigger guard/magazine housing. Remove the screw on the underside at the rear of the trigger guard, and separate the action from the stock. The trigger guard unit can be taken off downward.

7. The magazine box is easily detached from the underside of the receiver, and the spring and follower can be taken out of the box.

8. Position the safety snap washer so its opening is aligned with the stud on the detent spring, and push off the snap washer upward. Take off the detent spring, and take care not to lose the small steel ball in the side of the safety lever beneath the spring.

9. Push out the safety pivot toward the left, and remove the safety toward the rear and downward.

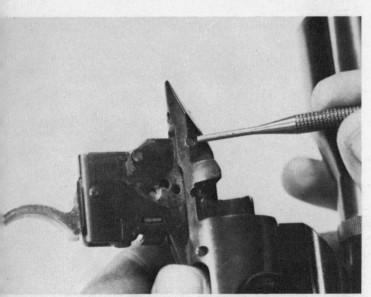

10. Drift out the rear trigger housing cross-pin toward the left, while restraining the sear at the top. When the pin is out, the sear spring will push the sear upward.

11. Drift out the front trigger housing cross-pin, and remove the trigger housing downward.

12. Remove the sear and sear spring from the top of the trigger housing.

13. The trigger housing should not be disassembled beyond this point in normal takedown. There are three trigger adjustment screws, two at the front and one at the rear, which are set and sealed with lacquer at the factory, and these should not be disturbed. A cross-pin retains the trigger and its connector, but removal requires that the two front screws be backed out.

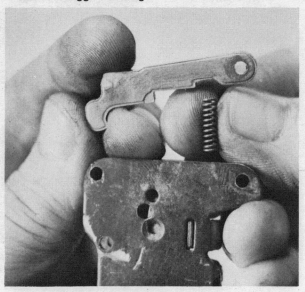

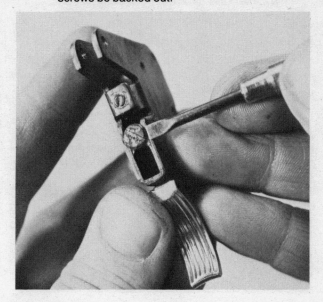

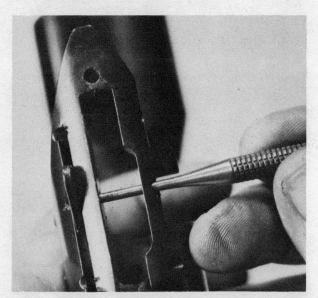

14. Removal of the bolt stop requires that its short pin be drifted out toward the left, and there is an access hole on the right side of the receiver through which a drift punch can be inserted to drive out the pin. The bolt stop and its spring are removed downward.

Reassembly Tips:

1. When replacing the trigger housing, start the two cross-pins in from the left, and be certain that the holes in the housing are aligned with the pins, to avoid deforming the housing. When the pins are just into the housing, but not into the center space, insert the sear from the rear, align its hole with the front cross-pin, and drive the pin across. Be sure the left tip of the cross-pin is clear of the bolt stop slot.

2. Insert the sear spring, being sure it is properly positioned to engage its recess on the underside of the sear, and swing the sear downward, keeping it depressed while the rear cross-pin is driven across.

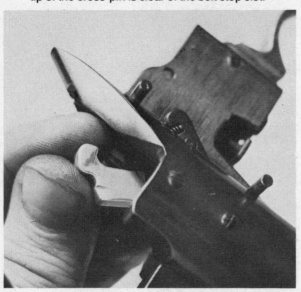

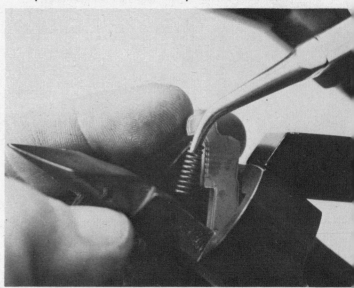

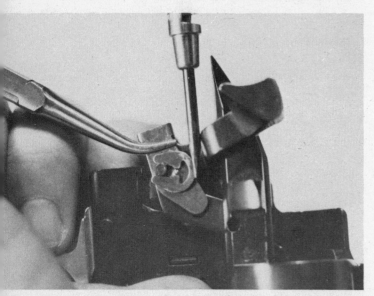

3. When replacing the safety system, be sure the pivot post is all the way through to the right when installing the detent spring and snap washer. Use pliers to compress the detent spring, and be sure the inside surfaces of the washer engage the groove in the top of the pivot post.

4. When removing the steel plate holding the striker, position the bolt endpiece as shown, so the released striker cocking piece will be in cocked position, and the bolt will be ready for re-insertion in the receiver.

Remington
600 Bolt Action Carbine

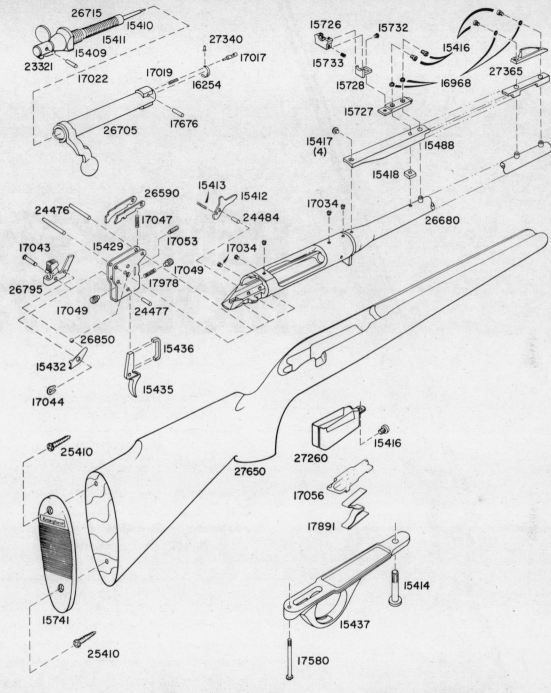

26880	Barrel	27365	Front Sight Assembly	15432	Safety Detent Spring
26705	Bolt Assembly	27260	Magazine	17043	Safety Pivot Pin
15409	Bolt Plug	17056	Magazine Follower	17044	Safety Snap Washer
15412	Bolt Stop	15416	Magazine Housing Screw	26590	Sear Safety Cam
24484	Bolt Stop Pin	17891	Magazine Spring	24476	Sear Pin
15413	Bolt Stop Spring	15411	Main Spring	17047	Sear Spring
15741	Buttplate	17580	Rear Guard Screw	15416	Sight Screw
25410	Buttplate Screws (2)	15727	Rear Sight Base	16968	Sight Washer
17017	Ejector	15733	Rear Sight Elevation Screw	27650	Stock
17676	Ejector Pin	15726	Rear Sight Eyepiece	15435	Trigger
17019	Ejector Spring	15728	Rear Sight Leaf	17049	Trigger Adjusting Screw
16254	Extractor	15418	Rear Sight Nut	15436	Trigger Connector
27340	Extractor Rivet	15732	Rear Sight Windage Screw	15437	Trigger Guard
15410	Firing Pin	17034	Receiver Plug Screw	15429	Trigger Housing
26715	Firing Pin Assembly	15488	Rib	24477	Trigger Pin
17022	Firing Pin Cross Pin	15417	Rib Screw	17978	Trigger Spring
23321	Firing Pin Head	26795	Safety Assembly	17053	Trigger Stop Screw
15414	Front Guard Screw	26850	Safety Detent Ball		

REMINGTON MODEL 788

Data:	Remington Model 788
Origin:	United States
Manufacturer:	Remington Arms Company Bridgeport, Connecticut
Cartridges:	222, 223, 22-250, 308, 243, 6mm Remington, and 44 Magnum
Magazine capacity:	4 rounds in 222, 3 in others
Over-all length:	41⅝ inches
Barrel length:	22 and 24 inches
Weight:	7 to 7½ pounds

A glance at the cartridges listed for the Model 788 may lead some to believe there's an error here, but the gun was actually offered for a short time in 44 Magnum chambering. The others listed are still available. For those who have the 44 Magnum version, it should be noted that their bolt is different, having a two-piece construction and a non-rotating bolt head. The Model 788 was introduced in 1967, and is still being offered by Remington.

Disassembly:

1. Remove the magazine. Open the bolt and move it toward the rear, while pushing the safety forward beyond its off-safe position. Remove the bolt from the rear of the receiver.

2. Insert a small-diameter drift punch into the tiny transverse hole in the bolt endpiece, being sure that it goes deep enough to enter the hole in the sriker head inside.

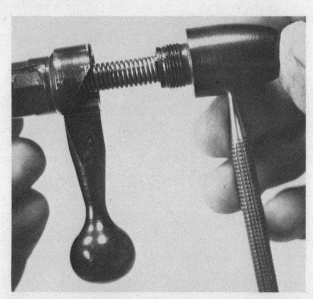

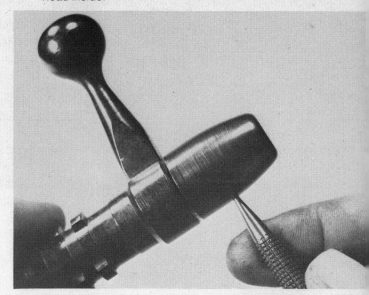

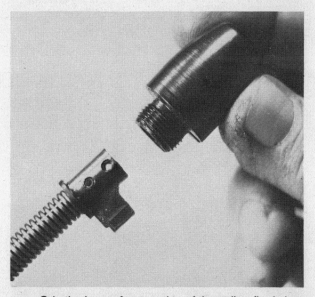

3. Leaving the drift punch in place, unscrew the bolt endpiece and striker assembly, removing it toward the rear.

4. Grip the heavy front portion of the striker firmly in a vise, and exert forward pressure on the endpiece while removing the drift punch from the hole. **Caution:** *The compressed spring is powerful, so keep a firm hold on the endpiece.* Slowly ease the endpiece off the rear of the striker assembly, and remove it toward the rear. The striker assembly can be taken apart by drifting out the retaining cross-pin in the striker head, but this is definitely not recommended in normal takedown.

5. Drifting out the cross-pin near the front of the bolt will release the ejector and its spring toward the front. **Caution:** *The spring is a strong one, so control the parts and ease them out.*

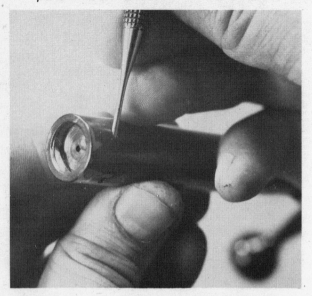

6. The extractor is retained inside the cartridge head recess in the bolt face by a tiny rivet, and in normal disassembly *its removal is not recommended,* as the extractor will almost invariably break. If removal of a broken extractor is necessary, drift out the rivet inward, using a small-diameter punch. Note that the ejector must be removed before this is done.

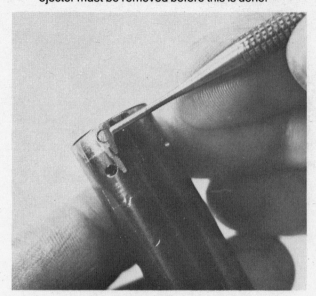

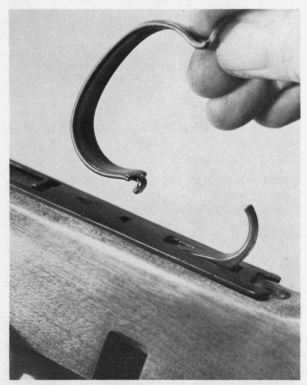

8. Remove the large vertical screw on the underside just forward of the magazine opening, and separate the action from the stock.

7. Remove the vertical screw at the rear of the trigger guard. Swing the guard downward and toward the front, and remove it.

9. The magazine guide bar and catch piece can be removed by backing out the vertical screw in its rear tail, on the underside of the receiver.

10. The trigger housing is retained by a single roll cross-pin at its top center. Use a roll pin punch to drift it out.

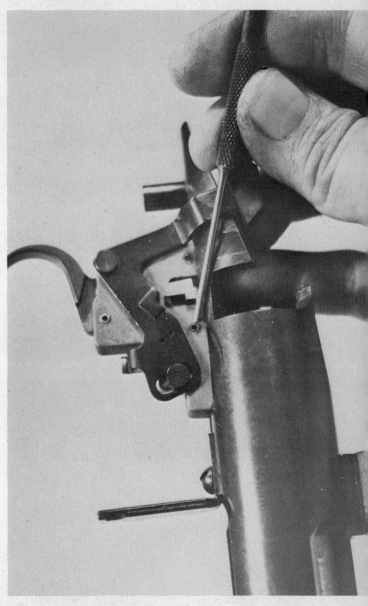

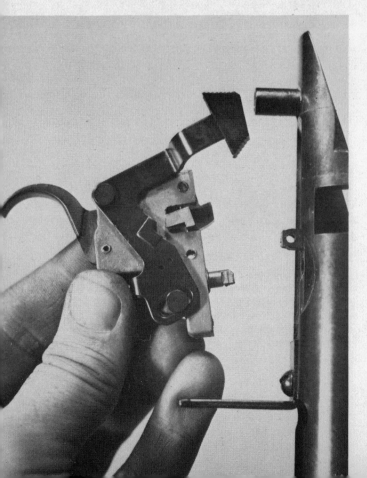

11. Remove the trigger housing downward.

12. Tipping the sear upward will allow removal of the combination sear and trigger spring.

13. Drift out the roll pin at the upper rear of the trigger housing, and remove the sear upward.

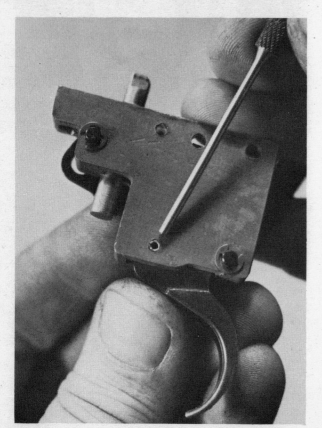

14. Drift out the roll cross-pin at the lower front of the trigger housing, and remove the trigger downward.

15. Remove the C-clip on the left side of the trigger housing at the front, and take out the forward safety guide pin toward the right. Hold the safety against the right side of the housing, as the positioning plunger and spring will tend to force it outward.

16. Remove the C-clip on the left side of the housing at the lower rear, and take out the safety pivot toward the right.

17. Restrain the bolt stop, and slowly ease the safety off toward the right.

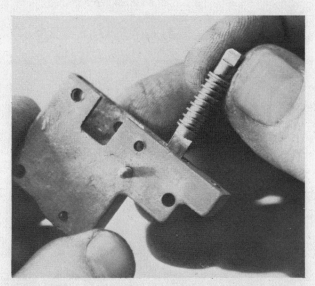

18. Remove the bolt stop and its spring from the top of the trigger housing.

19. Remove the safety positioning plunger and its spring from the right side of the housing.

20. The housing tension screw, located in the front lip of the unit, is staked in place and should not be disturbed unless the housing is loose when re-mounted.

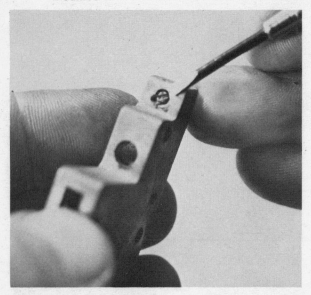

Reassembly Tips:

1. When the cocking piece is at the position shown, the drift punch can be re-inserted through the hole in the bolt endpiece to lock the striker assembly for replacement in the bolt.

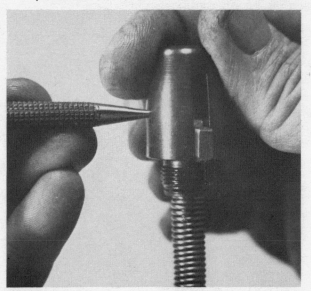

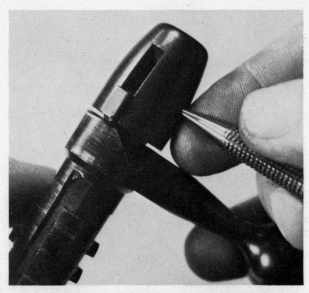

2. When turning the bolt endpiece and striker assembly back into the bolt, it should not be screwed down all the way. Stop it at the position shown, with the cocking lug aligned behind the full-cock detent notch, and withdraw the punch from the hole in the endpiece.

Remington
Model 788 Bolt Action Rifle

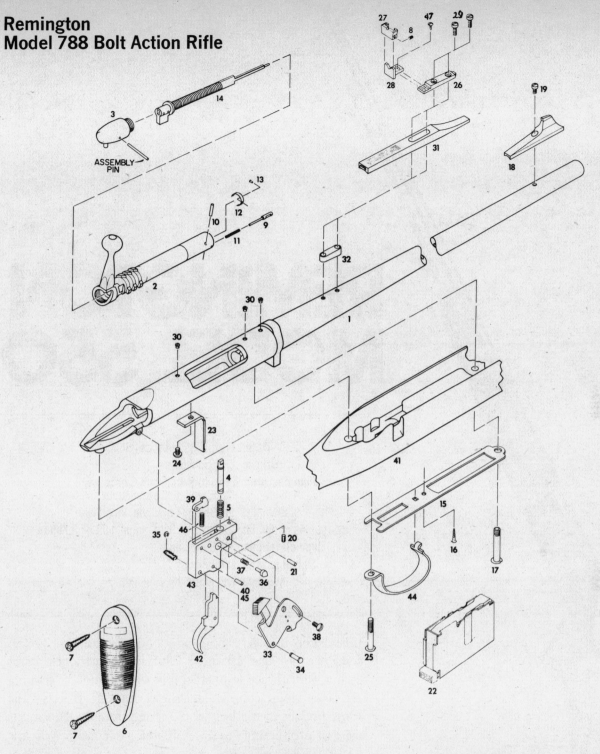

1	Barrel Assembly	**14** Firing Pin Assembly	**31** Rib (Rear Sight)
2	Bolt Assembly	**15** Floorplate	**32** Rib Spacer (Rear Sight)
3	Bolt Plug	**16** Floorplate Screw	**33** Safety Assembly
4	Bolt Stop	**17** Front Guard Screw	**34** Safety Pivot Pin
5	Bolt Stop Spring	**18** Front Sight	**35** Safety Pivot Pin Retaining Washer
6	Buttplate	**19** Front Sight Screw	**36** Safety Plunger
7	Buttplate Screws (2)	**20** Housing Lock Screw	**37** Safety Plunger Spring
8	Elevation Screw	**21** Housing Pin	**38** Safety Retaining Screw
9	Ejector	**22** Magazine Assembly	**39** Sear
10	Ejector Pin	**23** Magazine Guide Bar	**40** Sear Pin
11	Ejector Spring	**24** Magazine Guide Bar Screw	**41** Stock Assembly
12	Extractor	**25** Rear Guard Screw	**42** Trigger
13	Extractor Rivet	**26** Rear Sight Base	**43** Trigger Housing
		27 Rear Sight Aperture	**44** Trigger Guard
		28 Rear Sight Leaf	**45** Trigger Pin
		29 Rear Sight Screws (2)	**46** Trigger Spring
		30 Receiver Plug Screws (3)	**47** Windage Screw

REMINGTON MODEL 550

Data:	Remington Model 550
Origin:	United States
Manufacturer:	Remington Arms Company Bridgeport, Connecticut
Cartridge:	22 Short, Long, or Long Rifle
Magazine capacity:	22 Shorts, 17 Longs, 15 Long Rifles
Over-all length:	43½ inches
Barrel length:	24 inches
Weight:	6¼ pounds

Introduced in 1941, the Model 550 was the first 22-cal. semi-auto to use all three 22 rimfire cartridges interchangeably. It accomplished this with a unique "floating chamber" which allowed the Short cartridge to deliver the same impact to the bolt as the longer rounds. During its time of production several submodels were offered—the 550A, 550P, and so on, with different sight options. All of the 550 series guns are mechanically identical, and the same instructions will apply.

Disassembly:

1. Back out the stock mounting screw on the underside of the stock, and separate the action from the stock. If necessary, the stock screw can be removed by moving it out until its threads engage the threads in its escutcheon, then unscrewing it.

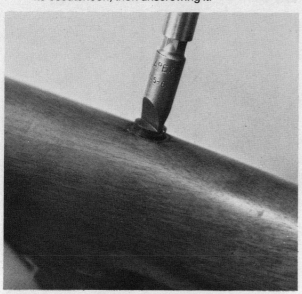

2. Pull the trigger to release the striker, so it will be in the fired position, and unscrew the receiver endcap at the rear of the receiver. If the endcap has been over-tightened, there is a large coin slot at the rear of its dome to aid in starting it. Remove the endcap and its attached spring guide, and the bolt spring and striker spring and guide toward the rear. The springs are under some tension, but not so much that the endcap can't be easily controlled. The springs are easily removed from the guide on the endcap, but the hollow guide is not removable. Take care not to lose the collar at the front of the bolt spring.

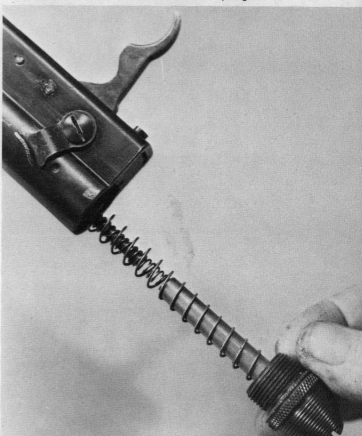

3. Move the bolt all the way to the rear, until the bolt handle aligns with the opening at the end of its track, and remove the bolt handle toward the right.

4. Use a small tool to push the bolt toward the rear, and remove it from the rear of the receiver.

5. Remove the striker (firing pin) from the rear of the bolt.

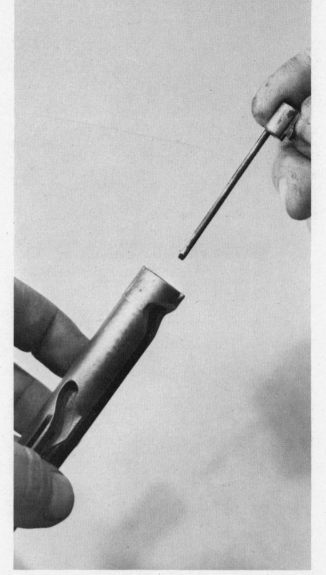

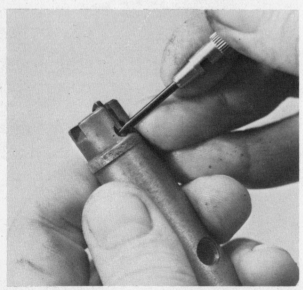

6. Use a small screwdriver to depress the extractor spring plunger, and lift the extractor out of its recess in the bolt. **Caution:** *Take care that the plunger and spring don't get away, as the compressed spring can propel the parts quite a distance.* They are very small and difficult to locate.

7. Remove the small screw and washer on the underside of the receiver near the rear edge, and take out the L-shaped endcap lockplate.

8. With the safety in the on-safe position, remove the safety screw, and take off the safety lever toward the right. The safety tumbler can then be moved inward, and removed toward the rear. As the tumbler is moved inward, the trigger spring will move its plunger upward, so control it and ease its tension slowly. Next, drift out the trigger pin and the trigger limit pin. The trigger will be freed, but can't be removed at this point because of its attached disconnector assembly.

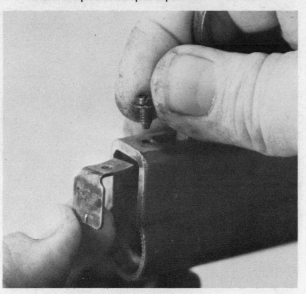

9. Drift out the cross-pin in the forward section of the receiver, and remove the carrier assembly and its spring downward. The two leaves of the carrier, the spacer bushing, and the spring are easily separated. This pin also is the sear pivot, and the sear can now be moved forward and taken out downward.

10. Remove the screw-slotted sear spring housing (looks like a large screw head) from the bottom center of the receiver, along with the sear spring is contains. The housing is often found staked in place, and some effort may be required to start it. **Caution:** *Never try to remove the housing while the sear is still in place on its cross-pin, or the parts are likely to be damaged.* The trigger assembly may now be moved upward into the receiver, then forward, and out the carrier opening. The disconnector system may be separated from the trigger by drifting out the small cross-pin, releasing the disconnector and its spring and plunger. However, the cross-pin is usually riveted in place, and during routine disassembly it is best left undisturbed.

11. Removal of the stock mounting base at the lower front of the receiver will give access to a small screw beneath it. Taking out this screw will allow removal of the outer magazine tube toward the front. This will also release the receiver insert, the subframe which forms the cartridge guide, and allows it to be pushed out toward the rear. The insert is often tight, and may require the use of a hammer and nylon drift to start it. Take care that it is not deformed during removal. The ejector is staked in place in the left wall of the receiver, and no attempt to remove it should be made during normal disassembly.

Reassembly Tips:

1. When replacing the striker in the bolt, be sure its slim forward portion enters its tunnel in the bolt, and that the striker goes all the way forward. This can be checked on the underside of the bolt, as shown.

2. When replacing the bolt handle, be sure the flat inner tip of the handle is at the top, as shown. Also, be sure the carrier is in its raised position (up at the front) before inserting the bolt in the receiver.

3. Before replacing the receiver endcap, be sure the springs are in the proper order, with the striker spring guide in the front of the spring, and the collar on the front of the bolt spring, as shown.

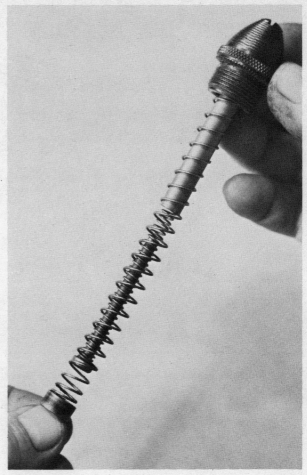

When installing the sear and sear spring system, put the sear and carrier system in place, and insert a smaller diameter rod or drift through the pin hole to keep them in general position. Then, install the sear spring housing, being sure the top of the spring enters its recess in the underside of the sear. Next, move the sear downward and toward the rear, engaging its rear lobe with the collar on the housing. When it is in position, insert the cross-pin, pushing out the smaller diameter rod or drift. This is the most difficult point in the reassembly of the Model 550.

Remington
Model 550-1 Automatic Rifle

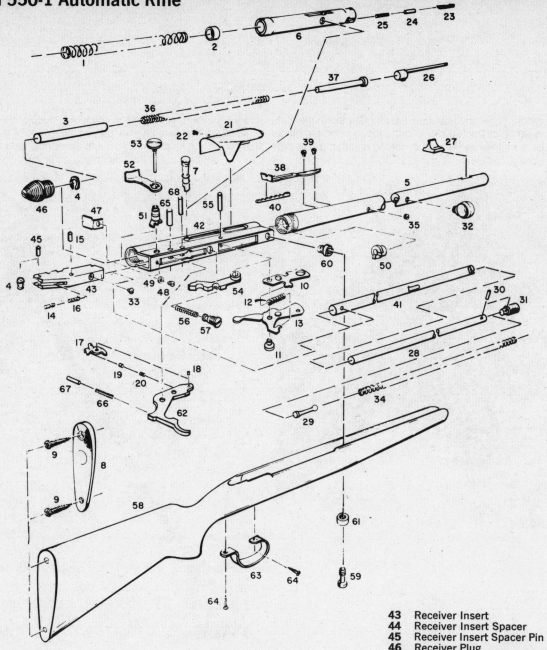

1	Action Spring	22	Deflector Screw
2	Action Spring Bushing	23	Extractor
3	Action Spring Guide	24	Extractor Plunger
4	Action Spring Guide Retainer	25	Extractor Spring
5	Barrel	26	Firing Pin
6	Bolt	27	Front Sight
7	Bolt Handle	28	Inner Magazine Tube
8	Buttplate	29	Magazine Follower
9	Buttplate Screws (2)	30	Magazine Pin
10	Carrier	31	Magazine Plug
11	Carrier Spacer Bushing	32	Magazine Ring
12	Carrier Tension Spring	33	Magazine Screw
13	Cartridge Stop	34	Magazine Spring
14	Cartridge Stop Detent	35	Magazine Tube Support Screw
15	Cartridge Stop Detent Pin	36	Main Spring
16	Cartridge Stop Detent Spring	37	Main Spring Plunger
17	Connector	38	Open Sight Leaf
18	Connector Pin	39	Open Sight Screws (2)
19	Connector Plunger	40	Open Sight Step
20	Connector Spring	41	Outer Magazine Tube
21	Deflector	42	Receiver Assembly

43	Receiver Insert
44	Receiver Insert Spacer
45	Receiver Insert Spacer Pin
46	Receiver Plug
47	Receiver Plug Retainer
48	Receiver Plug Retainer Screw
49	Receiver Plug Retainer Screw Lock Washer
50	Recoiling Chamber
51	Safety
52	Safety Lever
53	Safety Screw
54	Sear Assembly
55	Sear Pin
56	Sear Spring
57	Sear Spring Case
58	Stock
59	Take Down Screw
60	Take Down Screw Bushing
61	Take Down Screw Escutcheon
62	Trigger
63	Trigger Guard
64	Trigger Guard Screws (2)
65	Trigger Pin
66	Trigger Spring
67	Trigger Spring Plunger
68	Trigger Stop Pin

REMINGTON MODEL 742

Data: Remington Model 742

Origin: United States

Manufacturer: Remington Arms Company
Bridgeport, Connecticut

Cartridges: 6mm Rem., 243 Win., 280 Rem.,
308 Win., 30-06

Magazine capacity: 4 rounds

Over-all length: 42 inches

Barrel length: 22 inches

Weight: 7½ pounds

The original version of this gun, the Model 740, was first offered in 1955, and was made for only five years. It was redesigned in 1960 to become the Model 742, and in this form it is still in production. A carbine version is also available, with an 18½-inch barrel. Like its ancestor, the Model 740, the 742 is a difficult gun to take down. For simple repairs, such as a broken extractor or firing pin, the gun must be totally disassembled, including pulling the barrel. There are a few mechanical differences in the older Model 740, but otherwise the instructions can apply to certain shared systems.

Disassembly:

1. Remove the magazine, and cycle the action to cock the internal hammer. Push the safety across to the on-safe position. Use a drift punch to push out the two cross-pins in the receiver.

2. Move the trigger group forward, then take it off downward.

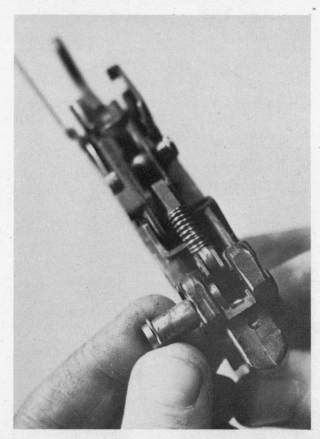

3. Push the safety to the off-safe position. Restrain the hammer, pull the trigger to release it, and ease it forward. Keeping the trigger pulled to the rear, push out the rear cross-pin sleeve toward the left.

4. Removal of the pin sleeve will allow the top of the trigger to move further toward the rear, easing the tension of the combination sear and trigger spring. This spring can now be flexed off its stud on the rear of the sear, and removed upward.

5. Drift out the trigger cross-pin toward the right.

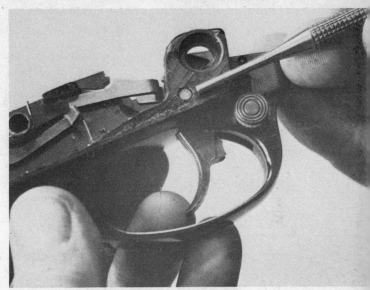

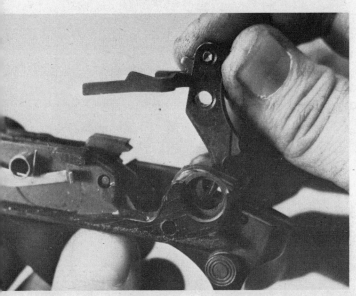

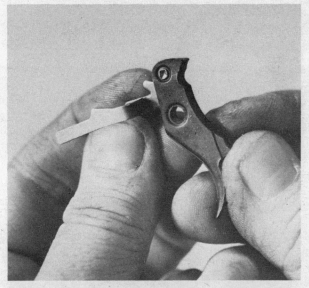

6. Remove the trigger assembly upward, turning it slightly to allow its left connector arm to clear the shelf on the trigger housing.

7. If necessary for repair, the right and left connector arms can be detached from the trigger by drifting out the cross-pin. However, its left tip is semi-riveted on the left side, and in normal disassembly it is best left in place. If removal is necessary, the pin must be drifted out toward the right, and take care that the parts are well-supported, to avoid deforming the top wings of the trigger.

8. Push out the small cross-pin at the upper rear of the trigger housing toward the right, holding a fingertip over the hole on top to restrain the released safety spring.

9. Remove the safety spring from its hole in the top, and, if possible, the detent ball beneath it. If the ball can't be shaken out at this time, it can be removed after the safety is taken out. Push out the safety toward either side, and if the detent ball has not been previously removed, insert a small drift into the hole at the top, and push the ball downward, into the safety tunnel. Take care to catch it as it rolls out.

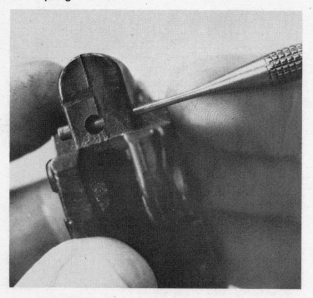

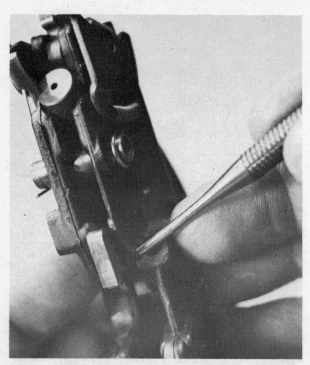

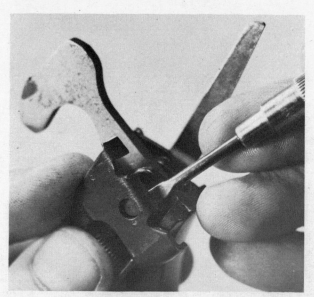

10. The sear pivot pin is accessible on the right side of the trigger housing by angling a small drift punch as shown. After it is started out it can be removed toward the left. The sear is then taken out upward.

11. The magazine catch is moved off its post on the trigger housing toward the right for removal. **Caution:** *The catch spring is compressed even when at rest, so control it during removal.* If the catch is very tight, it may have to be pried gently off its post.

12. Unhook the disconnector spring from its slot in the left end of the front cross-pin sleeve, and push out the sleeve toward the right.

13. Pull the hammer back to slightly depress the hammer spring plunger, and relieve tension on the disconnector, and push the hammer and disconnector pivot pin toward the right, just far enough to clear the disconnector.

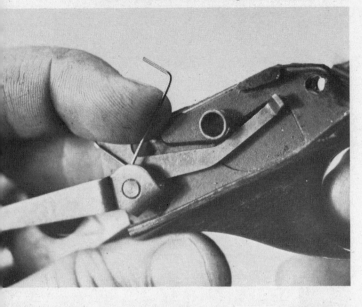

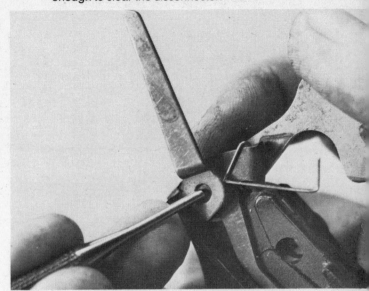

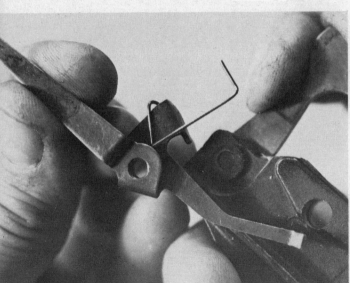

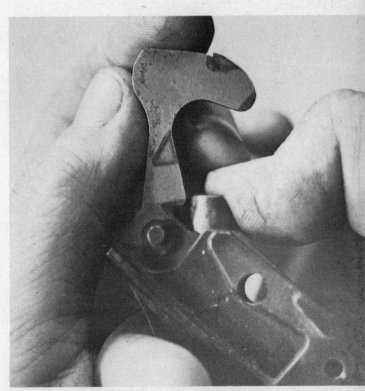

14. Remove the disconnector and its spring. Keep a firm grip on the hammer during this operation, with its spring plunger slightly depressed. The disconnector spring is easily separated from the disconnector after the part is removed.

15. Ease the hammer forward while holding and restraining the plunger, slowly releasing the tension of the spring.

16. Push the hammer pivot pin out toward the right, and take off the hammer. Remove the hammer plunger and spring from their recess in the trigger housing.

17. The buttstock is retained by a through-bolt from the rear, accessible by taking off the buttplate. Use a B-Square stock tool or a large screwdriver to unscrew the bolt, and remove the stock toward the rear. Take care not to lose the stock bearing plate, mounted between the stock and the receiver. The fore-end is retained by a large screw in its forward tip. Remove the screw, and take off the fore-end cap. The fore-end can then be slid forward and off.

18. Use a roll pin punch to drift out the action tube support pin, the large cross-pin in the gas tube housing.

19. Draw the bolt all the way to the rear, and move the action tube support bracket back off the gas tube housing. Tip the action tube downward, and slide it toward the front when it has cleared the lower edge of the gas tube housing. Take care not to release the bolt at this time, as it is very important to avoid damage to the gas tube.

20. Release the bolt very slowly as the action tube is withdrawn, easing the tension of the recoil spring. Remove the recoil spring from the rear of the action bar sleeve. It will still have some tension, so control it and ease it out.

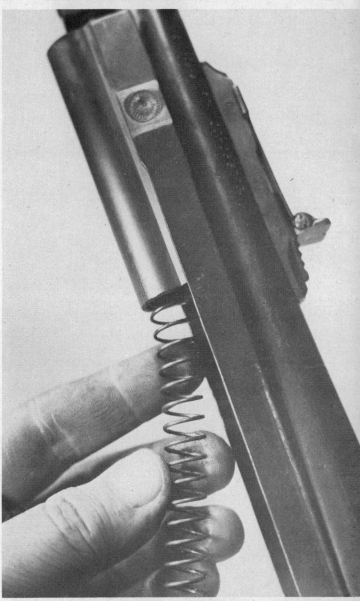

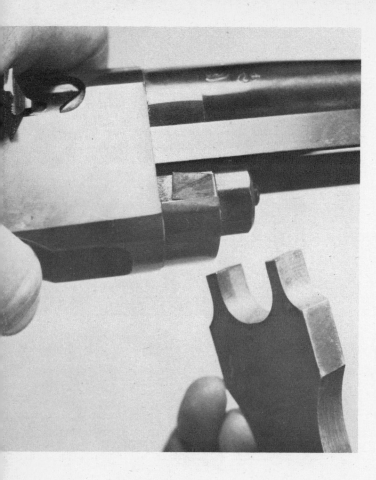

21a. With a Brownells wrench, as shown, or an open-end wrench of the proper size, turn the barrel nut counter-clockwise (front view) and remove it. Take off the fore-end stabilizer spring, mounted behind the nut.

21b. If the barrel nut has never been removed, it will be quite tight, and it may be necessary to rap the wrench handle with a hammer to start the nut.

22. Move the bolt partially toward the rear to clear its locking lugs from the barrel, and move the barrel forward out of the receiver. Move the bolt back to the front, to allow space between the action bars, and turn the barrel at a right angle to the receiver to clear its underlug projections from the action bars. Lift the barrel straight up and out of the action bars.

23. Position the bolt handle and the ejection port cover to give access to the bolt handle retaining pin, and drive out the pin downward. Remove the bolt handle toward the right.

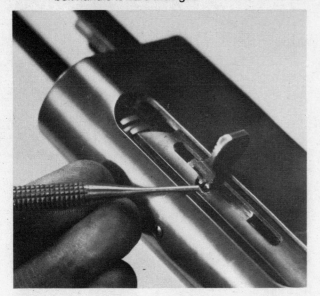

24. Remove the bolt and action bar assembly toward the front, taking off the ejection port cover as it emerges from the receiver.

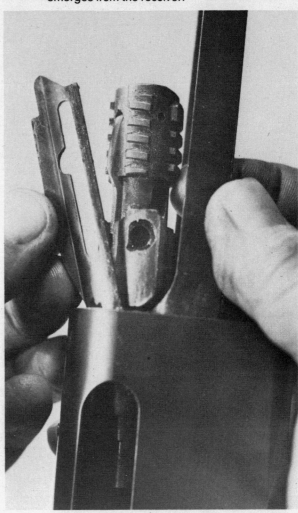

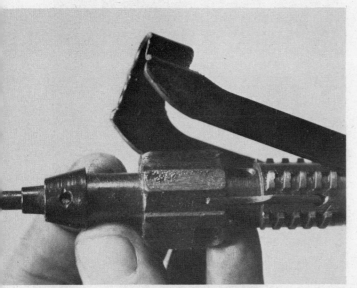

25. The bolt is easily detached from the action bar assembly by moving it downward, turning it slightly, and taking it off toward the rear.

26. The firing pin is retained in the bolt by a cross-pin at the rear, and the firing pin and its return spring are removed toward the rear.

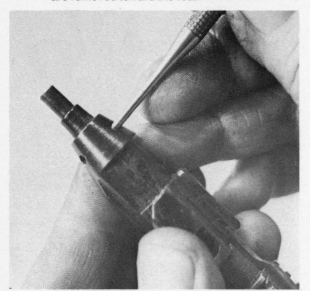

27. Insert a small screwdriver into the cam pin track at the front to lift the cam pin out of its hole in the bolt carrier. The bolt can then be separated from the carrier.

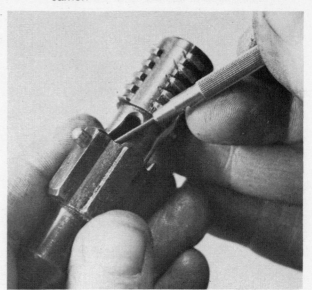

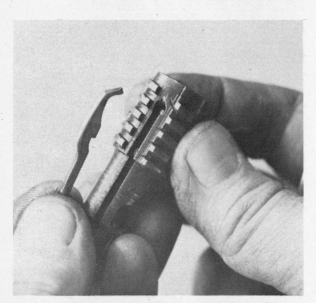

28. The bolt latch can now be moved toward the rear and upward for removal. Take care that the bolt latch pivot and plunger, and their springs, are not lost from their holes beneath the bolt latch—these are very small parts.

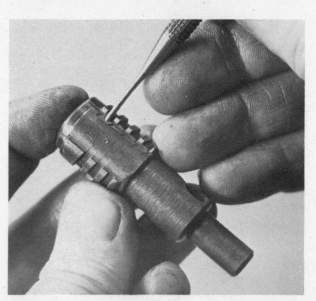

29. The ejector is removed by drifting out its cross-pin near the front of the bolt. **Caution:** *The ejector spring is quite strong, so restrain the ejector during removal, and ease it out.*

Reassembly Tips:

30. The extractor is mounted inside the cartridge head recess at the front of the bolt, and is held in place by a small rivet on the left side. Except for replacement of a broken extractor, this assembly should not be disturbed, as attempted removal will almost always break the extractor.

1. If the extractor has been removed for replacement of a broken one, installing and setting the new rivet can be very difficult, unless a tool such as the one shown is used. Newly available from B-Square, it is designed specifically for this job on all of the guns from Remington that have an extractor of this type.

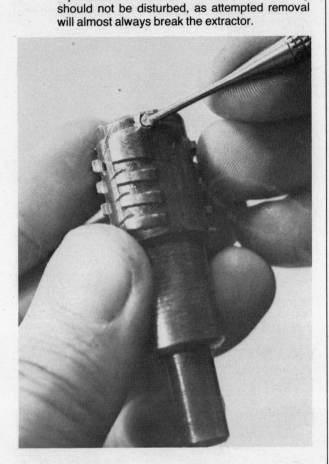

2. When replacing the bolt carrier on the rear of the bolt, note that there is a notch on the carrier which must align with the tail of the bolt latch. The bolt latch must be depressed slightly as the parts are rejoined.

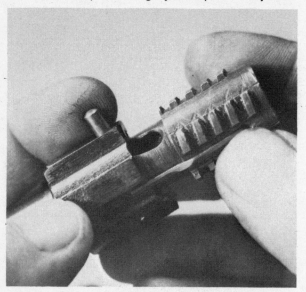

3. When replacing the bolt handle retaining pin, note that it has lengthwise stake marks at one end, and the opposite end should be inserted. Grip the pin with sharp-nosed pliers, insert it from inside the receiver, and drive it upward into place. Be sure the bolt handle is fully in place, and properly aligned with the hole, before driving in the pin.

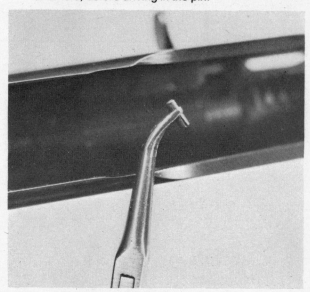

4. When replacing the barrel nut and fore-end stabilizer spring, be sure they are installed as shown, with the outer flanges of the stabilizer at the top, and the rebated nose of the barrel nut toward the rear.

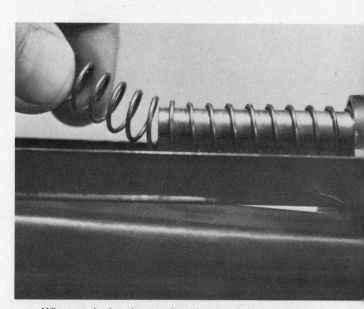

5. When replacing the recoil spring, partially insert the action tube, and slip the spring onto it from the rear, compressing the spring until its rear tip can be lifted onto its stud at the center of the barrel nut bolt. Then, push the action tube all the way to the rear. Once again, take care that the projecting gas tube is not damaged during replacement of the tube and its support bracket.

6. When replacing the front trigger group cross-pin sleeve, note that it must be oriented with its slot in the left end on the underside, so the disconnector spring can be hooked into the slot.

7. When replacing the safety spring, use a small screwdriver to depress the spring while inserting the cross-pin, pointed end first.

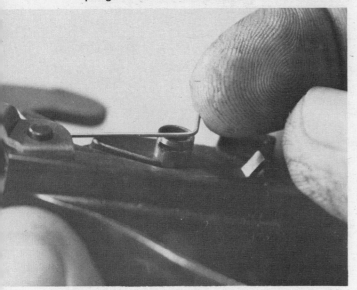

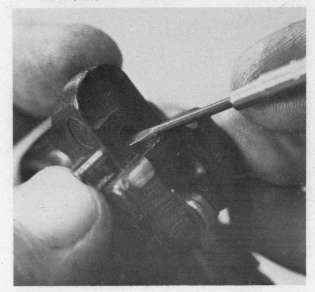

Remington
Model 742 Automatic Rifle, Carbine

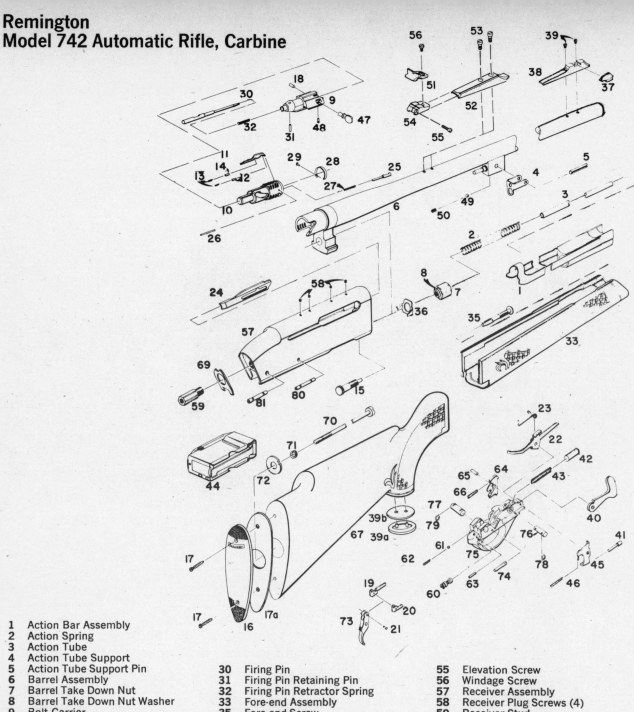

1	Action Bar Assembly	30	Firing Pin	55	Elevation Screw
2	Action Spring	31	Firing Pin Retaining Pin	56	Windage Screw
3	Action Tube	32	Firing Pin Retractor Spring	57	Receiver Assembly
4	Action Tube Support	33	Fore-end Assembly	58	Receiver Plug Screws (4)
5	Action Tube Support Pin	35	Fore-end Screw	59	Receiver Stud
6	Barrel Assembly	36	Fore-end Spring	60	Safety
7	Barrel Take Down Nut	37	Front Sight	61	Safety Detent Ball
8	Barrel Take Down Nut Washer	38	Front Sight Ramp	62	Safety Spring
9	Bolt Carrier	39	Front Sight Ramp Screws (2)	63	Safety Spring Retaining Pin
10	Breech Bolt Assembly	39a	Grip Cap	64	Sear
11	Bolt Latch	39b	Grip Cap Spacer	65	Sear Pin
12	Bolt Latch Pivot	40	Hammer	66	Sear Spring
13	Bolt Latch Spring	41	Hammer Pin	67	Stock
14	Bolt Latch Spring Plunger	42	Hammer Plunger	69	Stock Bearing Plate
15	Breech Ring Bolt	43	Hammer Spring	70	Stock Bolt
16	Buttplate	44	Magazine Assembly	71	Stock Bolt Lock Washer
17	Buttplate Screws (2)	45	Magazine Latch	72	Stock Bolt Washer
17a	Buttplate Spacer	46	Magazine Latch Spring	73	Trigger
18	Cam Pin	47	Operating Handle	74	Trigger Pin
19	Connector, Left	48	Operating Handle Retaining Pin	75	Trigger Plate, Right Hand
20	Connector, Right	49	Orifice Ball	76	Trigger Plate Pin Bushing, Front
21	Connector Pin	50	Orifice Screw	77	Trigger Plate Pin Bushing, Rear
22	Disconnector	51	Rear Sight Aperture	78	Trigger Plate Pin Detent Spring, Front
23	Disconnector Spring	52	Rear Sight Base	79	Trigger Plate Pin Detent Spring, Rear
24	Ejector Port Cover	53	Rear Sight Base Screw	80	Trigger Plate Pin, Front
25	Ejector	54	Rear Sight Slide	81	Trigger Plate Pin, Rear
26	Ejector Retaining Pin				
27	Ejector Spring				
28	Extractor				
29	Extractor Rivet				

REMINGTON MODEL 700

Data: Remington Model 700
Origin: United States
Manufacturer: Remington Arms Company
Bridgeport, Connecticut
Cartridges: Most popular calibers from 222 to 458
Magazine capacity: 4 rounds (3 in magnum calibers)
Over-all length: 41½ to 44½ inches
Barrel length: 22 or 24 inches
Weight: 7 to 7½ pounds

When Remington discontinued the Model 721, 722, and 725 rifles in 1962, the successor was the excellent Model 700. Although the basic mechanical features were essentially the same, there were a number of small mechanical improvements. Since its introduction, the Model 700 has been offered in several sub-models, each having various special features. From a takedown viewpoint, the only notable difference would be the version with a blind magazine, lacking a separate magazine floorplate. Otherwise, the same instructions will apply.

Disassembly:

1. Open the bolt, and push upward on the bolt release, located inside the trigger guard, just forward of the trigger. Remove the bolt toward the rear.

2. Grip the underlug of the cocking piece firmly in a vise, and pull the bolt body toward the front to clear the front projection of the cocking piece from the rear of the bolt. Unscrew the bolt from the sleeve and striker assembly counter-clockwise (front view).

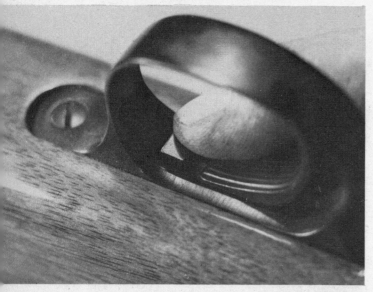

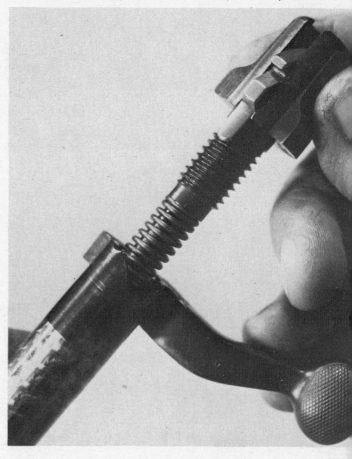

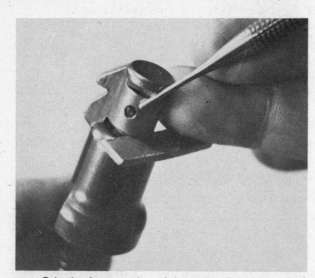

3. Grip the front portion of the striker firmly in a vise, taking care to exert no side pressure, and push the bolt sleeve forward until a small piece of steel (at least 1/16-inch thickness) can be inserted between the front of the cocking piece and the rear of the sleeve. Grip the cocking piece in a vise, hold firmly to the striker and spring, and drift out the cross-pin in the cocking piece. **Caution:** *The striker spring is fully compressed, and is quite strong, so keep it under control.* When the pin is out, slowly release the spring tension, and remove the striker, spring, and bolt sleeve toward the front.

4. Drifting out the cross-pin at the front of the bolt will release the ejector and its spring for removal toward the front. **Caution:** *The ejector spring is partially compressed, even when at rest. Control it, and ease it out.*

5. The extractor is retained inside the cartridge head recess in the front face of the bolt by a tiny rivet, and removal in normal disassembly is definitely *not* recommended, as this will usually break the extractor. If removal is necessary to replace a broken extractor, use a small-diameter drift punch to drive the rivet inward. Note that the ejector *must* be removed before this is done.

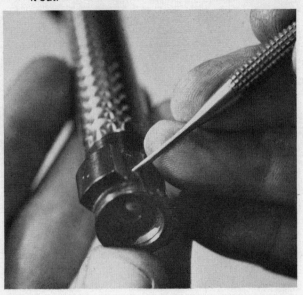

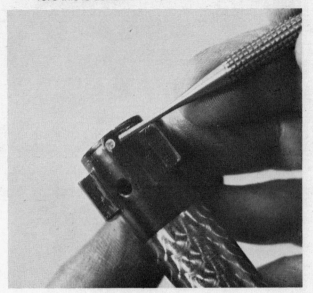

6. Remove the large vertical screw at the rear of the trigger guard. Remove the large vertical screw on the underside of the stock, forward of the trigger guard. Remove the vertical screw at the front of the trigger guard, and take the action out of the stock upward. The trigger guard can be taken off downward.

7. The magazine spring and follower will be released for removal as the action is taken out of the stock. The magazine box is retained by a small vertical screw through a tab at the rear, on the right underside of the receiver.

8. Drift out the front trigger housing cross-pin toward the right.

9. Note that the rear trigger housing cross-pin is also the retainer and pivot for the bolt stop and its spring, and the spring should be restrained while the pin is drifted out.

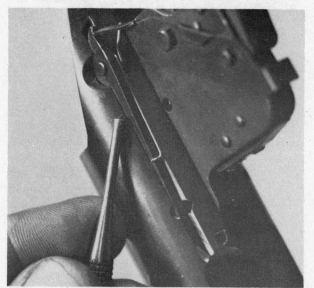

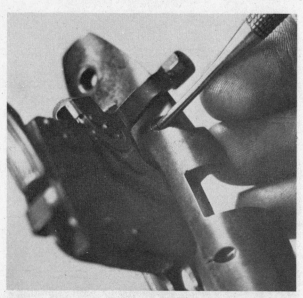

10. Set the safety lever in the on-safe position, and drift out the rear trigger housing cross-pin. Remember that the bolt stop and its spring will be released as the pin clears their position.

11. Remove the trigger housing downward.

12. Remove the bolt stop and its spring.

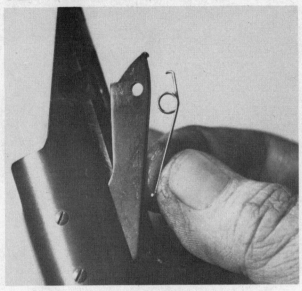

13. Remove the sear and its spring from the top of the trigger housing.

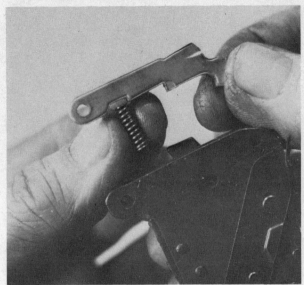

14. Remove the C-clip from the end of the safety pivot post on the right side of the housing, and take out the pivot post toward the left. The safety detent spring can then be pivoted downward and removed. Take care not to lose the small detent ball, which will be released as the spring is removed. The safety can now be moved out toward the rear. Removal of the pivot post will also free the bolt stop release from the left side of the housing.

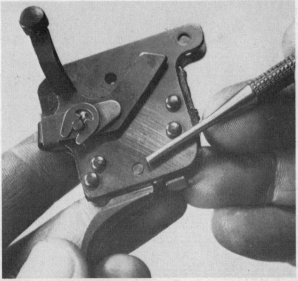

15. Drifting out the trigger cross-pin will release the trigger and trigger connector for removal. The other four cross-pins hold the housing together, and are riveted in place. Removal of these pins is not recommended.

Reassembly Tips:

1. Before the bolt can be replaced in the receiver, the striker must be in the cocked position, as shown.

2. If a broken extractor is being replaced, a new extractor rivet should be used. Clinching the new rivet is difficult, as its inner head must be well supported while the outer tip is peened and spread. With a new tool from B-square, shown in the photo, the job is much less difficult.

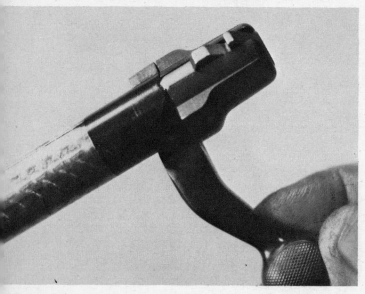

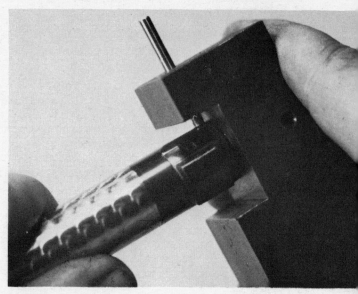

Remington
Model 700 Bolt Action Rifle

1	Barrel Assembly	23	Floorplate Pivot Pin	45	Safety Assembly
2	Bolt Assembly	24	Front Guard Screw	46	Safety Detent Ball
3	Bolt Plug	25	Front Guard Screw Bushing	47	Safety Detent Spring
4	Bolt Stop	26	Front Sight	48	Safety Pivot Pin
5	Bolt Stop Pin	27	Front Sight Ramp	49	Safety Snap Washer
6	Bolt Stop Release	28	Front Sight Ramp Screw	50	Sear Safety Cam
7	Bolt Stop Spring	29	Front Sight Hood	51	Sear Pin
8	Buttplate	30	Front Swivel Nut	52	Sear Spring
9	Buttplate Screw	31	Front Swivel Screw	53	Sling Strap Assembly
10	Center Guard Screw	32	Magazine	54	Stock
11	Ejector	33	Magazine Follower	55	Swivel Assembly
12	Ejector Pin	34	Magazine Spring	56	Trigger
13	Ejector Spring	35	Main Spring	57	Trigger Adjusting Screw
14	Extractor	36	Rear Guard Screw	58	Trigger Connector
15	Extractor Rivet	37	Rear Sight Aperture	59	Trigger Engagement Screw
16	Firing Pin	38	Rear Sight Base	60	Trigger Guard
17	Firing Pin Assembly	39	Rear Sight Base Screws (2)	61	Trigger Guard, BDL Grade
18	Firing Pin Cross Pin	40	Rear Sight Slide	62	Trigger Housing Assembly
19	Floorplate	41	Elevation Screw	63	Trigger Pin
20	Floorplate Latch	42	Windage Screw	64	Trigger Spring
21	Floorplate Latch Pin	43	Rear Swivel Screw	65	Trigger Stop Screw
22	Floorplate Latch Spring	44	Receiver Plug Screws (6)		

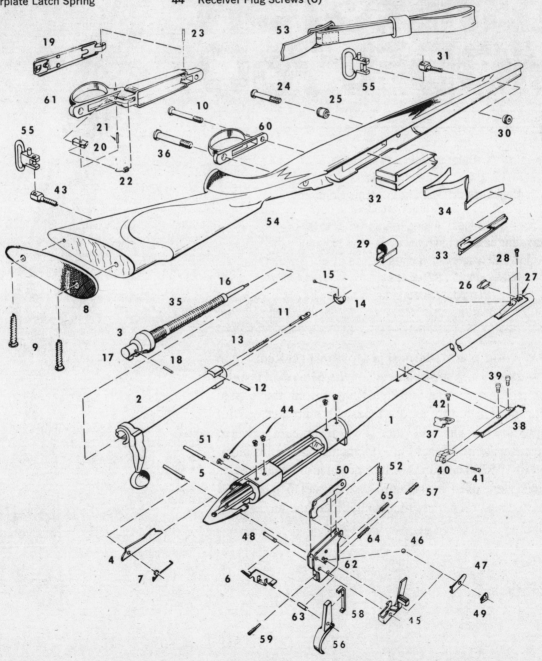

REMINGTON MODEL 760

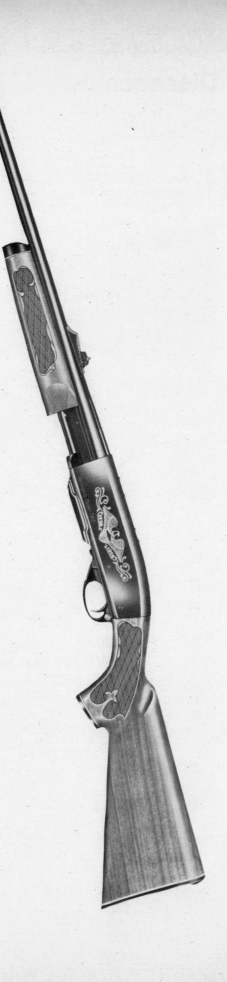

Data:	Remington Model 760
Origin:	United States
Manufacturer:	Remington Arms Company
	Bridgeport, Connecticut
Cartridges:	A long list, from 222 to 30-06
Magazine capacity:	4 rounds
Over-all length:	42 inches
Barrel length:	22 inches
Weight:	7½ pounds

Before World War II, the design department at Remington was working on a replacement for the Model 141 slide-action rifle, something with a locking system that would handle modern high-pressure loads. This project was interrupted by the war, and when it was resumed afterward, the result was the Model 760 "Gamemaster" rifle, introduced in 1952. The gun is still in production. Many of its features were used in the semi-auto Model 740 and 742 rifles, and several parts will actually interchange.

Disassembly:

1. Remove the magazine, and cycle the action to cock the internal hammer. Push out the large and small cross-pins in the lower rear area of the receiver.

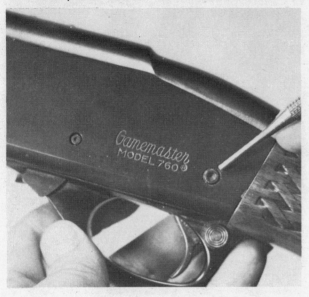

2. Move the trigger group forward, then remove it downward.

3. Grip the magazine catch firmly to control its spring tension, and push it off its post toward the right.

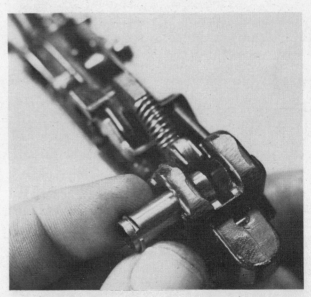

4. Restrain the hammer against the tension of its spring, and pull the trigger. Ease the hammer down beyond its normal fired position. The hammer spring plunger will be stopped by the inner arm of the disconnector. With the trigger still depressed, push out the rear cross-pin sleeve toward the left, and remove it.

5. Removal of the sleeve will allow the top of the trigger to move further toward the rear than its normal position, and will relieve the tension of the combination sear and trigger spring. Detach the spring from its stud on the back of the sear, and remove it upward.

6. Drift out the trigger pin toward the left, and remove it.

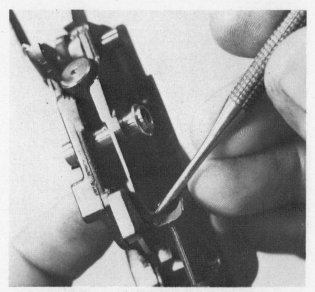

7. Remove the trigger and its attached connector arms upward. It will be necessary to turn the trigger slightly toward the left to clear the left arm past the upper shelf on the housing. The connector arms can be separated from the trigger by drifting out the cross-pin, but this is not advisable in normal takedown. If necessary for replacement of a broken arm, the pin must be drifted out toward the right.

8. The right end of the sear pin is accessible to an angled drift punch, and the pin is usually lightly staked on the left side. Nudge it toward the left, then use smooth-jawed pliers to remove it.

9. Remove the sear upward.

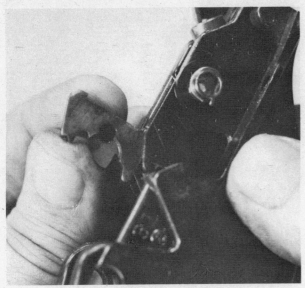

10. Unhook the rear arm of the action slide latch spring from its slot in the underside of the front guard cross-pin sleeve, and allow it to swing over forward, relieving its tension.

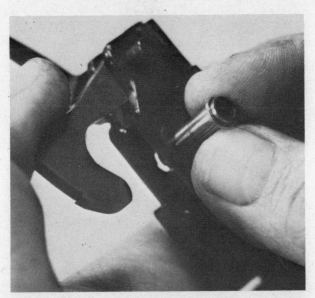

11. Depress the hammer spring plunger to relieve tension on the slide latch, and move its rear arm downward to clear the cross-pin sleeve. Remove the sleeve toward the right.

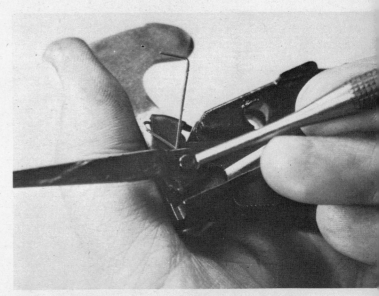

12. Push the hammer and latch pivot pin toward the right, just enough to clear the latch. During this operation, keep the hammer pushed back far enough to slightly depress the hammer spring plunger, taking pressure off the latch.

13. Keeping the hammer under control, remove the action slide latch and its spring upward.

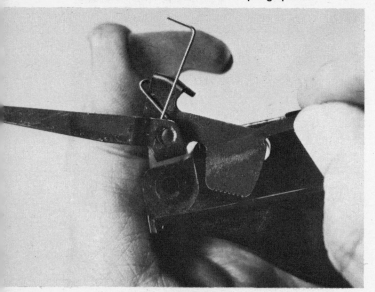

14. Restrain the hammer spring plunger, and ease the hammer over forward, slowly releasing the tension of the plunger and spring. Remove the plunger and spring upward and toward the front.

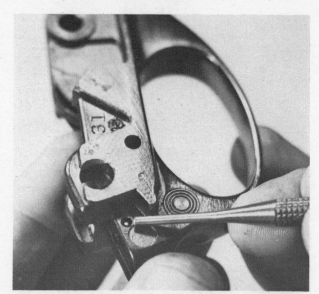

16. Push out the small cross-pin at the upper rear of the trigger group, holding a fingertip over the hole at the top to restrain the safety spring. Take out the spring upward. If the detent ball can be shaken out the top, remove it, too.

15. Push the hammer pivot pin out toward the right, and remove the hammer upward.

17. Remove the safety toward either side. If the detent ball was not previously removed, it can now be pushed downward into the safety tunnel and taken out.

18. Remove the large screw in the front of the fore-end, and slide the fore-end wood off toward the front.

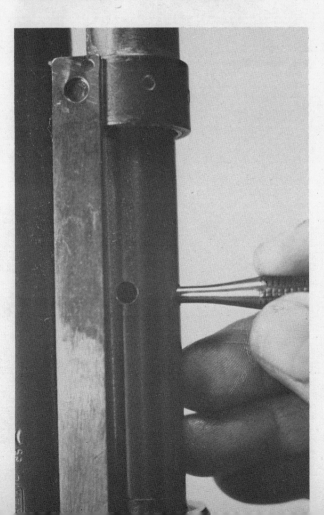

19. Insert a large drift punch through the holes in the action tube, and unscrew it counter-clockwise (front view). When the tube has cleared its threads, move it forward, into the action slide tube.

20. Move the barrel and action slide assembly forward out of the receiver. During this operation, take care that the ejection port cover is not damaged.

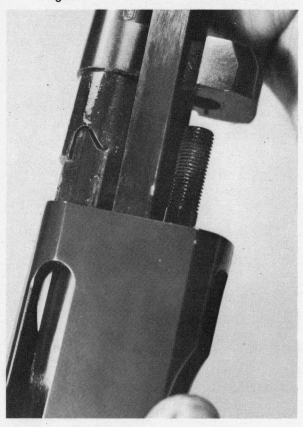

21. Move the slide assembly toward the rear, to clear the bolt from the barrel. Move the bolt assembly downward, out of the rear arch of the slide bars, tilt it to clear the bars, and remove it downward.

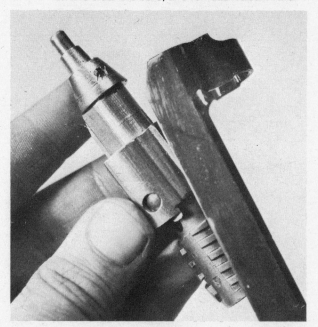

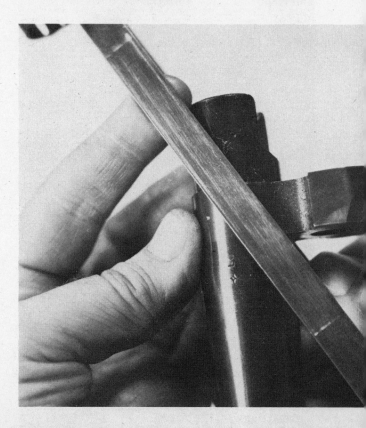

22. Position the rear end of the barrel at midpoint between the action slide bars, spread the bars just enough for clearance, and move them upward over the rear of the barrel. Remove the action slide assembly toward the front.

23. Insert a small screwdriver from the front to lift the small cam pin out of the bolt carrier, and remove it. Repeat the operation on the opposite side, lifting the larger cam pin out of the carrier, and remove it.

24. Remove the bolt from the carrier, toward the front.

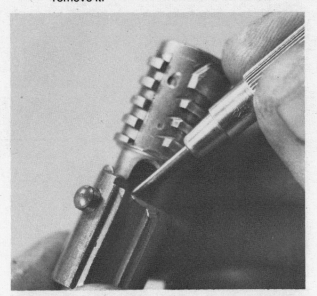

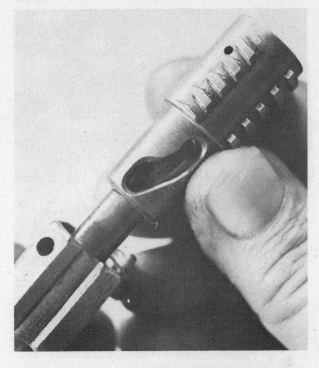

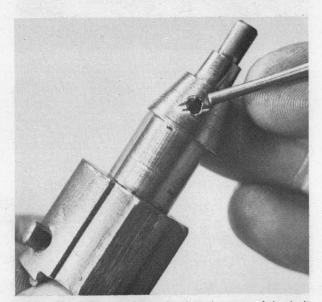

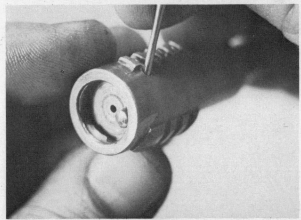

25. The firing pin is retained at the rear of the bolt carrier by a cross-pin, and is removed toward the rear. The bolt carrier tension spring can be removed from the front of the carrier.

26. The ejector is retained by a cross-pin near the front of the bolt, and is removed toward the front. **Caution:** *The ejector spring is under tension. Ease it out after removing the pin.*

27. The extractor is retained inside the bolt face recess by a small rivet, and should never be removed except for replacement of a broken part. If it must be taken out, the ejector must first be removed, then the rivet is driven inward with a small-diameter punch.

28. The buttstock is retained by a through-bolt from the rear, accessible by removing the buttplate. Use a B-Square stock tool or a long screwdriver to back out the bolt, and remove the stock toward the rear. If the stock is tight, bump the front of the comb with the heel of the hand to free it. Take care not to lose the bearing plate between the stock and receiver.

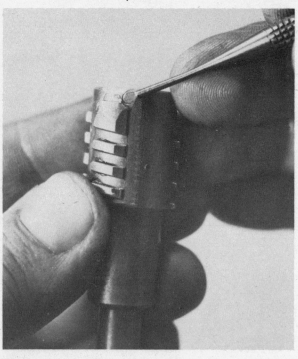

Reassembly Tips:

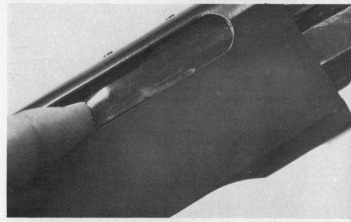

1. When replacing the ejection port cover, as the bolt and slide assembly are moved toward the rear, be sure the top edge of the cover enters the groove in the top of the receiver at the edge of the ejection port. The cover is easily broken.

2. When replacing the front cross-pin sleeve, note that the slot in its left tip must be positioned at the bottom, to engage the rear arm of the bolt latch spring.

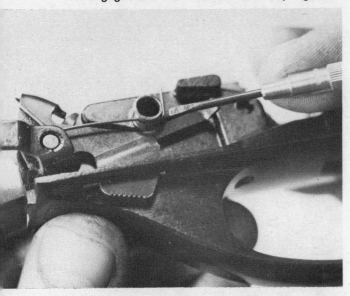

3. When replacing the trigger, note that its left connector arm must be installed *above* the rear arm of the slide latch, as shown.

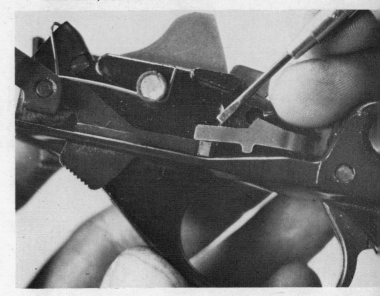

4. When replacing the trigger group in the receiver, remember to insert it forward of its position, then move it back to align with the cross-pins.

Remington
Model 760 Slide Action Rifle, Carbine

1	Action Bar Assembly	24	Firing Pin	47	Receiver Plug Screws (4)
2	Action Bar Lock	25	Firing Pin Retaining Pin	48	Receiver Stud
3	Action Bar Lock Spring	26	Fore-end Assembly	49	Safety
4	Action Tube Assembly	27	Fore-end Cap Screw	50	Safety Detent Ball
5	Action Tube Ring	28	Front Sight	51	Safety Spring
6	Barrel Assembly	29	Front Sight Ramp	52	Safety Spring Retaining Pin
7	Barrel Bracket Bolt	30	Front Sight Ramp Screws (2)	53	Sear
8	Bolt Carrier	31	Grip Cap	54	Sear Pin
9	Bolt Carrier Spring	32	Grip Cap Spacer	55	Sear Spring
10	Breech Bolt Assembly	33	Hammer	56	Stock
11	Buttplate	34	Hammer Pin	57	Stock Bearing Plate
12	Buttplate Screws (2)	35	Hammer Plunger	58	Stock Bolt
13	Cam Pin (lg.)	36	Hammer Spring	59	Stock Bolt Lock Washer
14	Cam Pin (sm.)	37	Magazine Assembly	60	Stock Bolt Washer
15	Connector, Left	38	Magazine Latch	61	Trigger
16	Connector, Right	39	Magazine Latch Spring	62	Trigger Pin
17	Connector Pin (16a Buttplate spacer)	40	Rear Sight Aperture	63	Trigger Plate, R.H.
18	Ejection Port Cover	41	Rear Sight Base	64	Trigger Plate Pin Bushing, Front
19	Ejector	42	Rear Sight Base Screw	65	Trigger Plate Pin Bushing, Rear
20	Ejector Retaining Pin	43	Rear Sight Slide	66	Trigger plate Pin Detent Spring, Front
21	Ejector Spring	44	Elevation Screw	67	Trigger Plate Pin Detent Spring, Rear
22	Extractor	45	Windage Screw	68	Trigger Plate Pin, Front
23	Extractor Rivet	46	Receiver Assembly	69	Trigger Plate Pin, Rear

REMINGTON NYLON 66

Data: Remington Nylon 66
Origin: United States
Manufacturer: Remington Arms Company
Bridgeport Connecticut
Cartridge: 22 Long Rifle
Magazine capacity: 14 rounds
Over-all length: 38½ inches
Barrel length: 19⅝ inches
Weight: 4 pounds

Around 1959, when the Remington Nylon 66 first arrived on the scene, many firearms traditionalists sneered at its DuPont Zytel stock/receiver, stamped-steel parts, and expansion-type springs. Over the years, they have found that it works, and keeps working, uncleaned, mistreated, and abused. The back-window rack in nearly every pickup truck in the country now carries a Nylon 66, a tribute to Wayne Leek and the design team at Remington. For those not familiar with its mechanism, though, the Nylon 66 can be a disassembly/reassembly nightmare.

Disassembly:

1. Remove the inner magazine tube from the stock. Grip the bolt handle firmly and pull it straight out toward the right.

2. Back out the two cross-screws, located near the lower edge of the receiver cover, and remove them toward the right.

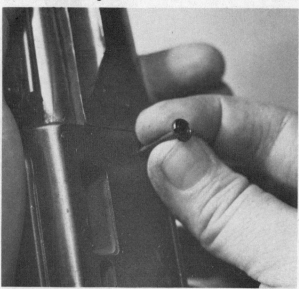

3. Remove the receiver cover assembly upward. The internal cartridge guide spring and the rear sight base are riveted on the cover, and removal is not advisable in normal disassembly.

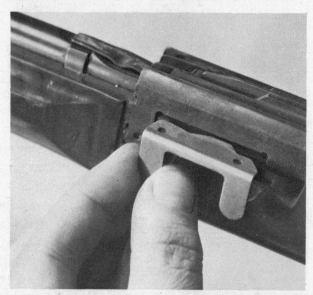

4. Remove the ejector from its recess in the left side of the receiver.

5. Loosen the large cross-slotted screw on the underside of the stock, just forward of the trigger guard, then push it upward to raise the barrel retaining piece until its upper cross-bar clears its recess on top of the barrel. Slide the barrel out toward the front.

6. The front sight is retained on top of the barrel by two screws, one at each end.

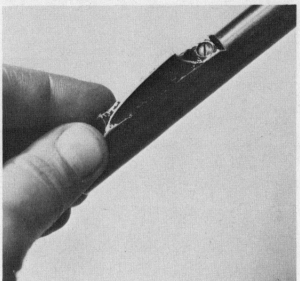

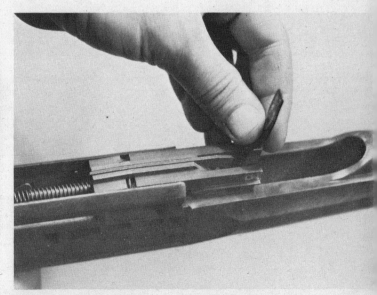

7. Take out the cross-slotted screw from the bottom of the stock, and lift the barrel retainer and its front plate out of their recess in the top of the stock.

8. Be sure the hammer is in its cocked position (at the rear), and the safety in the on-safe position. Grasp the cartridge guide, and move the bolt forward out of its tracks in the receiver. Remove the bolt spring and its guide toward the front.

9. Move the safety to the off-safe position, restrain the hammer against the tension of its spring, and pull the trigger to release the hammer. Ease the spring tension slowly, and move the hammer forward out of its tracks in the receiver. Remove the hammer spring and its guide.

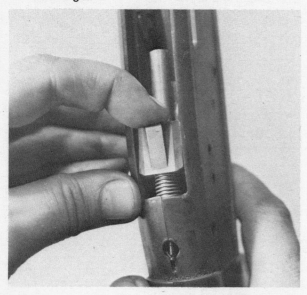

10. Push out the cross-pin located in the receiver just above the forward end of the trigger guard (arrow). Tip the trigger guard downward at the front, disengage its rear hook from inside the receiver, and remove the guard downward.

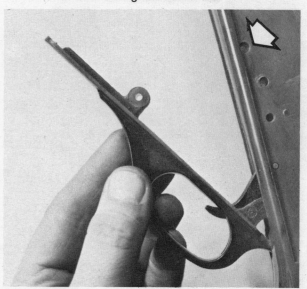

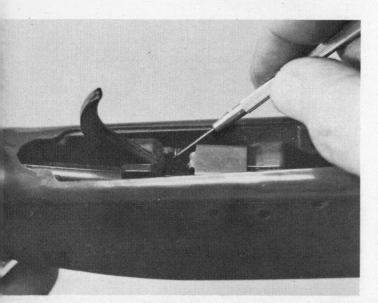

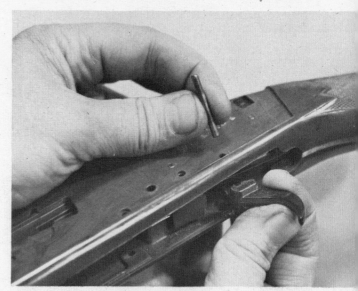

11. Use a small tool to unhook the trigger spring from its groove on the front of the trigger.

12. Push out the trigger cross-pin, and remove the trigger downward.

13. Push out the cross-pin just below the ejector recess (arrow), and remove the cartridge stop and its flat spring from the bottom of the receiver.

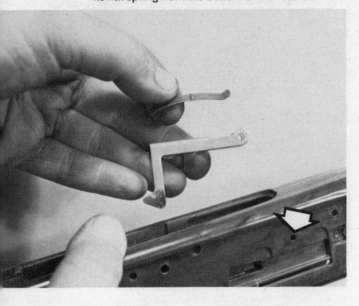

14. Use a tool to push the front of the cartridge feed throat (insert) downward, and tip it out of its recess for removal from the bottom of the receiver.

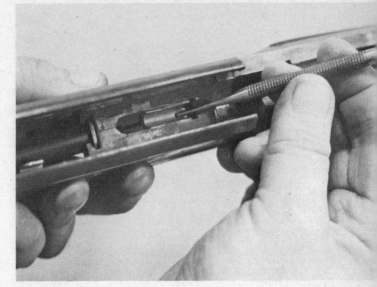

15. Use a small tool to lift the magazine tube retainer from its recess inside the receiver, and remove it from the top. Take out the magazine tube toward the rear.

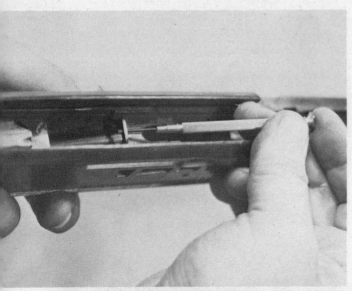

16. Restrain the sear at the top of the receiver against its spring tension, and push the disconnector pivot at the bottom of the receiver to release the sear. Allow the sear to pivot upward, slowly releasing the tension of its spring.

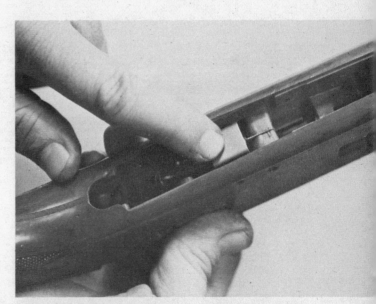

17. Use a tool to disengage the hook of the disconnector pivot spring from the receiver cross-piece at the bottom.

18. Push out the disconnector pivot points, one on each side of the receiver. After one has been removed, the other may be pushed out from the inside, using one of the other cross-pins already removed, or a drift punch.

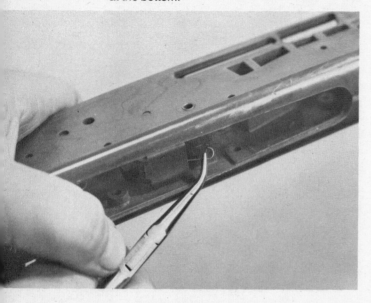

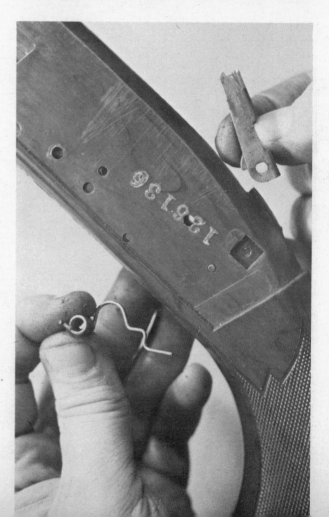

19. Depress the sear slightly to clear the rear arm of the disconnector, and remove the disconnector assembly from the top of the receiver. The disconnector is easily separated from its pivot by squeezing the sides of the pivot inward just enough to detach the lugs from the holes in the disconnector. The springs are also easily detached by turning their ends out of the holes in the parts.

20. Push out the sear pivot pin, and remove the sear and its spring from the top of the receiver (actually, the spring will usually fall from the bottom as the pin is taken out).

21. Push out the safety lever cam pin, the last cross-pin at the rear of the receiver. This will allow the safety lever to drop, and the safety and its attached lever can then be removed upward.

22. Use a fingernail or a small tool to move the safety detent spring retaining pin out toward the rear. The pin has a groove at its rear tip to aid removal. The detent spring is not under heavy tension, but it can flip the pin as it is removed, so restrain it with a fingertip during removal. Take out the detent spring and the ball bearing from their hole in the top of the receiver, and take care that the bearing isn't lost.

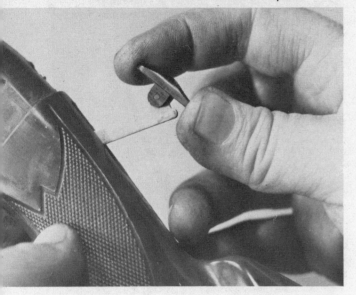

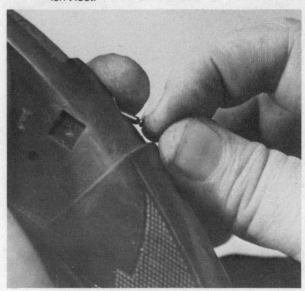

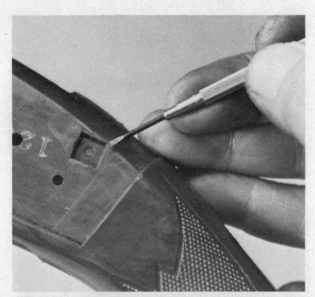

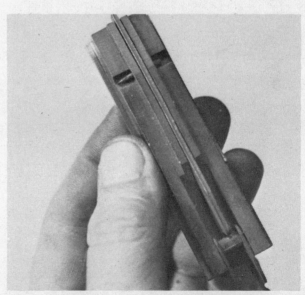

23. The two internal cross-screws with square nuts on the left side do not retain parts, and their removal is neither necessary nor advisable during normal takedown.

24. The firing pin is retained in the bolt by a cross-pin on top, near the rear of the bolt. The retaining pin is bent down on each side to lock it in place, and one end must be pried upward before the pin is drifted out. The firing pin is then removed toward the rear.

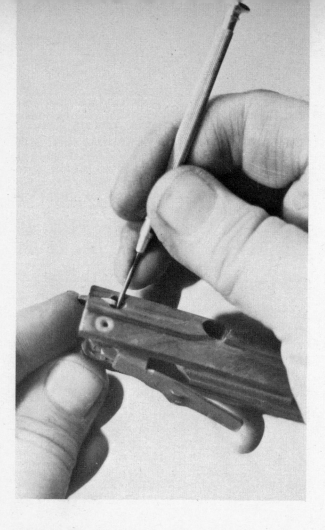

25. Insert a small screwdriver between the rear of the extractor and its plunger, and depress the plunger while lifting the extractor out of its recess. **Caution:** *The spring is under compression, so take care it doesn't get away.* Ease it out, and remove the plunger and spring.

26. A roll pin across the top front of the bolt retains the cartridge guide. Drifting out the pin will release the guide for removal. Be sure to use a roll pin punch, to avoid deforming the pin.

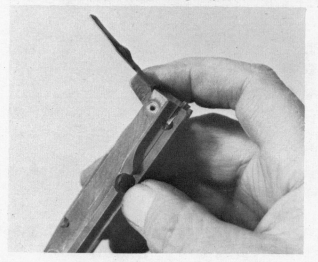

Reassembly Tips:

1. When replacing the disconnector assembly, remember that the sear (arrow) must be tipped forward to allow the rear arm of the disconnector to go behind the sear.

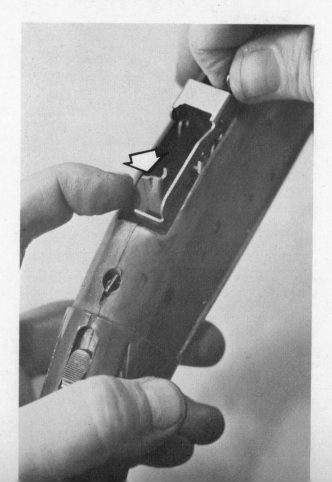

2. Remember that the cartridge feed throat ("cartridge insert") must be put in from below. Insert its rear tip first, then swing its front wings upward into the recesses, while holding the rear tip in place with a tool, as shown. When the cartridge feed throat is in place, invert the gun so the feed throat will not fall back into the stock before installation of the cartridge stop (the front tip of the stop spring holds the feed throat in place). Installation of the cartridge feed throat is the single most difficult point in the reassembly of the Nylon 66.

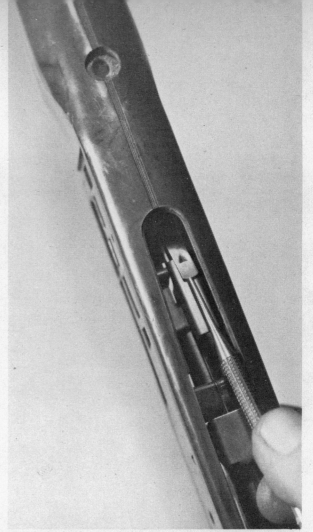

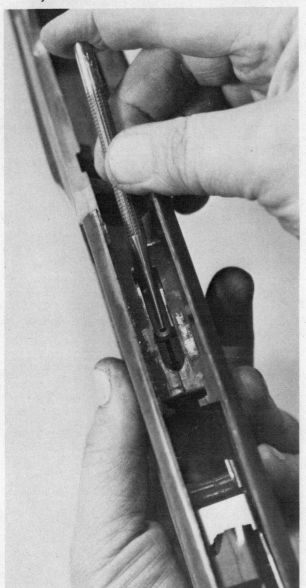

3. Do not attempt to install the cartridge stop and its flat spring at the same time. Install the stop, then insert the spring, with its forward end going under the pin (remember, the gun is inverted), and push the spring forward until its indented catch locks on the front edge of the cartridge stop.

4. When properly installed, the front lip of the sear (arrow) should be under the front cross-piece of the disconnector, as shown.

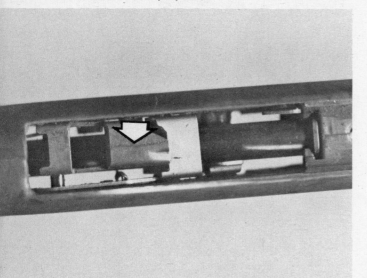

When reinstalling the hammer assembly, it is necessary to use a small tool to depress the sear while holding the trigger back, allowing the hammer to move to the rear. When the hammer is moved back to the cocked position, set the safety in the on-safe position to prevent release of the hammer while the bolt is installed.

When installing the barrel retainer, note that the front plate goes at the front of the retainer, and that the plate has an oblong slot which mates with a stud on the retainer.

Before replacing the receiver cover, be sure the ejector is in place in its recess on the left side. This part is often left out during reassembly, or drops off if the gun is tilted toward the left during replacement of the cover.

Before replacing the cover, be sure the cartridge guide is flipped over forward, to lie on top of the barrel.

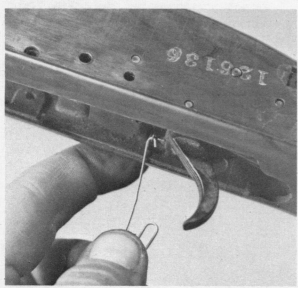

5. It is very difficult to reattach the trigger spring to the front of the trigger without a small hooked tool. The one shown was made from an opened paper clip.

Remington
Nylon 66 Automatic Rifle

1	Action Spring	19	Ejector	37	Magazine Spring

Remington
Models 580, 581, 582 Bolt Action Rifles

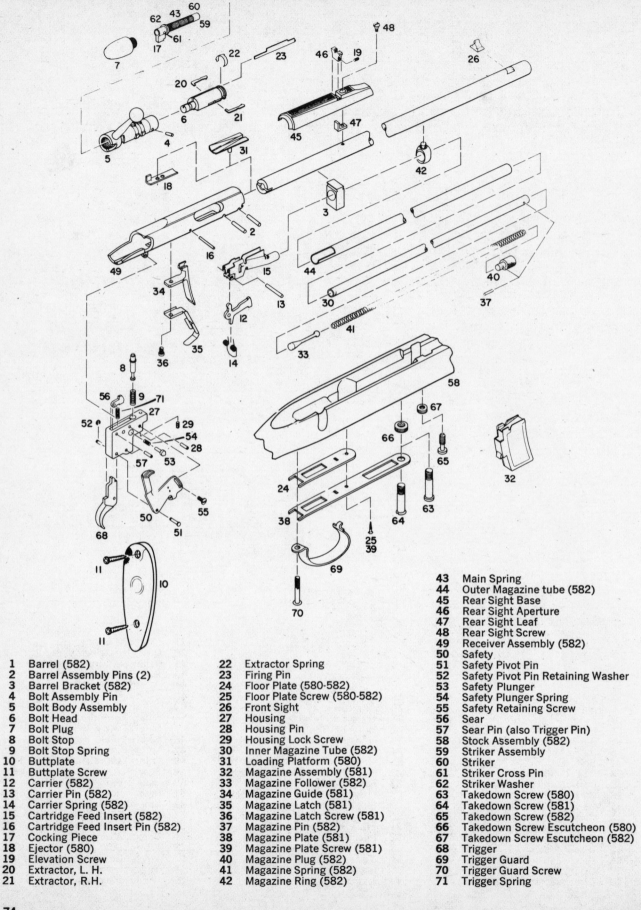

1	Barrel (582)	**22**	Extractor Spring	**43**	Main Spring
2	Barrel Assembly Pins (2)	**23**	Firing Pin	**44**	Outer Magazine tube (582)
3	Barrel Bracket (582)	**24**	Floor Plate (580-582)	**45**	Rear Sight Base
4	Bolt Assembly Pin	**25**	Floor Plate Screw (580-582)	**46**	Rear Sight Aperture
5	Bolt Body Assembly	**26**	Front Sight	**47**	Rear Sight Leaf
6	Bolt Head	**27**	Housing	**48**	Rear Sight Screw
7	Bolt Plug	**28**	Housing Pin	**49**	Receiver Assembly (582)
8	Bolt Stop	**29**	Housing Lock Screw	**50**	Safety
9	Bolt Stop Spring	**30**	Inner Magazine Tube (582)	**51**	Safety Pivot Pin
10	Buttplate	**31**	Loading Platform (580)	**52**	Safety Pivot Pin Retaining Washer
11	Buttplate Screw	**32**	Magazine Assembly (581)	**53**	Safety Plunger
12	Carrier (582)	**33**	Magazine Follower (582)	**54**	Safety Plunger Spring
13	Carrier Pin (582)	**34**	Magazine Guide (581)	**55**	Safety Retaining Screw
14	Carrier Spring (582)	**35**	Magazine Latch (581)	**56**	Sear
15	Cartridge Feed Insert (582)	**36**	Magazine Latch Screw (581)	**57**	Sear Pin (also Trigger Pin)
16	Cartridge Feed Insert Pin (582)	**37**	Magazine Pin (582)	**58**	Stock Assembly (582)
17	Cocking Piece	**38**	Magazine Plate (581)	**59**	Striker Assembly
18	Ejector (580)	**39**	Magazine Plate Screw (581)	**60**	Striker
19	Elevation Screw	**40**	Magazine Plug (582)	**61**	Striker Cross Pin
20	Extractor, L. H.	**41**	Magazine Spring (582)	**62**	Striker Washer
21	Extractor, R.H.	**42**	Magazine Ring (582)	**63**	Takedown Screw (580)
				64	Takedown Screw (581)
				65	Takedown Screw (582)
				66	Takedown Screw Escutcheon (580)
				67	Takedown Screw Escutcheon (582)
				68	Trigger
				69	Trigger Guard
				70	Trigger Guard Screw
				71	Trigger Spring

REMINGTON MODEL 581

Data:	Remington Model 581
Origin:	United States
Manufacturer:	Remington Arms Company Bridgeport, Connecticut
Cartridge:	22 Short, Long, or Long Rifle
Magazine capacity:	5 rounds
Over-all length:	42⅜ inches
Barrel length:	24 inches
Weight:	4¾ pounds

Remington's current moderately-priced bolt-action 22 rifle, the Model 581, was introduced in 1967. For today's shooters, it serves the same purpose as the 512 and 513 did for an earlier generation. The 581 is also supplied with a single-shot adapter, a useful accessory when teaching youngsters to shoot. It is also available in a left-handed version, the mechanical details being the same.

Disassembly:

1. Remove the magazine, and use a wide, thin-bladed screwdriver to back out the main stock mounting screw, on the underside just forward of the magazine well. Separate the action from the stock.

2. To remove the bolt, open it and move it toward the rear while pushing the safety lever forward, beyond its normal off-safe position. Withdraw the bolt from the rear of the receiver.

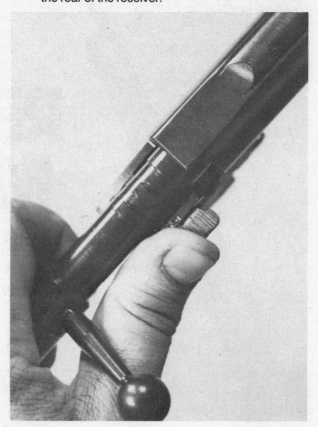

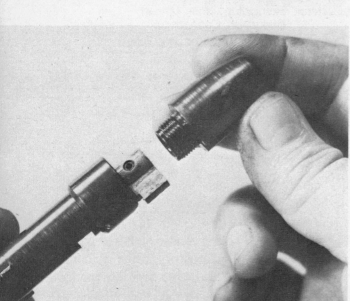

3. Grip the underlug of the striker head, at the rear of the bolt, in a sharp-edged bench vise, and be sure it is firmly held. Push forward on the bolt endpiece, against the tension of the striker spring, and unscrew the forward portion of the bolt from the endpiece. **Caution:** *The powerful spring is under heavy tension, so control the bolt as the threaded section is cleared.*

4. Remove the striker and its captive spring assembly from the rear of the bolt. The striker head may be separated from the front portion of the striker by drifting out the roll cross-pin. This will release the striker spring with force, so proceed with caution. In normal disassembly, this unit is best left intact. If it is taken apart, take care not to lose the compression washer, located between the spring and the striker head.

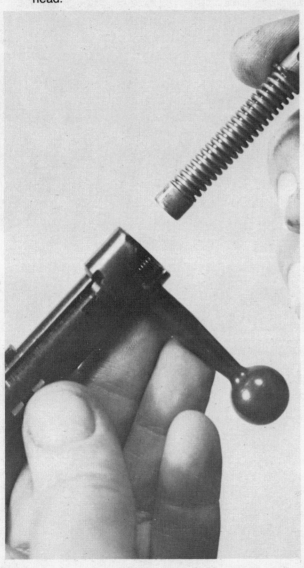

5. A solid cross-pin near the forward end of the bolt body retains the breechblock on the front of the bolt. Drifting out the cross-pin will allow the breechblock to be taken off toward the front.

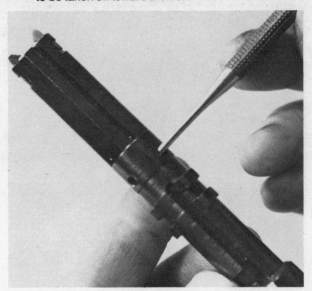

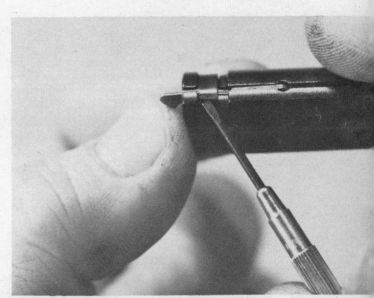

6. Use a small screwdriver to gently pry the left end of the semi-circular spring-clip at the front of the bolt upward. Flexing the left extractor very slightly outward will make insertion of the screwdriver tip easier. Take care to lift the clip only enough to slip it off, as it will break if flexed too far.

7. After the spring clip has been removed, the extractors are easily removed from their recesses on each side, and the firing pin can be taken out of its slot in the top. Note that the extractors are not identical, and each must be returned to the proper side in reassembly.

8. The safety lever is mounted on the trigger housing by its pivot post at the rear and a guide post at the front, and these posts are retained on the left side of the housing by C-clips. Carefully remove the C-clips, guarding against their loss, and take out the two mounting posts toward the right.

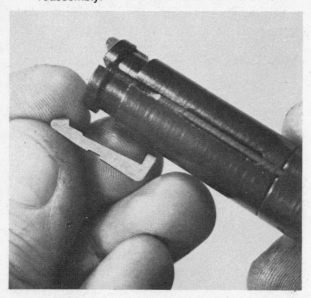

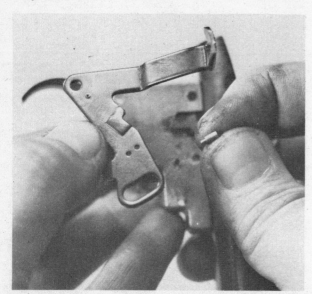

9. Remove the safety lever toward the right. **Caution:** *As the safety lever is removed, the safety plunger and spring will be released from their cross-hole in the housing.* Control them during removal, and take them out of the housing.

10. The safety plunger and spring will usually come out of the housing together. If not, it may be necessary to use a small screwdriver to lift out the spring.

11. The large pin at the upper rear of the trigger housing is the sear pivot pin. It is sometimes mistaken for the trigger group retaining pin, and is drifted out in error. This will release the sear within the housing, and the housing must then be removed to replace the sear and its spring in proper order.

12. The trigger housing retaining pin is a roll pin at the upper center of the housing. Drifting out this cross-pin will allow the trigger housing to be taken off downward. When the housing is removed, the bolt stop and its spring can be lifted from their well in the top of the housing, and the sear is easily removed by drifting out its cross-pin.

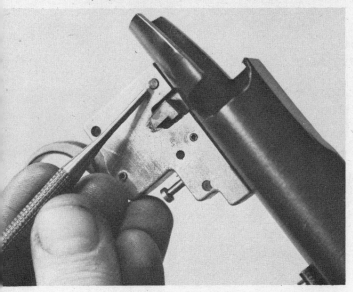

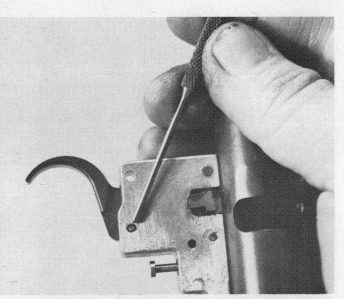

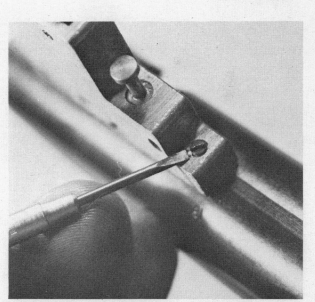

13. The trigger is retained by a roll cross-pin at the lower edge of the housing, and is removed downward. The same coil spring powers both the sear and the trigger.

14. The housing tension screw at the extreme front edge of the housing can be backed out if the housing mounting pin is unusually tight, as this will ease tension on the cross-pin.

15. Backing out the single screw at the rear of the magazine catch will allow removal of the magazine catch and magazine guide downward. The ejector is an integral part of the magazine guide.

16. Removal of the large screw just forward of the rear sight will allow the sight and sight base to be taken off upward.

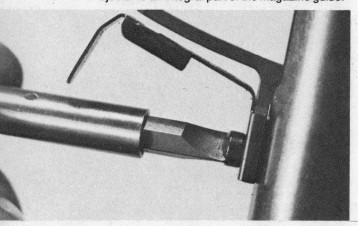

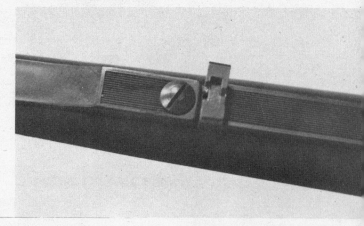

Reassembly Tips:

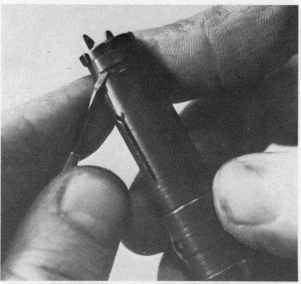

1. When replacing the safety lever, seat the tip of the safety spring plunger in the larger, dished-out recess on the inside of the lever while pushing the safety into place. In this position, the plunger will be less likely to slip out during installation.

2. When replacing the semi-circular spring clip at the front of the bolt that retains and powers the extractors, note that the small central projection at its top must go toward the front, and its split wing toward the left. Use a small screwdriver to guide its lower end over the extractor as it is pushed into place

When replacing the extractors, note that the one with the sharp beak must be placed on the right.

WINCHESTER MODEL 70

Data:	Winchester Model 70
Origin:	United States
Manufacturer:	Winchester Repeating Arms Company New Haven, Connecticut
Cartridges:	From 222 to 458, including several magnum rounds
Magazine capacity:	Varies with cartridges
Over-all length:	42½ to 44½ inches
Barrel length:	22 and 24 inches
Weight:	About 7½ pounds

The original Model 70 first appeared in 1936, and was made until 1963. An "economy" version was made between 1964 and 1972, and since that time the original quality was resumed, with some of the innovations of the 1964 version retained. Collectors, and some shooters, treasure the pre-1964 "originals," but in some ways, the later guns, as now currently made, are mechanically superior. A list of the calibers and model variations of the Model 70 would nearly fill an entire page. The gun covered here is a late standard model. On the pre-1964 guns, the bolt detail is quite similar to the standard Mauser pattern.

Disassembly:

1. To remove the bolt, the safety must be in the off-safe position. Open the bolt, and depress the bolt stop, located at the left rear of the receiver. Hold it down, and withdraw the bolt toward the rear. For clarity, the bolt stop is indicated with a drift punch in the photo. It is depressed with a fingertip.

2. Remove the screws on the underside at the front and rear of the trigger guard. Note that on some Model 70 guns the magazine is a through-type, with a hinged cover-plate. The one shown in the photos is a closed type, with a solid stock underside. After the guard screws are removed, the guard can be taken off downward.

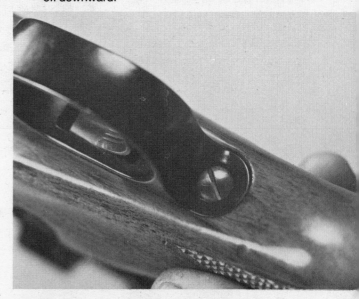

3. Remove the main stock mounting screw, on the underside below the chamber area. If the gun is a through-magazine type, this screw will be in the forward base of the magazine floorplate. When all three screws are removed, the action can be taken out of the stock.

4. If the gun is a blind-magazine type, the magazine follower, spring, and internal floorplate can be taken out upward. If the gun has an external floorplate, the floorplate and front hinge plate can be taken off downward. The plate is attached to its base with a cross-pin. A cross-pin also retains the floorplate catch and its spring in the front of the trigger guard.

5. The magazine box, or housing, is usually a tight press fit on the bottom of the receiver, and can be removed by exerting downward pressure while working it gently from side to side.

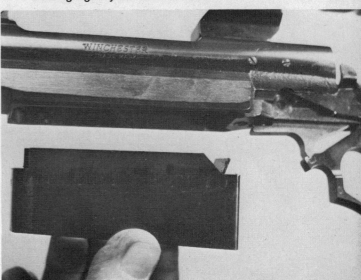

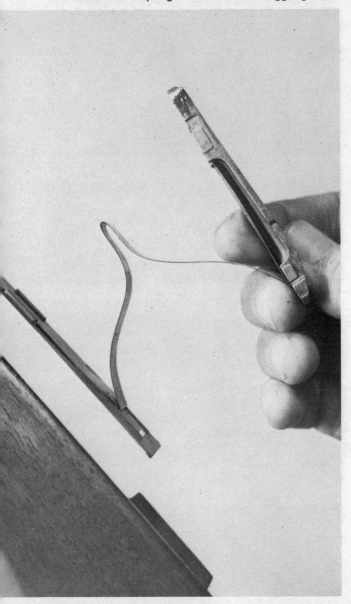

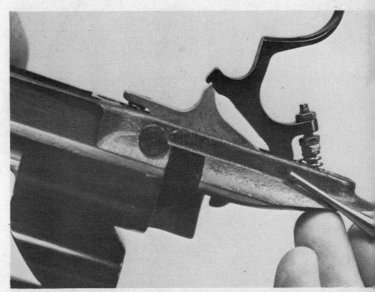

6. A cross-pin retains the trigger assembly on the underside of the receiver. Note that the trigger, its spring, and adjustment system can be removed downward without disturbing the adjustment. The cross-pin must be drifted out toward the left.

7. Note that the trigger pin has an enlarged head on the left side, and is also the pivot and retainer for the bolt stop and its spring. Before removal, note the relationship of the bolt stop, its spring, and the trigger, to aid reassembly. Restrain the spring as the pin is drifted out, and ease it off.

8. The bolt stop is moved downward and toward the rear for removal.

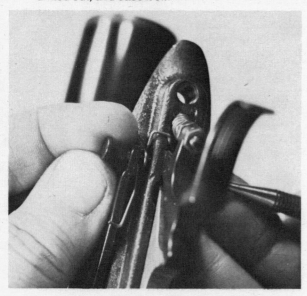

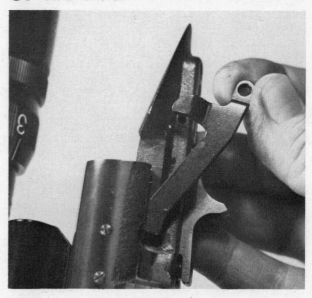

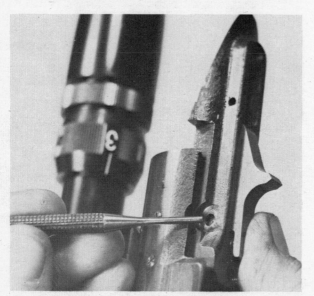

9. The sear is retained on the underside of the receiver by a cross-pin which must be drifted out toward the right. Restrain the sear against the tension of its strong spring, and remove the sear and spring downward.

10. Grip the lower lug of the cocking piece firmly in a vise, and move the bolt forward until the safety can be turned back to the safe position. Depress the bolt sleeve lock plunger, located on the left side of the bolt, and unscrew the rear section, the bolt sleeve. During this operation, take care that the safety is not tripped to the fire position.

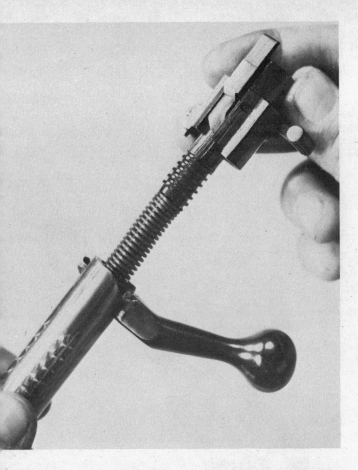

11. When the sleeve and striker assembly has cleared its internal threads, withdraw it toward the rear.

12. Grip the forward portion of the striker firmly in a vise, with the spring retaining C-clip and compression washer just above the vise jaws. Pry the compression washer upward, remove the C-clip, and allow the washer and spring to come down on the vise. With a firm hold on the bolt sleeve, open the vise, and slowly ease the assembly upward, releasing the tension of the spring. Take care not to lose the compression washer. If the gun is an older one, spring removal is done by simply pulling the firing pin sleeve slightly toward the rear, giving it a quarter-turn in either direction, and easing it off toward the front. After the tension is relieved, take off the spring toward the front.

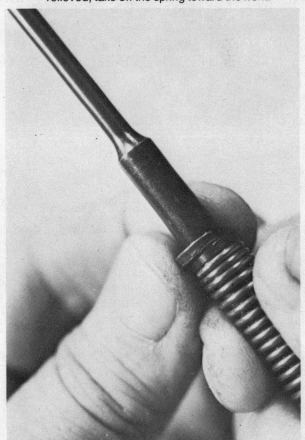

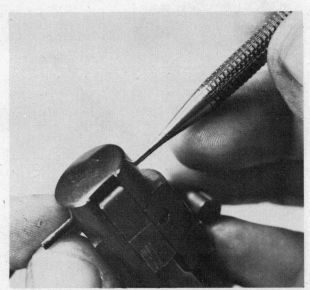

13. Drift out the cross-pin in the bolt end-piece, at the rear of the bolt sleeve.

14. Remove the bolt end-piece toward the rear. If it is tight, it can be tapped off by sliding the striker assembly against it.

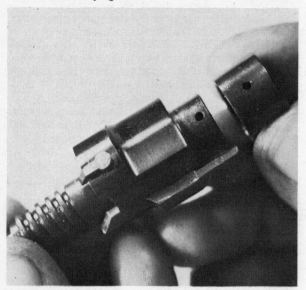

15. Remove the striker assembly from the rear of the bolt sleeve.

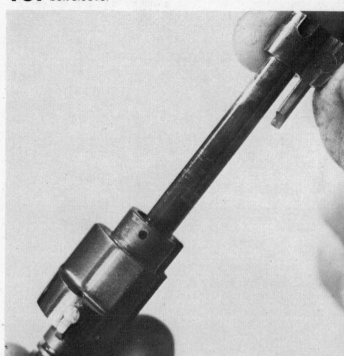

16. To remove the bolt sleeve lock plunger and spring, push out the retaining pin, which runs lengthwise in the sleeve, and take off the plunger and spring toward the side.

17. Use a very small drift punch to push the small pin beside the safety inward, into the interior of the bolt sleeve. The safety lever should be in the off-safe position.

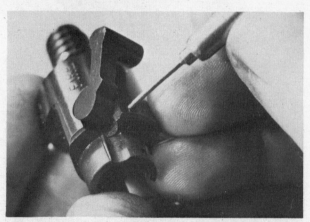

18. Turn the safety around toward the rear, then move it upward and out of the bolt sleeve. **Caution:** *The safety positioning spring and plunger will be released as the safety clears the sleeve, so restrain them and ease them out.*

19. To remove the ejector, drift out the angled cross-pin at the front of the bolt. **Caution;** *The strong ejector spring will expel the ejector as the drift is removed, so ease the ejector out toward the front, and remove the spring.*

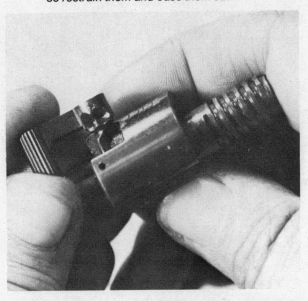

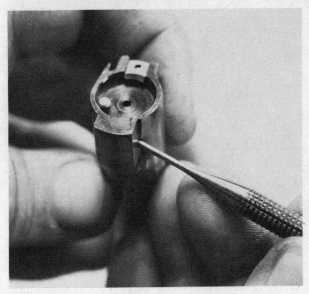

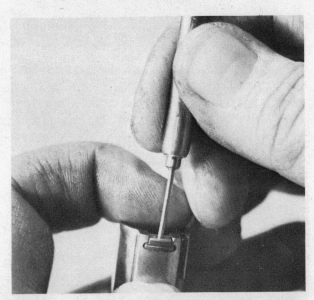

20. To remove the extractor, use a small-diameter drift punch to depress the extractor plunger, accessible through a small hole in the front face of the extractor. While keeping the plunger depressed, move the extractor out of its T-slot in the bolt lug. **Caution:** *Restrain the plunger and spring, and ease them out.* If the gun is an older one, it will have a long external Mauser-style extractor. For removal details on this type, see the Mauser or Springfield section.

Reassembly Tips:

1. When replacing the striker spring, note that the retaining C-clip has a recess on one side. This side must go toward the front. With the forward part of the striker gripped in a vise (as in disassembly), this means that the recess on the C-clip should be installed downward, toward the vise jaws.

2. Before the bolt sleeve and striker assembly can be reinstalled in the bolt body, the striker must be locked to the rear by placing the safety in the on-safe position. Grip the lower lug of the striker firmly in a vise, push the bolt sleeve toward the front, and set the safety. When the sleeve and striker assembly are back in the bolt body, the safety must be released to the off-safe position before the bolt can be re-inserted in the receiver.

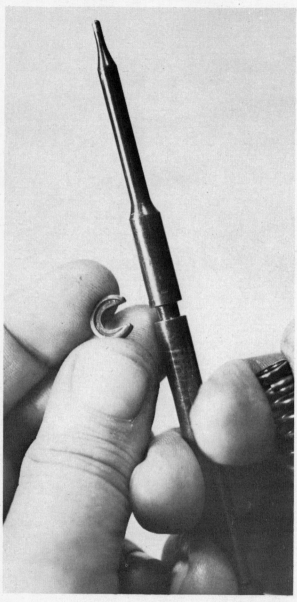

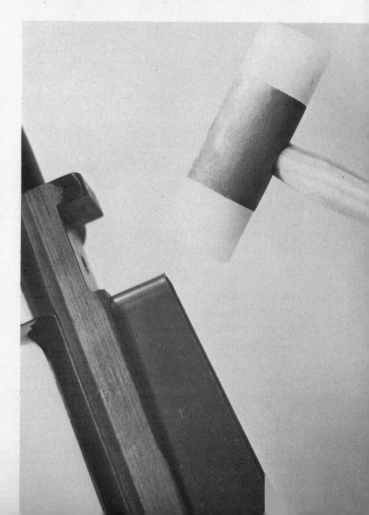

3. If the magazine housing has been removed, insert its rear edge into the recess first, then tap the front gently inward and toward the rear until it is in place.

Winchester
New Model 70 Bolt Action Rifle

COMPONENT PARTS FOR MODEL 70'S SERIALLY NUMBERED ABOVE 1,050,000

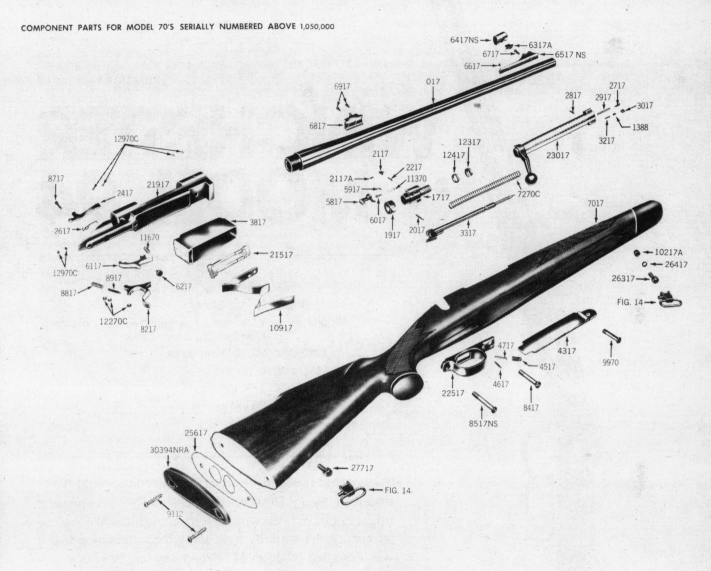

		7270C	Firing Pin Spring	**6217**	Sear Pin	
017	Barrel	**12317**	Firing Pin Spring Retainer	**11670**	Sear Spring	
23017	Breech Bolt—(Regular)	**12417**	Firing Pin Spring Washer	**6317A**	Sight, Front	
	Anti-Bind	**26317**	Fore-end Screw Eye	**6417NS**	Sight Cover, Front	
1717	Breech Bolt Sleeve	**26417**	Fore-end Screw Eye Washer	**6517NS**	Sight Ramp, Front	
1917	Breech Bolt Sleeve Cap	**10217A**	Fore-end Screw Eye	**6617**	Sight Ramp Screw, Front,	
2017	Breech Bolt Sleeve Cap		Escutcheon		(Short)	
	Pin	**3817**	Magazine	**6717**	Sight Ramp Screw, Front,	
2117	Breech Bolt Sleeve Lock	**4317**	Magazine Cover		(Long)	
2117A	Breech Bolt Sleeve Lock	**4517**	Magazine Cover Catch	**6817**	Sight, Rear—(Standard	
	Pin	**4617**	Magazine Cover Catch Pin		Barrel Only)	
2217	Breech Bolt Sleeve Lock	**4717**	Magazine Cover Catch	**6917**	Rear Sight Screws (2)	
	Spring		Spring	**27717**	Stock Swivel Stud	
2417	Breech Bolt Stop	**9970**	Magazine Cover Hinge	**7017**	Stock	
30394NRA	Butt Plate		Plate Screw	**12970C**	Telescope Sight Base	
25617	Butt Plate Spacer	**21517**	Magazine Follower		Plug Screws (6)	
9112	Butt Plate Screws (2)	**10917**	Magazine Spring	**8217**	Trigger	
2717	Ejector	**Fig. 14**	Quick Detachable Swivel	**22517**	Trigger Guard	
2817	Ejector Pin	**21917**	Receiver	**8417**	Trigger Guard Screw, Front	
2917	Ejector Spring	**5817**	Safety	**8517NS**	Trigger Guard Screw, Rear	
3017	Extractor	**5917**	Safety Pin	**8717**	Trigger Pin	
1388	Extractor Plunger	**6017**	Safety Plunger	**8817**	Trigger Spring	
3217	Extractor Spring	**11370**	Safety Plunger Spring	**8917**	Trigger Stop Screw	
3317	Firing Pin	**6117**	Sear	**12270C**	Trigger Stop Screw Nuts (3)	

WINCHESTER MODEL 94

Data:	Winchester Model 94
Origin:	United States
Manufacturer:	Winchester Repeating Arms Company New Haven, Connecticut
Cartridge:	30-30 Winchester
Magazine capacity:	6 rounds
Over-all length:	37¾ inches
Barrel length:	20 inches
Weight:	6½ pounds

To say that this gun needs no introduction would be an understatement. However, since some younger readers might not have been with us long enough to have learned its history, let's briefly pass along the information that it was designed by John M. Browning, and has been produced continuously by Winchester since 1894. It was originally chambered for two blackpowder loads, but for most of its production life the calibers have been the 30-30 and 32 Winchester Special, the latter recently discontinued. There have been several slight internal design changes along the way, but the instructions will generally apply to all 94s.

Disassembly:

1. Use a screwdriver with a wide, thin blade to remove the lever pin cover screw, located on the left side of the receiver at the upper front.

2. Use a drift punch to push out the lever pin toward the left. This is accessible through a small hole on the right side of the receiver, just above the front of the loading gate.

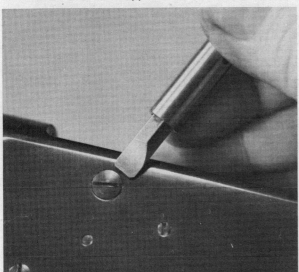

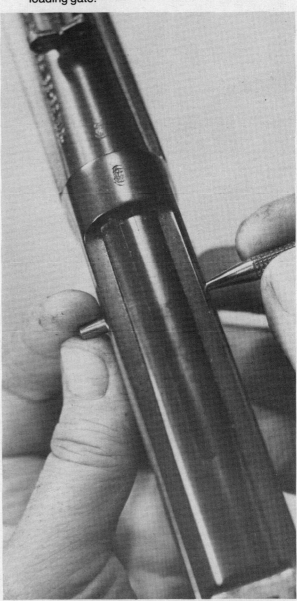

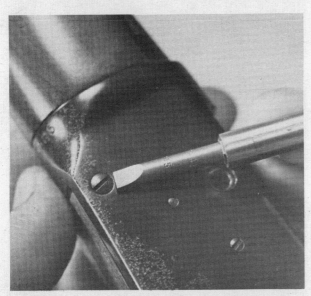

3. Remove the cross-screw that pivots the link plate at the lower left front of the receiver.

4. Move the lever downward, along with the attached link, then move them forward, disengaging the rear of the link from the locking block. The lever and link assembly are then removed downward.

5. Drifting out the large cross-pin in the link plate will release the lever for removal. Drifting out the small cross-pin at the rear of the link plate will release the plate latch plunger and its spring toward the rear. The spring is under tension, so restrain the plunger and ease it out.

6. Remove the carrier pivot screw toward the left. Note that on early guns, there are two separate screws, one on each side of the receiver.

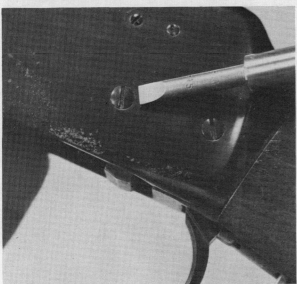

7. Remove the carrier downward.

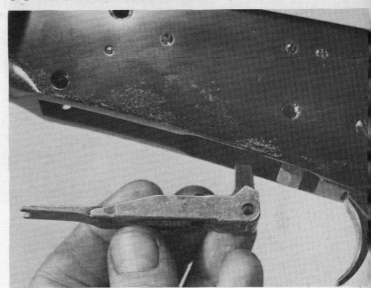

8. It should be noted that removal of the lever will have released the firing pin (in late guns), and if it needs to be taken out for repair, this can be done without further disassembly. In early guns, a firing pin retaining pin at the lower rear of the bolt must also be removed. Also, the extractor can be taken out by moving the bolt to the rear and drifting out its cross-pin or cross-pins (later guns have two).

9. Remove the vertical screw at the rear of the upper tang, and take off the stock toward the rear. If the stock is tightly fitted, bump the front of the comb with the heel of the hand to start it.

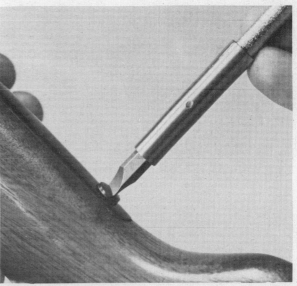

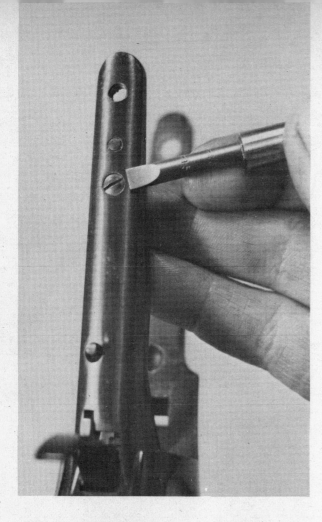

10. With the hammer lowered to the fired position, remove the hammer spring screw, located on the inside of the lower tang at the rear. This will be made easier by first backing out or removing the hammer spring strain screw, as shown.

11. Removal of the hammer spring screw will require an offset screwdriver, or one with an angled tip, as shown. After the screw is removed, the spring and its angled base are taken out toward the rear.

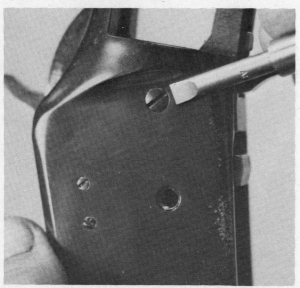

12. Remove the cross-screw that retains both the hammer and the lower tang/trigger housing. Remove the hammer upward and toward the rear.

13. Remove the lower tang/trigger housing unit toward the rear. If this assembly is tight, use a drift punch of nylon or some other non-marring material to nudge it out.

14. The locking block can now be removed downward. Drifting out the roll cross-pin near the top of the locking block will allow removal of the short firing pin striker.

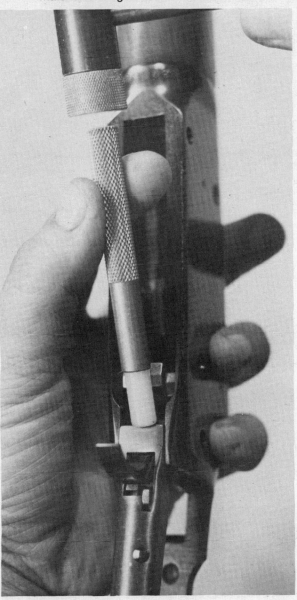

15. The breechblock (bolt) can now be moved straight out of the receiver toward the rear.

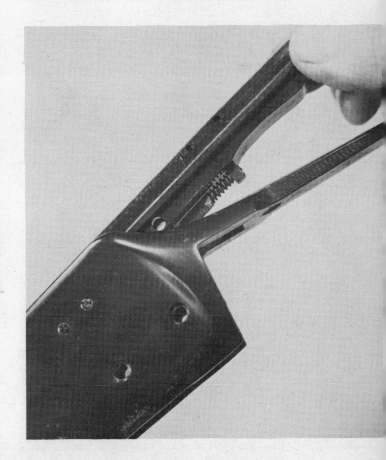

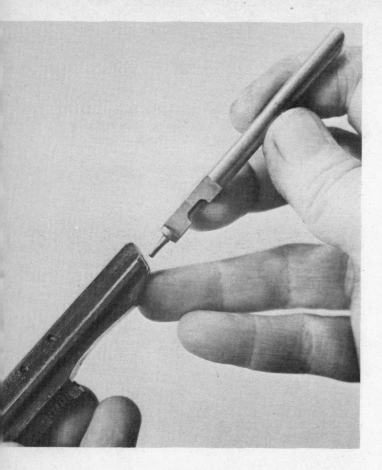

16. If it has not been previously removed, the firing pin can now be taken out of the bolt toward the rear. In early guns, a small retaining cross-pin at the lower rear of the bolt must be driven out to release the firing pin.

17. The extractor is retained in the top of the bolt by a single solid cross-pin (early guns), or by two roll cross-pins (late guns). After these are drifted out, the extractor is removed upward.

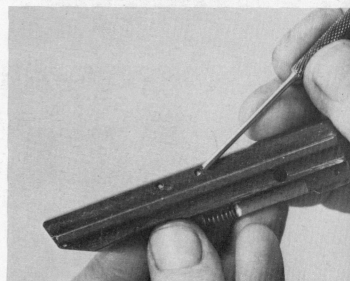

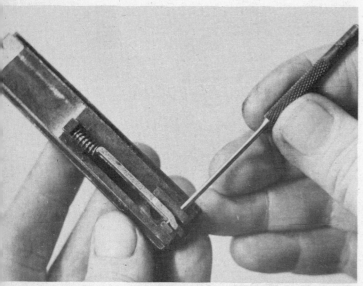

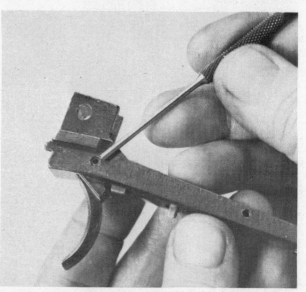

18. The ejector and its spring are retained on the underside of the bolt by a single cross-pin at the lower front. Use a roll pin drift to remove the pin, and take out the ejector and its spring toward the front.

19. The trigger and sear are retained in the trigger housing by a roll cross-pin that is the pivot for both parts. After the pin is drifted out, the trigger is removed downward, the sear toward the front.

20. A cross-pin at the center of the lower tang unit retains both the trigger stop and the combination spring that powers the stop and the sear. Drift out the pin toward the left, so the spring will be released first.

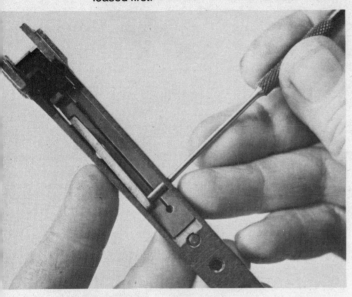

21. Remove the screw on the right side of the receiver directly to the rear of the loading gate, and take out the loading gate from inside the receiver.

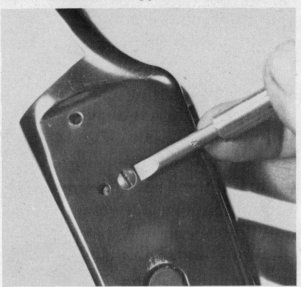

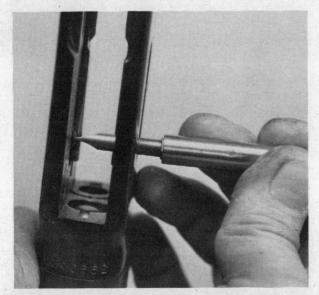

22. With the loading gate removed, the screw that retains the carrier spring will be accessible through the front portion of the loading port. Remove the screw, and take out the spring from inside the receiver.

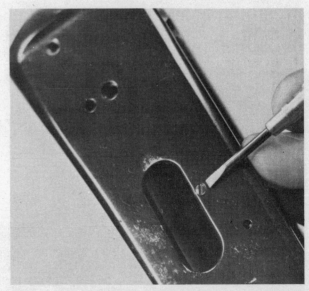

23. There are two small screws, one on each side of the receiver, the one on the right being just above the loading port. These retain the right and left cartridge guides inside the receiver. In normal takedown, these are best left in place, as any slight misalignment during reassembly can cause problems, one of which is possible stripping of the screws.

24. Removal of the vertical screw at the forward end of the magazine tube will allow the magazine plug, magazine spring, and follower to be taken out toward the front. **Caution:** *The magazine spring is under some tension, so control it and ease it out.*

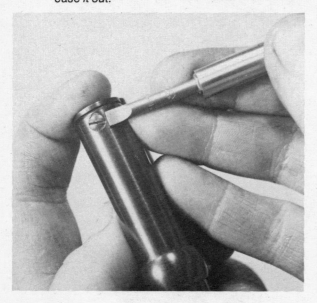

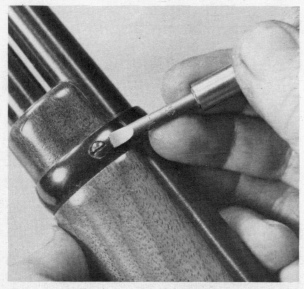

25. Remove the cross-screw from the front barrel band. Remove the cross-screw from the rear barrel band, and slide the barrel band forward, off the front of the fore-end wood. The magazine tube can now be moved out toward the front, and the fore-end can be moved slightly forward and taken off downward.

Reassembly Tips:

1. When replacing the locking block in the receiver, note that the upper wings of the block must be toward the rear.

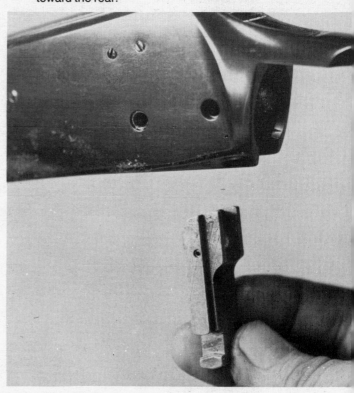

When replacing the firing pin in the breechblock, note that it must be oriented for insertion of the lever, with its front recess on the left side—see step number 16.

When replacing the loading gate, hold it in position inside the receiver with a fingertip, centering the hole for insertion of the screw. To align the screw for proper start, allow the front tip of the gate to protrude from the loading port. As soon as the screw is started, though, be sure to depress the front of the gate inside the port before tightening the screw.

Winchester
New Model 94 Lever Action Carbine

COMPONENT PARTS FOR MODEL 94's SERIALLY NUMBERED ABOVE 2,700,000

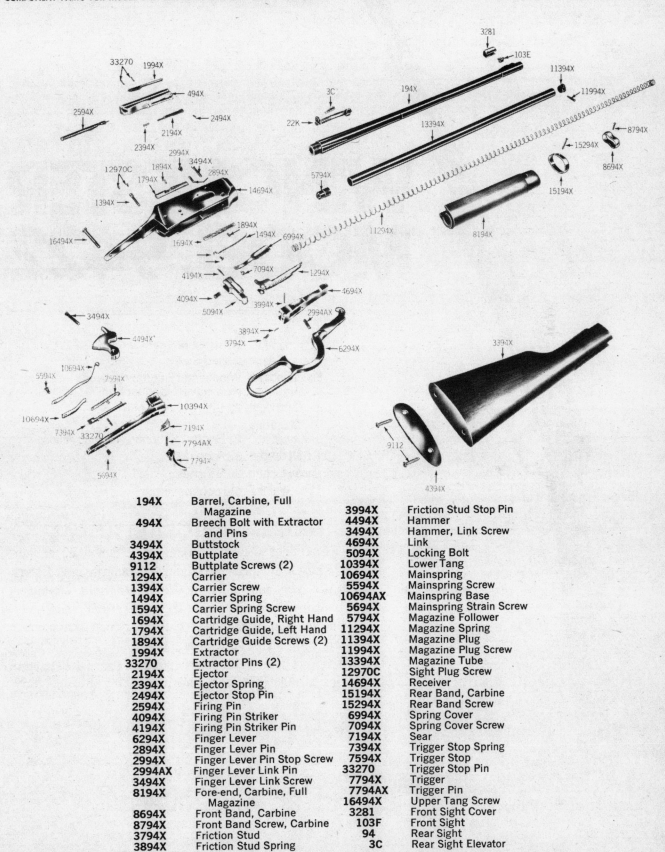

194X	Barrel, Carbine, Full Magazine	**3994X**	Friction Stud Stop Pin
494X	Breech Bolt with Extractor and Pins	**4494X**	Hammer
3494X	Buttstock	**3494X**	Hammer, Link Screw
4394X	Buttplate	**4694X**	Link
9112	Buttplate Screws (2)	**5094X**	Locking Bolt
1294X	Carrier	**10394X**	Lower Tang
1394X	Carrier Screw	**10694X**	Mainspring
1494X	Carrier Spring	**5594X**	Mainspring Screw
1594X	Carrier Spring Screw	**10694AX**	Mainspring Base
1694X	Cartridge Guide, Right Hand	**5694X**	Mainspring Strain Screw
1794X	Cartridge Guide, Left Hand	**5794X**	Magazine Follower
1894X	Cartridge Guide Screws (2)	**11294X**	Magazine Spring
1994X	Extractor	**11394X**	Magazine Plug
33270	Extractor Pins (2)	**11994X**	Magazine Plug Screw
2194X	Ejector	**13394X**	Magazine Tube
2394X	Ejector Spring	**12970C**	Sight Plug Screw
2494X	Ejector Stop Pin	**14694X**	Receiver
2594X	Firing Pin	**15194X**	Rear Band, Carbine
4094X	Firing Pin Striker	**15294X**	Rear Band Screw
4194X	Firing Pin Striker Pin	**6994X**	Spring Cover
6294X	Finger Lever	**7094X**	Spring Cover Screw
2894X	Finger Lever Pin	**7194X**	Sear
2994X	Finger Lever Pin Stop Screw	**7394X**	Trigger Stop Spring
2994AX	Finger Lever Link Pin	**7594X**	Trigger Stop
3494X	Finger Lever Link Screw	**33270**	Trigger Stop Pin
8194X	Fore-end, Carbine, Full Magazine	**7794X**	Trigger
8694X	Front Band, Carbine	**7794AX**	Trigger Pin
8794X	Front Band Screw, Carbine	**16494X**	Upper Tang Screw
3794X	Friction Stud	**3281**	Front Sight Cover
3894X	Friction Stud Spring	**103F**	Front Sight
		94	Rear Sight
		3C	Rear Sight Elevator

WINCHESTER MODEL 9422

Data:	Winchester Model 9422
Origin:	United States
Manufacturer:	Winchester Repeating Arms New Haven, Connecticut
Cartridge:	22 Short, Long, Long Rifle
Magazine capacity:	21 Shorts, 17 Longs, 15 Long Rifles
Over-all length:	37⅛ inches
Barrel length:	20½ inches
Weight:	6½ pounds

Introduced in 1972, the Model 9422 is the 22 caliber counterpart of the popular Model 94 centerfire gun. Externally it is very much like the Model 94, but the internal mechanism is quite different. The feed system is similar to the one used in the Model 61, making malfunctions extremely unlikely. The Model 9422 is fairly simple for a lever action, and with the exception of the cartridge stop and its spring, takedown and reassembly are relatively easy.

Disassembly:

1. Remove the magazine tube, and take out the large coin-slotted cross-screw at the rear of the receiver. A nickel fits the slot best. Separate the two sections of the gun, moving the rear portion down and toward the rear.

2. Remove the bolt assembly from the receiver toward the rear.

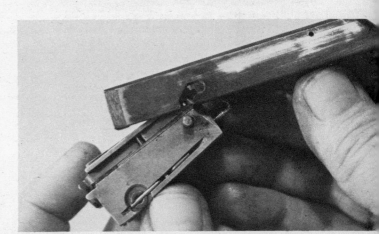

3. Separate the bolt from the bolt slide, and take out the bolt cam pin which crosses the bolt at the rear. The cam pin does not fit tightly, and can fall out, so take care that it isn't lost during disassembly.

4. Use a roll pin punch to drift out the cross-pin in the bolt slide, and remove the firing pin striker upward.

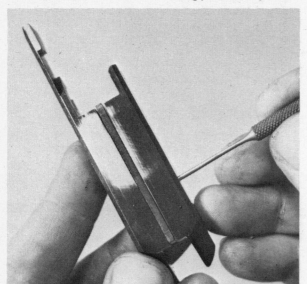

5. The firing pin is retained in the bolt by a roll pin across the upper rear, and the firing pin and its return spring are removed toward the rear.

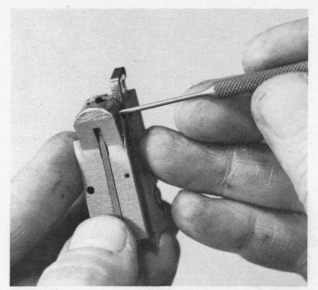

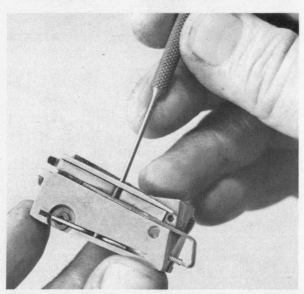

6. A vertical pin on the left side of the bolt retains three parts—the left extractor, the ejector, and the carrier pawl retainer. The extractor and pawl retainer are removed toward the left, and the ejector is moved out toward the rear. Take care that the small coil springs with the ejector and inside the carrier pawl are not lost.

7. The right extractor is retained by a vertical roll pin on the right side of the bolt. The pin is accessible through a hole in the bottom right of the bolt, and is driven out upward. The extractor and its coil spring are taken off toward the right.

8. The lower extractor, part of the feed system, is retained by a vertical roll pin, accessible through a hole in the top of the bolt on the right side, and the pin is driven out downward. The lower extractor and its spring are then removed toward the right. Keep the spring with the lower extractor, and don't get it confused with the upper one, as they are not interchangeable.

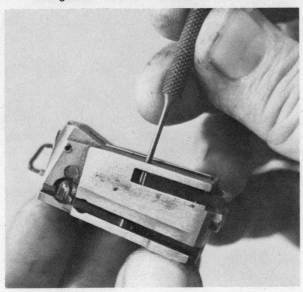

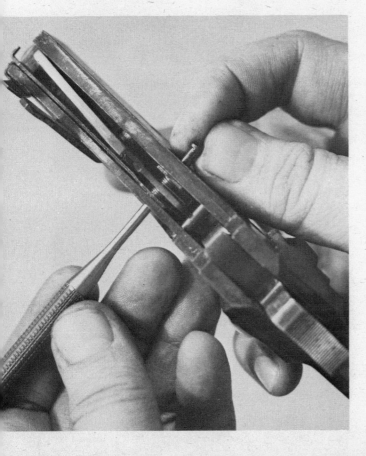

9. Remove the buttplate, and use a B-square stock bolt tool, or a long screwdriver, to take out the stock retaining bolt. When the bolt is out, take off the buttstock toward the rear.

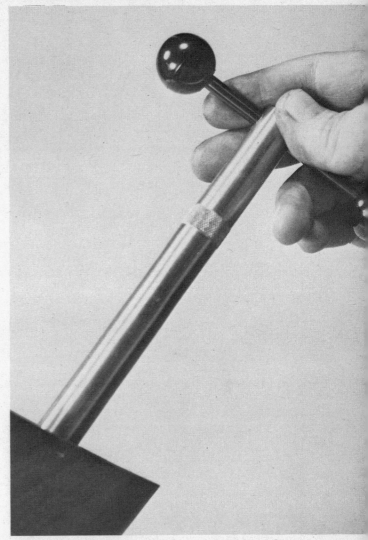

10. Before removing the carrier and cartridge stop, carefully note the position and relationship of the combination spring which powers these parts, to aid in reassembly. Push out the cross-pin which pivots and retains the cartridge stop, carrier, and the spring. All are removed upward, but the cartridge stop must be moved slightly forward before being lifted out. **Caution:** *The spring is under some tension, so keep the parts under control when pushing out the cross-pin.*

11. Use a roll pin punch to drift out the hammer stop pin, located just forward of the hammer. Set the hammer on its safety step while the stop pin is drifted out.

12. Restrain the hammer against its spring tension, pull the trigger to release it, and ease the hammer forward, past its normal down position. This will relieve the tension of the hammer spring, and the spring and its guide strut can then be removed at the rear, toward either side.

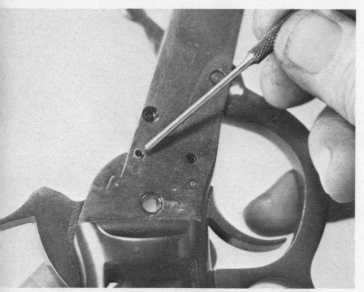

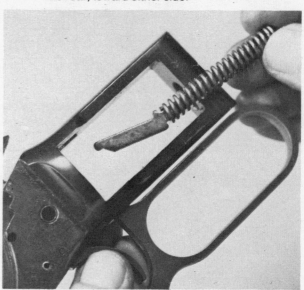

13. The hollow hammer pivot is now easily pushed out toward either side, and the hammer is removed upward. If the hammer pivot is tight, use a non-marring tool as large as its diameter, and take care not to deform its end edges.

14. With an Allen wrench of the proper size, take out the screw that retains the lever tension spring and its plate, and remove the plate and spring upward.

15. Push out the lever pivot pin toward the left, and remove the lever downward. Tip the upper lever arm toward the left as it is lifted out of its semi-circular opening, and remove it.

16. Drifting out the solid cross-pin above the trigger will release the trigger downward. The trigger spring is retained by a roll pin, just forward of the trigger pin.

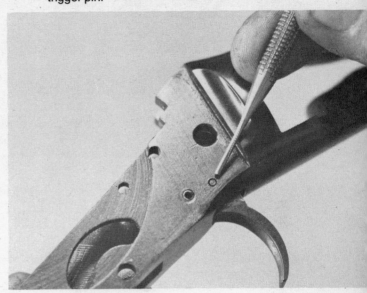

17. Remove the cross-screw in the rear barrel band, and slide the band off toward the front. If the band is very tight, it will be necessary to nudge it with a nylon drift and hammer. Nudge it equally, on alternate sides, to avoid binding.

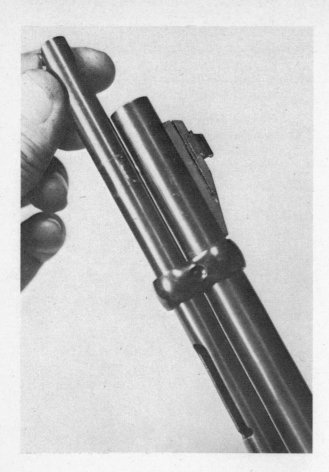

18. Remove the cross-screw from the front barrel band, and slide the outer magazine tube out toward the front.

19. Remove the fore-end forward and downward.

20. The barrel is retained in the receiver by a cross-pin that is riveted on the right side. The pin must be driven out toward the left. The barrel can then be gripped in a padded vise and the receiver driven off with a wood or nylon mallet. In normal disassembly, however, the barrel is best left in place.

Reassembly Tips:

1. When replacing the outer magazine tube, be sure it is installed to its proper depth, and that the shallow groove in its top is aligned with the cross-screw hole in the front barrel band.

2. To install the carrier, cartridge stop, and combination spring without great difficulty will require the use of a slave pin, a short length of rod stock to hold the parts together while they are positioned for insertion of the cross-pin. The photo shows the proper arrangement of the parts and the spring, with the slave pin in place. The longer left arm of the spring goes below the hammer stop pin.

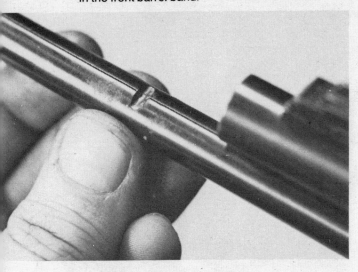

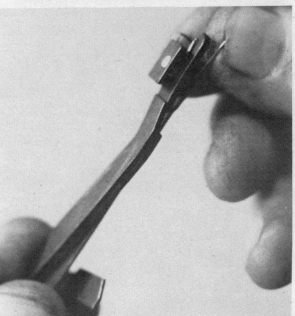

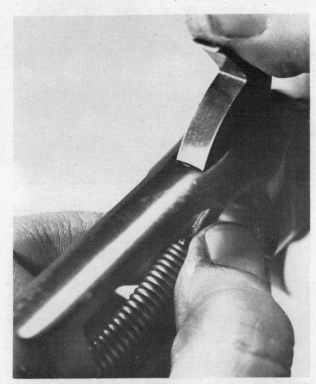

3. When replacing the hammer strut and spring, guide the spring at the rear to position the rear tip of the strut in alignment with its hole in the rear vertical bar of the trigger group. Be sure the front tip of the strut enters its recess on the rear of the hammer as the hammer is drawn back to the safety step.

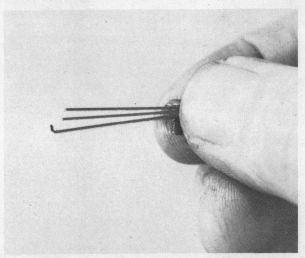

4. When replacing the lever tension system in the front of the trigger group, note that the single or double spring leaves go on top, and the L-shaped plate on the bottom, with the short arm of the "L" upward.

5. When replacing the lever, note that the upper arm of the lever must be in position in the trigger group before the lever is moved into place.

6. When replacing the bolt assembly in the receiver, the bolt and bolt slide should be engaged as shown, with the bolt in the unlocked position, as the assembly is moved into the rear of the receiver.

Winchester
Model 9422 Lever Action Carbine

149	Barrel, Carbine	3049	Firing Pin Spring
249	Barrel Retaining Pin	3149	Firing Pin Retainer Pin
349	Breech Bolt	3249	Firing Pin Striker
549	Bolt Cam Pin	3349	Firing Pin Striker Retaining
649	Bolt Guide With Pad		Pin
749	Bolt Slide	3449	Fore-end
949	Buttstock	3549	Front Band
14102	Buttstock Bolt	3649	Front Band Screw
15102	Buttstock Bolt Washer	3749	Finger Lever
694X	Buttplate	3849	Finger Lever Arm
9112	Buttplate Screws (2)	3949	Finger Lever Pin
1049	Carrier	4049	Finger Lever Spring
1149	Carrier Pawl	4149	Finger Lever Spring Plate
1249	Carrier Pawl Retainer	4249	Finger Lever Spring Screw
1349	Carrier Pawl Retainer Pin	4349	Frame
1449	Carrier Pawl Spring	4449	Hammer
1549	Carrier Pin	4549	Hammer Pivot Bushing
1649	Carrier Spring	4649	Hammer Spring
1749	Cartridge Cut Off	4749	Hammer Spring Guide Rod
1849	Ejector	4849	Hammer Stop and Trigger
1949	Ejector/Extractor Left and		Spring Pins (2)
	Extractor Lower Pins (2)	4949	Magazine Tube Inside
2049	Ejector Spring		Assembly
2149	Extractor Left	5049	Magazine Tube Outside
2249	Extractor Lower	5149	Rear Band
2349	Extractor Right Upper	15294X	Rear Band Screw
2449	Extractor Lower Spring	5249	Receiver
2549	Extractor Lower Helper	103H	Sight — Front
	Spring	3281	Sight — Front — Cover
2649	Extractor Right Upper	94	Sight — Rear
	Spring	3C	Sight Rear Elevator
2749	Extractor Right Upper	5449	Take Down Screw
	Helper Spring	5549	Trigger
2849	Extractor Right Upper Pin	5649	Trigger Pin
2949	Firing Pin	5749	Trigger Spring

BROWNING AUTOLOADER

Data: Browning Autoloader
Origin: Belgium
Manufacturer: Browning Arms Company
Morgan, Utah
(Made for Browning by FN in Belgium)
Cartridge: 22 Long Rifle
Magazine capacity: 11 rounds
Over-all length: 37 inches
Barrel length: 19¼ inches
Weight: 4¾ pounds

This neat little semi-auto rifle was first produced in 1914 by Fabrique Nationale in Belgium, and in 1922 the production rights for the U.S. were leased to the Remington company. It was made by them as the Model 24 and Model 241 until 1951. In 1956, an altered version of the original gun was introduced by Browning, and it is still in production. Through all of this time, some 65 years, the internal mechanism has been essentially unchanged. Except for minor variations in the extractor and cartridge guide systems, the instructions will apply to all of the guns by FN, Remington, and Browning.

Disassembly:

1. The takedown latch is located on the underside of the fore-end, at its rear edge. Push the latch forward into its recess in the fore-end.

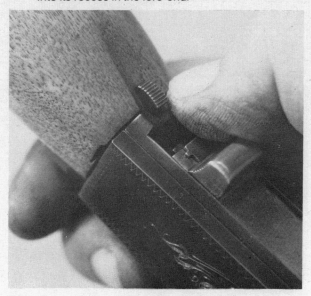

2. Retract the bolt slightly, and turn the barrel assembly clockwise (rear view) until it stops. Then, remove the barrel assembly toward the front.

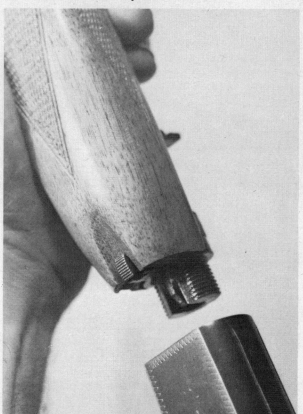

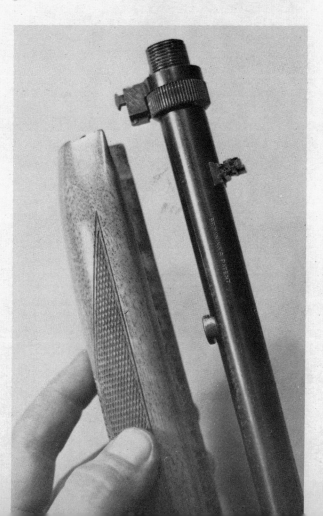

3. Remove the screw on the underside of the fore-end, and take off the fore-end downward.

4. Slide the takedown latch forward out of its base at the rear of the barrel. **Caution:** *Two plunger-and-spring assemblies will be released, and must be restrained to prevent loss.* The first will be the positioning plunger and spring at the rear of the latch, and the second will be the wedge-shaped plunger under the latch which bears on the barrel adjustment nut serrations. Ease both of these out, and take care that these small parts aren't lost.

5. Remove the takedown latch base ring toward the rear. Unscrew the knurled barrel adjustment nut and remove it toward the rear.

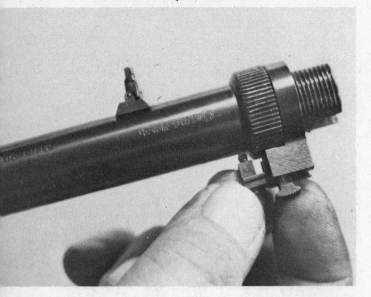

7. Pull the trigger to release the striker into the bolt, then move the front of the bolt upward out of the guard unit and ease it off forward. **Caution:** *Both the bolt spring and the striker spring are under some tension, so take care that they don't get away.* Remove the springs and their guides from the rear of the bolt.

6. Insert a finger through the trigger guard, place the thumb on the bolt handle, and retract the bolt to the rear while exerting forward pressure on the guard. The trigger group and bolt assembly can now be moved forward together and removed downward.

8. Remove the striker from the rear of the bolt.

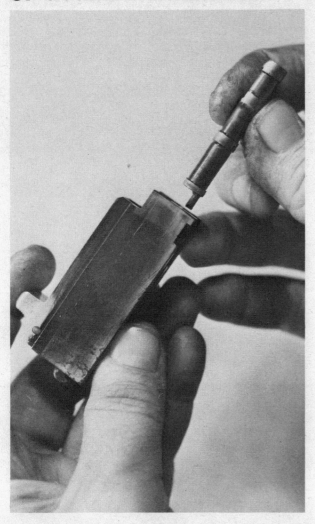

9. Drifting out the cross-pin at the lower front of the bolt will release the extractor retainer and allow removal of the extractor and its spring downward.

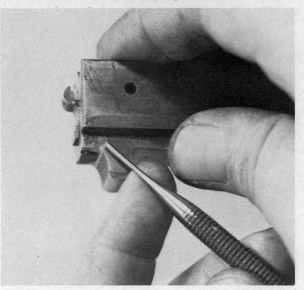

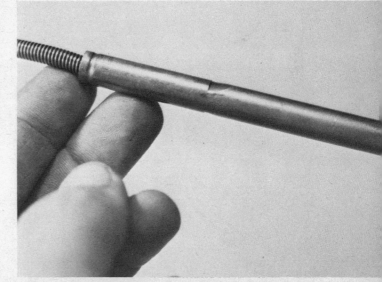

10. To remove the inner magazine tube, pull it out until it stops, then turn it 180 degrees to clear its side steps from the detents in the outer tube and take it out toward the rear.

11. Drifting out the locking cross-pin at the head of the inner magazine tube will allow removal of the handle piece, spring, feed cable, and follower.

12. Use a very wide screwdriver or a special shop-made tool to remove the nut at the rear of the buttstock, and its lock-washer, and take off the stock toward the rear. The outer magazine tube can now be unscrewed from the rear of the receiver. **Caution:** *Avoid gripping it too tightly and deforming it.*

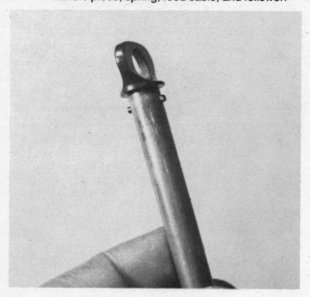

13. Swing the cartridge stop toward the inside wall of the receiver to clear its inner arm and lift it out of its privot-hole in the roof of the receiver. It should be noted that on older guns that have seen a lot of use, the cartridge stop may fall out when the bolt and trigger assembly are removed, so be sure it isn't missed and lost.

14. Removal of the cartridge guide spring in the top front of the receiver will release the cartridge guide to be taken out toward the front. To remove the spring, use a small tool to pry its rear loop from beneath its flange in the receiver.

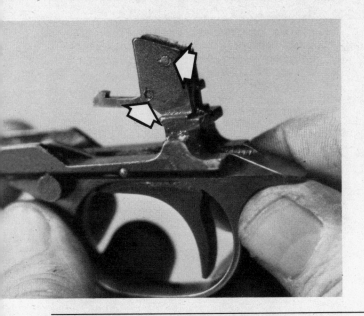

15. Drifting out the small cross-pin (upper arrow) at the top of the vertical trigger group extension will release the sear spring and plunger for removal upward. Drifting out the sear pivot pin (lower arrow) will allow the sear to be taken out toward the front. The trigger and disconnector pivot on the same pin, and are removed as a unit, along with the disconnector spring. The disconnector can be separated from the trigger by drifting out the short pin that mounts it in the trigger. To remove the safety, use a small screwdriver to depress the plunger and spring inside, at the center, under the safety, and move the safety out toward the right. **Caution:** *Control the compressed spring and plunger and ease them out.*

Reassembly Tips:

1. When replacing the striker in the bolt, note that the striker has a guide lug on its left side that mates with a track inside the bolt.

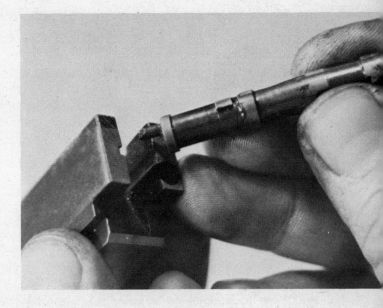

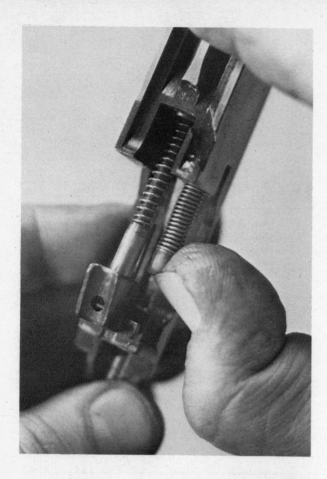

2. When replacing the bolt in the trigger group, carefully compress the recoil spring on its guide, then use a fingertip to hold the spring and guide in place on the bolt while fitting the bolt into place, inserting the tip of the striker spring guide into its hole in the vertical extension. Then, fit the rear bracket of the bolt spring guide onto its lug on the extension. **Caution:** *While the bolt spring is compressed, keep it aimed away from your eyes, in case the finger should slip.*

3. When reassembling the takedown latch system, be sure the small wedge-tipped plunger on the underside of the latch is oriented so the wedge tip aligns with the serrations on the adjustment nut. Use a small screwdriver to depress the two plungers alternately as the latch is moved into place.

4. To readjust the barrel nut, install the barrel on the gun before replacing the fore-end, lock the takedown latch in place, and turn the knurled adjustment nut until the ring is snug against the receiver. Then, reinstall the fore-end.

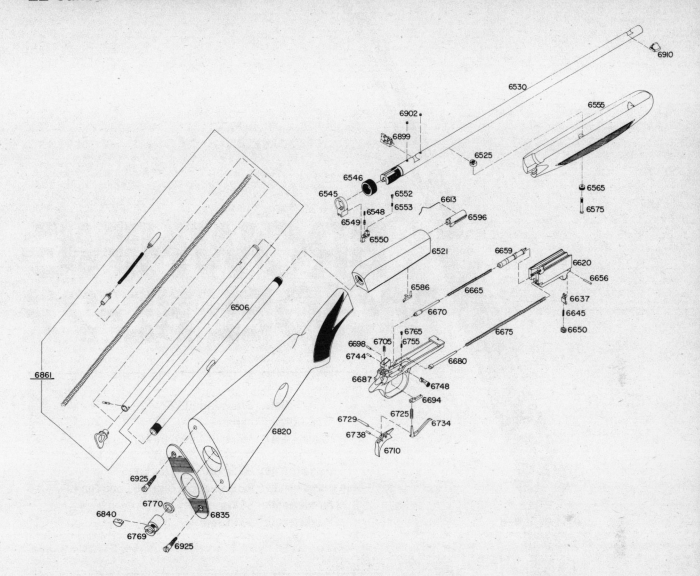

6506	Magazine Tube, Outer	6675	Recoil Spring
6521	Receiver	6680	Recoil Spring Guide
6525	Fore-end Retaining Stud	6687	Trigger Guard
6530	Barrel	6694	Sear
6545	Barrel Lock Ring	6698	Sear Pin
6546	Barrel Adjusting Ring	6705	Sear Spring
6548	Barrel Lock Spring	6710	Trigger
6549	Barrel Lock Spring Plunger	6725	Trigger Spring
6550	Barrel Lock	6729	Trigger Pin
6552	Barrel Adj. Ring Follower	6734	Disconnector
6553	Barrel Adj. Ring Follower Spring	6738	Disconnector Pin
6555	Fore-end	6744	Sear Spring Pin
6565	Fore-end Escutcheon	6748	Safety, Right & Left Hand
6575	Fore-end Screw	6755	Safety Spring
6586	Cartridge Stop	6765	Safety Spring Plunger
6596	Cartridge Guide	6769	Stock Nut
6613	Cartridge Guide Spring	6770	Stock Nut Washer
6620	Breech Block	6820	Buttstock
6637	Extractor	6925	Buttplate Screws (2)
6645	Extractor Spring	6835	Buttplate
6650	Extractor Spring Retainer	6840	Magazine Tube Stop Spring
6656	Extractor Spring Retainer Pin	6861	Magazine Assembly
6659	Firing Pin	6899	Rear Sight Assembly
6665	Firing Pin Spring	6902	Scope Mount Base Filler Screws (2)
6670	Firing Pin Spring Guide	6910	Front Sight

BROWNING MODEL BL-22

Data: Browning BL-22
Origin: Japan
Manufacturer: Made in Japan by Miroku for Browning Arms, Morgan, Utah
Cartridge: 22 Short, Long, or Long Rifle
Magazine capacity: 22 Short, 17 Long, 15 Long Rifle
Over-all length: 36¾ inches
Barrel length: 20 inches
Weight: 5 pounds

Browning's neat little lever action 22 has been made by Miroku of Tokyo for the past ten years, and it will probably be around for many years to come. It is unique among currently-made 22-cal. lever actions in having the trigger mounted in the lever, rather than in the receiver. It also has a very short lever arc that allows operation of the action without removing the hand from the wrist of the stock. For the nonprofessional, some elements of the takedown and reassembly can be rather difficult.

Disassembly:

1. Remove the inner magazine tube, and set the hammer on its safety step. Partially open the action. Take out the large cross-screw at the rear of the receiver.

2. Move the sub-frame and buttstock assembly straight out toward the rear. Move it slowly, and insert a fingertip through the ejection port to restrain the ejector, as it will be released as the front of the bolt clears it.

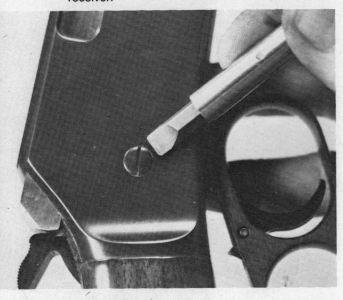

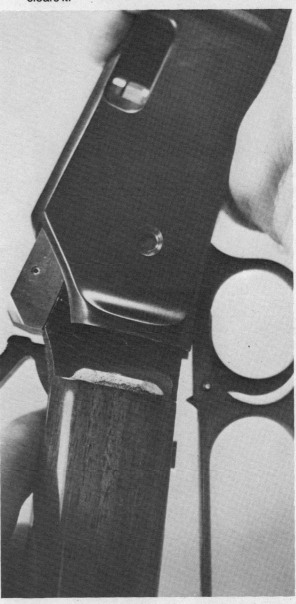

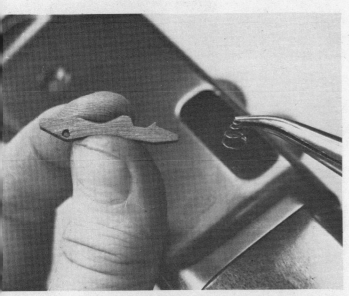

3. Remove the ejector spring from its recess in the left inner wall of the receiver. Move the ejector downward off its fixed pivot post, and take it out.

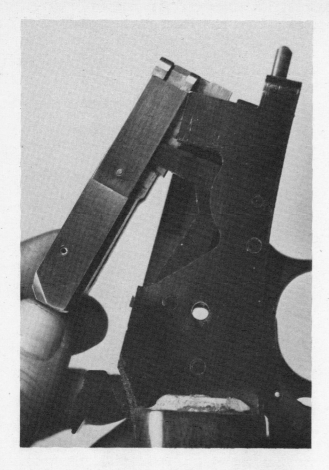

4. Tip the bolt upward at the rear, and move it a short distance toward the front.

5. Bring the rear of the bolt back down parallel with the top of the sub-frame, then lift the bolt off upward.

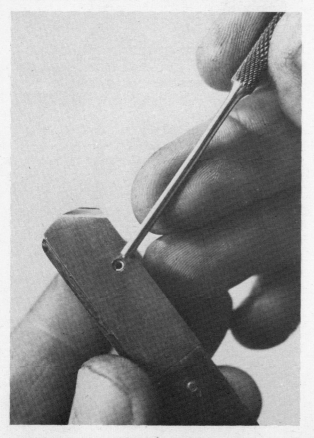

6. The firing pin and its return spring are retained in the bolt by a roll cross-pin. Drift out the pin, and remove the firing pin and spring toward the rear.

7. The bolt cover plate on the right side is taken off by prying it gently outward at the rear, equally at the top and bottom, until it snaps off its fixed mounting pin.

8. Insert a screwdriver blade between the extractor and its plunger, depress the plunger, and remove the extractor from its recess in the bolt. **Caution:** *Take care that the screwdriver doesn't slip, and ease out the plunger and spring.*

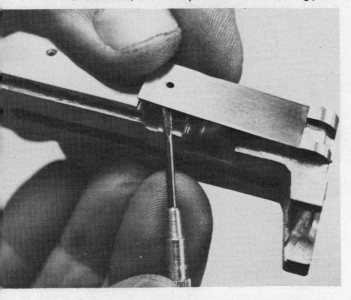

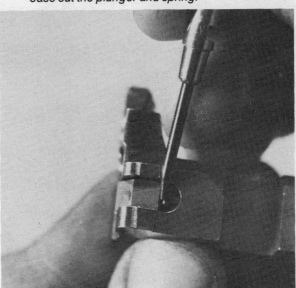

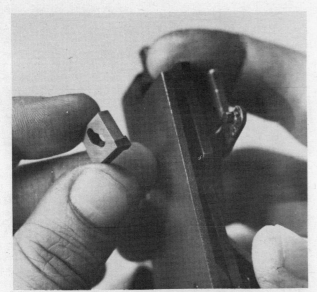

9. Depress the carrier, and remove the locking block from the lever link toward the left.

10. Unhook the carrier spring and allow its front arm to swing upward, relieving its tension.

11. Drift out the carrier pivot pin toward the right, and remove the carrier and its spring upward.

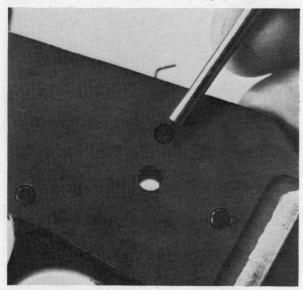

12. Removal of the carrier pin will also release the hammer stop block, and it can now be removed upward.

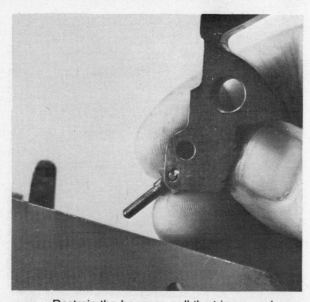

13. Restrain the hammer, pull the trigger, and ease the hammer down beyond its normal forward position, relieving the tension of its spring. Drift out the hammer pivot pin toward the right, and remove the hammer and its attached spring guide upward. The guide pin is staked in place, and should not be removed in normal takedown.

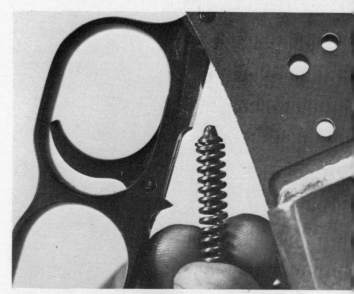

14. Open the lever, and remove the mainspring and its lower guide downward.

15. Drift out the lever link pivot pin.

16. Removal of the pin will allow the lever to be pivoted downward beyond its normal position, and the link can then be removed toward the right.

17. Drift out the lever pivot pin, and remove the lever downward.

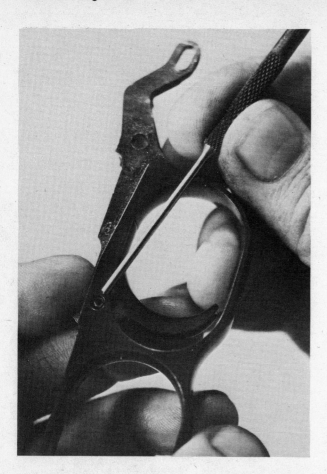

18. Drift out the roll cross-pin at the rear of the trigger, restrain the sear link, and remove the link and its spring upward.

19. Drift out the trigger cross-pin and remove the trigger and its spring upward.

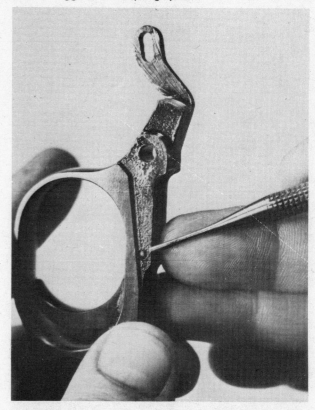

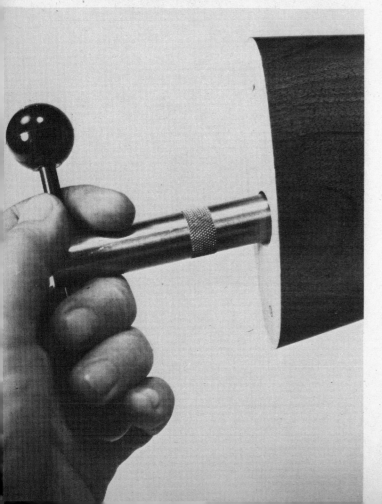

20. Remove the buttplate, and use a B-Square stock tool or a long screwdriver to remove the stock bolt. Take off the stock toward the rear.

21. Push out the cross-pin that retains the sear, and remove the sear and its spring downward.

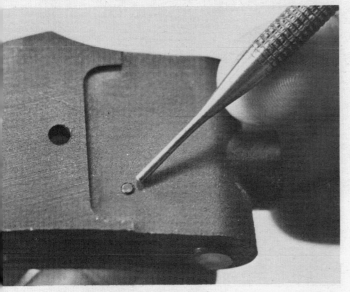

22. Remove the cross-screw in the front barrel band.

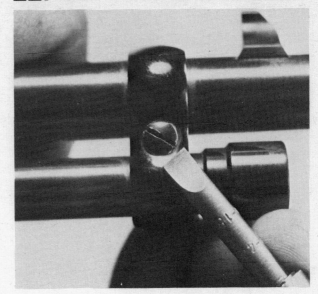

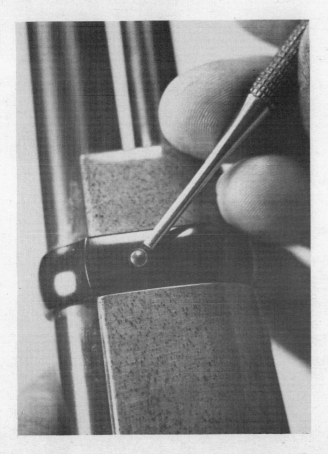

23. Drift out the cross-pin in the rear barrel band, and slide the band off the fore-end toward the front. Remove the outer magazine tube toward the front, and take off the fore-end downward. The front barrel band can be removed only after the front sight is drifted out of its dovetail.

Reassembly Tips:

1. After the sear is installed, flip it over and insert the spring, then rotate it back into position, and insert a tool from the top to nudge the spring onto its plate inside the frame.

2. After the hammer is installed, tip its spring guide upward, and fit the spring and lower guide onto it.

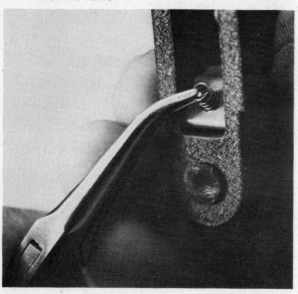

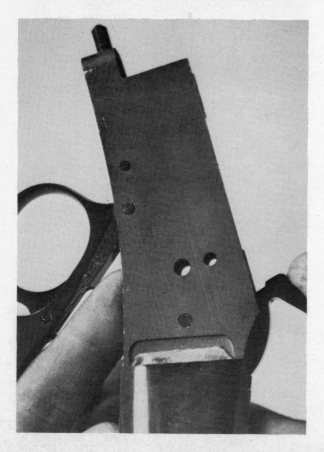

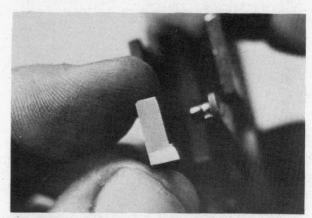

4. When replacing the locking block on the lever link, note that its side projection must be at the right rear, as shown.

3. Swing the mainspring assembly downward, with the lever in closed position. Pull the trigger to release the hammer, and tip it forward beyond its normal lowered position. Snap the nose of the lower spring guide into its recess on the lever. Open the lever, and insert a fingertip to support the underside of the spring while slowly cocking the hammer. **Caution:** *If solid resistance is felt, stop and be sure that the spring is being kept straight (it will tend to bow downward).*

Browning
BL-22 Lever Action Rifle

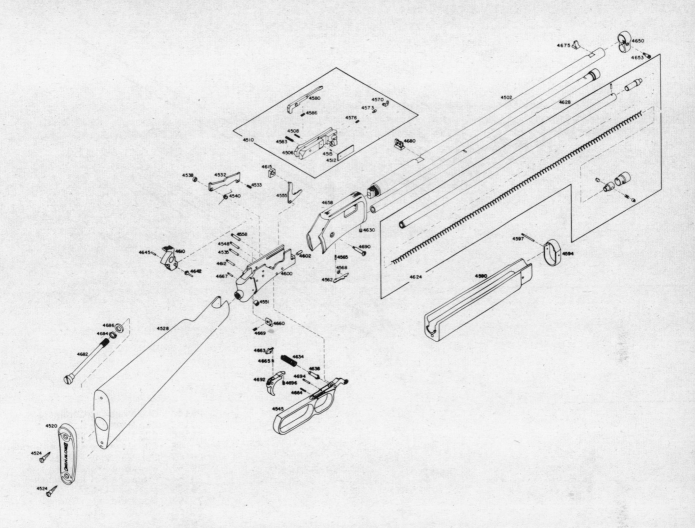

4502	Barrel	4600	Frame
4506	Bolt	4602	Frame Insert Pin
4508	Bolt Actuating Pin	4610	Hammer
4510	Bolt Assembly	4612	Hammer Pin
4512	Bolt Cover Plate	4615	Locking Block
4515	Bolt Cover Pin	4624	Magazine Assembly
4520	Buttplate	4628	Magazine Tube, Outer
4524	Buttplate Screws (2)	4630	Magazine Tube Retaining Screw
4528	Butt Stock	4634	Mainspring
4532	Carrier	4638	Mainspring Follower
4533	Carrier Guide Pin	4642	Mainspring Guide
4535	Carrier Pin	4645	Mainspring Guide Pin
4538	Carrier Spacer	4650	Muzzle Clamp
4540	Carrier Spring	4653	Muzzle Clamp Screw
4545	Cocking Lever	4658	Receiver
4548	Cocking Lever Pin	4660	Sear
4551	Cocking Lever Stop Screw	4663	Sear Link
4555	Cocking Lever Link	4664	Sear Link Pin
4558	Cocking Lever Link Pin	4665	Sear Link Spring
4562	Ejector	4667	Sear Pin
4565	Ejector Pin	4669	Sear Spring
4568	Ejector Spring	4675	Sight Front
4570	Extractor	4680	Sight Assembly, Rear
4573	Extractor Plunger	4682	Stock Bolt
4576	Extractor Spring	4684	Stock Bolt Lock Washer
4580	Firing Pin	4686	Stock Bolt Washer
4583	Firing Pin Retaining Pin	4690	Take-Down Screw
4586	Firing Pin Spring	4692	Trigger
4590	Fore-end	4694	Trigger Pin
4594	Fore-end Band	4696	Trigger Spring
4597	Fore-end Band Pin		

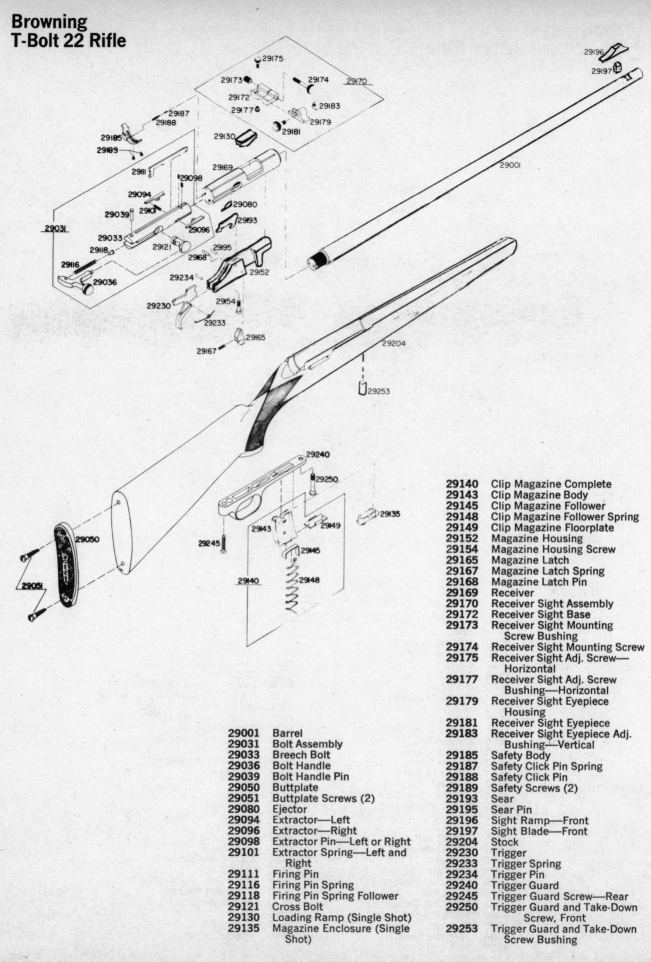

29140	Clip Magazine Complete
29143	Clip Magazine Body
29145	Clip Magazine Follower
29148	Clip Magazine Follower Spring
29149	Clip Magazine Floorplate
29152	Magazine Housing
29154	Magazine Housing Screw
29165	Magazine Latch
29167	Magazine Latch Spring
29168	Magazine Latch Pin
29169	Receiver
29170	Receiver Sight Assembly
29172	Receiver Sight Base
29173	Receiver Sight Mounting Screw Bushing
29174	Receiver Sight Mounting Screw
29175	Receiver Sight Adj. Screw— Horizontal
29177	Receiver Sight Adj. Screw Bushing—Horizontal
29179	Receiver Sight Eyepiece Housing
29181	Receiver Sight Eyepiece
29183	Receiver Sight Eyepiece Adj. Bushing—Vertical
29185	Safety Body
29187	Safety Click Pin Spring
29188	Safety Click Pin
29189	Safety Screws (2)
29193	Sear
29195	Sear Pin
29196	Sight Ramp—Front
29197	Sight Blade—Front
29204	Stock
29230	Trigger
29233	Trigger Spring
29234	Trigger Pin
29240	Trigger Guard
29245	Trigger Guard Screw—Rear
29250	Trigger Guard and Take-Down Screw, Front
29253	Trigger Guard and Take-Down Screw Bushing

29001	Barrel
29031	Bolt Assembly
29033	Breech Bolt
29036	Bolt Handle
29039	Bolt Handle Pin
29050	Buttplate
29051	Buttplate Screws (2)
29080	Ejector
29094	Extractor—Left
29096	Extractor—Right
29098	Extractor Pin—Left or Right
29101	Extractor Spring—Left and Right
29111	Firing Pin
29116	Firing Pin Spring
29118	Firing Pin Spring Follower
29121	Cross Bolt
29130	Loading Ramp (Single Shot)
29135	Magazine Enclosure (Single Shot)

BROWNING T-BOLT

Data:	Browning T-Bolt
Origin:	Belgium
Manufacturer:	Fabrique Nationale, Herstal (for Browning Arms, Morgan, Utah)
Cartridge:	22 Long Rifle
Magazine capacity:	5 rounds
Over-all length:	39¼ inches
Barrel length:	22 inches
Weight:	5½ pounds

The unusual "straight pull" bolt of this fine little gun is a masterpiece of good engineering, and works beautifully. Unfortunately, the average American shooter has never been fond of unusual actions, and the T-Bolt was imported for less than ten years, from 1965 to 1973. In addition to the plain T-1 model, a T-2 was offered, with 24-inch barrel and fancy stock. The gun was also available in a left-hand version. An accessory single-shot adapter would allow the use of 22 Short or Long, as well as Long Rifle. Except for the reversal of some directions in the left-hand model, the instructions will apply to all of them.

Disassembly:

1. Remove the magazine, and remove the main stock mounting screw, on the underside just forward of the magazine well. Separate the action from the stock.

2. Removal of the wood screw at the rear of the trigger guard unit will allow the guard to be taken off downward.

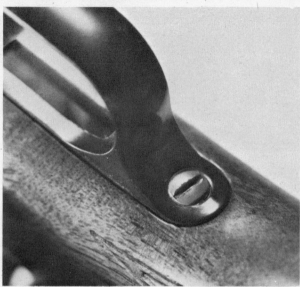

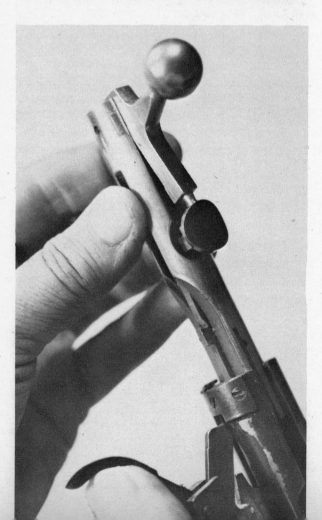

4. With the bolt handle in the closed (locked) position, push the vertical pin at the rear of the bolt upward, and remove it.

3. To remove the bolt, hold the trigger to the rear, and move the bolt out the rear of the receiver.

5. Remove the bolt handle toward the rear.

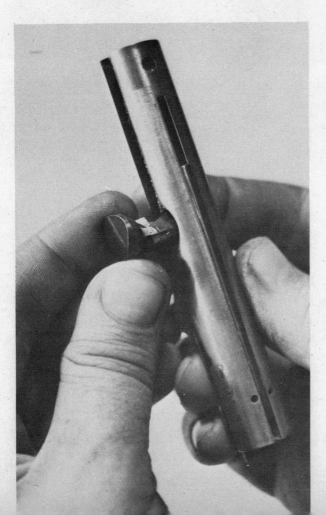

6. Remove the striker spring and its plunger toward the rear.

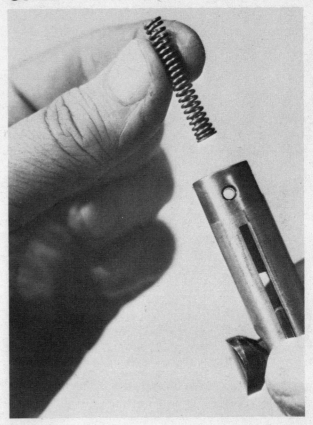

7. Turn the locking block ("cross-bolt") slightly to raise the firing pin out of its inside shoulder, and remove the locking block toward the right.

8. Remove the firing pin from its channel in the top of the bolt.

9. The twin extractors are retained by two vertical roll pins at the front of the bolt. Use a roll pin punch to drift out the pins, and remove the extractors from each side, along with the single transverse coil spring that powers both.

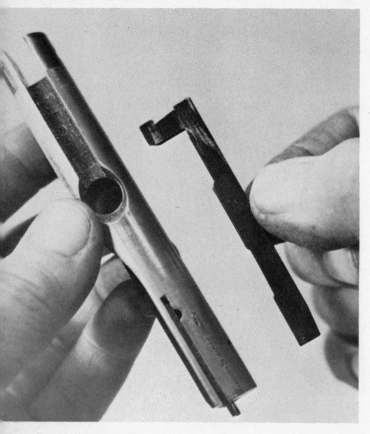

10. Push out the magazine catch cross-pin, and remove the magazine catch and its coil spring downward.

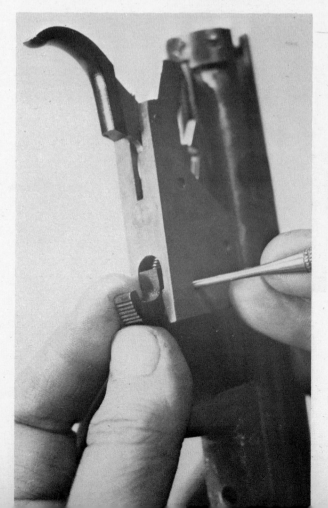

11. Removal of the magazine catch will give access to the magazine housing screw, which is taken out downward.

12. Remove the magazine housing downward.

13. Push out the cross-pin at the top of the magazine housing, and remove the sear upward and toward the front.

14. Note the relationship of the trigger and its spring before removal, to aid in reassembly. Push out the cross-pin at the lower rear of the magazine housing, and remove the trigger and its spring toward the rear and downward. Take care that the trigger spring isn't lost. Restrain it, and ease it out.

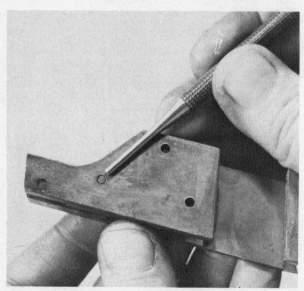

15. The trigger stop pin can also be drifted out, but can be left in place, as it retains no part.

16. The ejector is easily pushed from its slot in the underside of the receiver for removal.

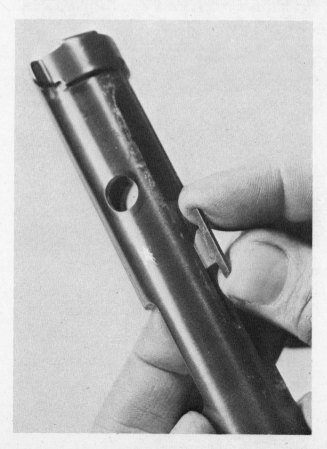

17. Removal of the two screws in the outer band of the safety catch at the rear of the receiver will allow the catch to be taken off. **Caution:** *Removal of the safety will release the safety positioning plunger and spring, so restrain them and ease them out.*

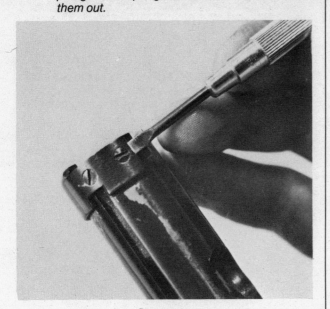

Reassembly Tips:

1. When replacing the ejector in its slot in the underside of the receiver, be sure its vertical face is toward the front, and its angled end toward the rear, as shown.

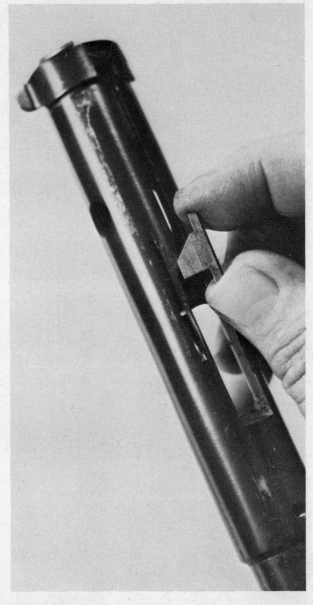

2. When replacing the trigger and its spring, taking out the trigger stop pin will make this operation easier. Insert the cross-pin from the right, just far enough to hold the spring in position, then put in the trigger, and move the cross-pin the rest of the way across. Be sure the front arm of the spring is against its shoulder or shelf inside the housing.

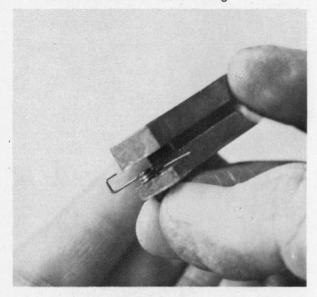

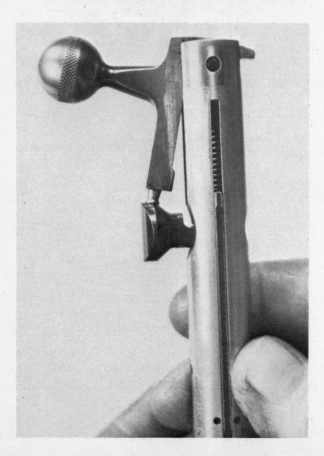

3. When replacing the locking cross-bolt in the body of the bolt, note that the face with the deep cut and hole must be oriented toward the rear, and install the locking bolt before the firing pin is returned to its channel.

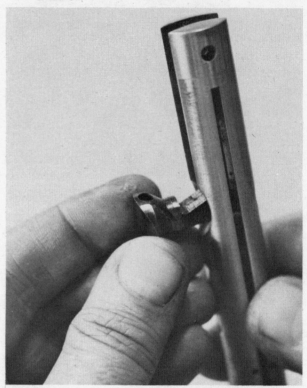

4. When replacing the bolt handle, be sure its front projection enters the hole in the rear face of the locking bolt, and note that the handle must be in the unlocked position, as shown, when the bolt is inserted into the receiver.

BROWNING BAR

Data: Browning BAR
Origin: Belgium
Manufacturer: Fabrique Nationale, Herstal, for Browning, Morgan, Utah
Cartridges: 243, 270, 30-06, 308, 7mm Remington Magnum, 300 Winchester Magnum
Magazine capacity: 4 rounds (3 in magnum)
Over-all length: 43 and 45 inches
Barrel length: 22 and 24 inches
Weight: 7⅜ and 8⅜ pounds

The factory designation of this gas-operated semiauto sporter has caused a little confusion, as the famed military selective-fire gun was also called the ''BAR.'' The sleek sporting rifle was introduced in 1967, and it is still in production. The gun is offered in several grades, the price depending on the extent of stock checkering, carving, engraving, and inlay work. Regardless of the grade, the mechanical details are the same, and the instructions will apply.

Disassembly:

1. With the empty magazine in place, pull back the cocking handle to lock the bolt in open position. With a small wrench or a pair of smooth-jawed pliers, unscrew the front sling swivel base, on the underside of the fore-end near the forward end.

2. Tip the front of the fore-end downward until firm resistance is felt, then move it forward and off. Do this carefully, and use no extreme force, or the fore-end will be damaged.

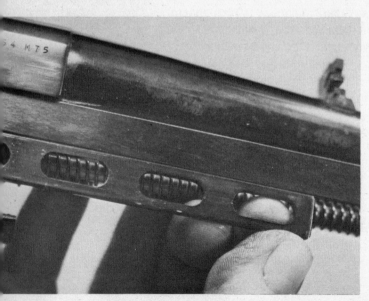

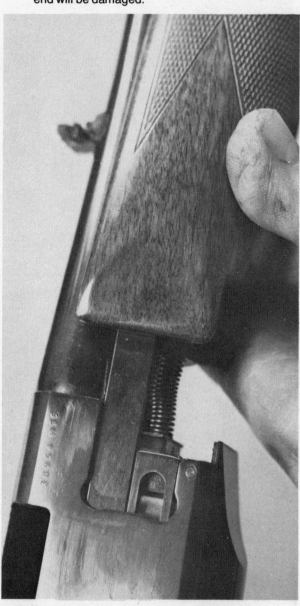

3. Slide the right and left action rod support rails out of the receiver toward the front, and remove them.

4. Disengage the forward ends of the action bars from the studs on the sides of the intertia block, and take the bars out toward the front.

5. Remove the gas regulator from the front end of the gas cylinder. A ⅝-inch open-end wrench will fit the side flats of the regulator, and it is simply unscrewed. Be sure the wrench is properly engaged to prevent marring. Take care not to lose the lock washer behind the gas regulator.

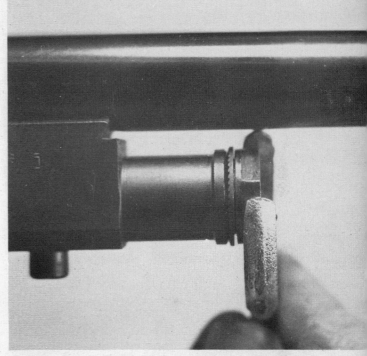

6. Remove the gas piston toward the front. If the piston is very tight, it may have to be nudged from the rear with a drift punch. If this is necessary, be very careful, as any burrs raised will cause the system to malfunction. If the piston won't move with the use of reasonable force, soak it for a time in a good powder solvent or penetrant.

7. Firmly grip the action spring guide at the rear, and lift its rear tip out of its seat in the front of the receiver. Remove the guide, spring, and inertia block toward the rear. **Caution:** *Keep a firm grip on the partially compressed spring, and ease it off.*

8. Open the magazine floorplate, and insert a small screwdriver at the rear of the magazine to pry it away from the floorplate. Remove the magazine from the floorplate.

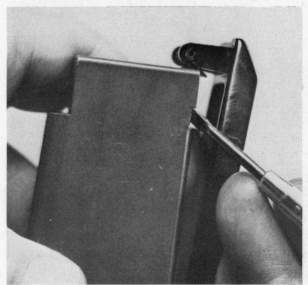

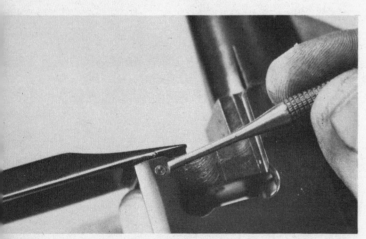

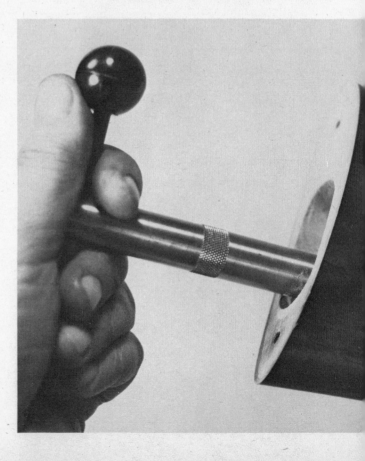

9. The magazine retaining spring is mounted on the end of the floorplate by a cross-pin, and is easily removed. The floorplate is attached to the receiver by a cross-pin, and the floorplate spring is mounted around the pin. Restrain the spring when drifting out the cross-pin, and remove the floorplate downward.

10. Remove the buttplate to give access to the stock mounting bolt. Use a B-Square stock tool or a long screwdriver to remove the stock mounting bolt, and take off the stock toward the rear. If it is very tight, bump the front of the comb with the heel of the hand to start it.

11. Insert a drift punch into the hole in the stock mounting plate at the rear of the receiver, and lift the plate upward, then tip it and remove it toward the rear.

12. Slide the trigger group out of the receiver toward the rear.

13. Restrain the hammer, pull the trigger, and ease the hammer down to the fired position. Drift out the trigger cross-pin.

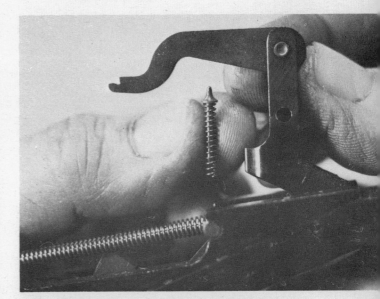

14. Remove the trigger and the attached disconnector upward, and take out the disconnector spring and its plunger. The cross-pin that joins the disconnector to the trigger is riveted in place, and should be removed only for repair or replacement purposes.

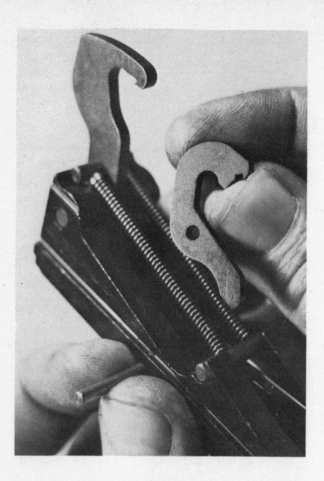

15. Push out the sear cross-pin, move the sear forward, then remove it upward.

16. Insert a screwdriver behind the base for the twin hammer springs and lever it forward and upward, out of its seats in the trigger group. **Caution:** *Grip the ends of the base firmly during this operation, and control its movement, as the semi-compressed double springs are quite strong.* Remove the spring base, springs, guide rods, and the front base in the hammer.

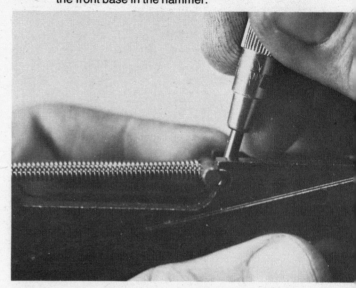

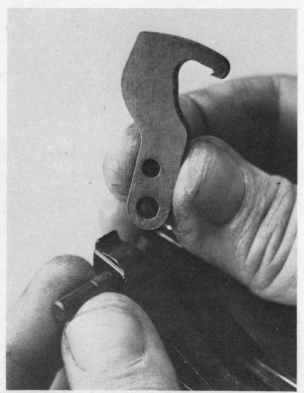

17. Push out the hammer cross-pin, and take out the hammer upward.

18. The magazine floorplate latch is retained in the receiver by a vertical roll pin, and this pin need not be drifted completely out to free the latch and spring. Just drift it upward enough to clear the latch, and take out the latch and spring toward the front.

19. A roll cross-pin at the rear of the trigger group retains the safety plunger and spring. Restrain the spring at the top when drifting out the pin, and remove the spring and plunger upward. Remove the safety toward either side.

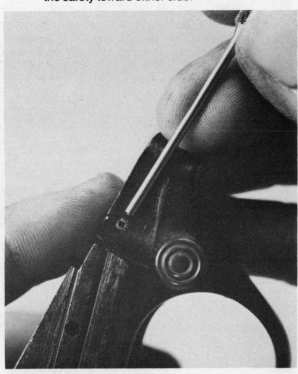

20. Move the bolt so the operating handle is accessible in the ejection port, and insert a small screwdriver to lift the handle latch outward. Move the handle forward, out of its recess in the bolt.

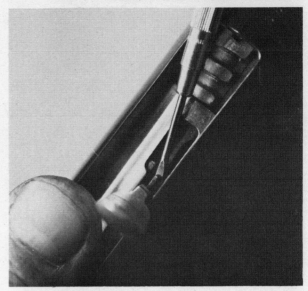

21. Move the operating handle to the wider opening in the bolt cover, and remove the handle toward the right. The latch and spring are retained in the handle by a very small cross-pin, and are easily removed. In normal takedown, they are best left in place.

22. After the handle is removed, move the bolt assembly about half-way to the rear, bring it downward from the roof of the receiver, and take it out toward the rear.

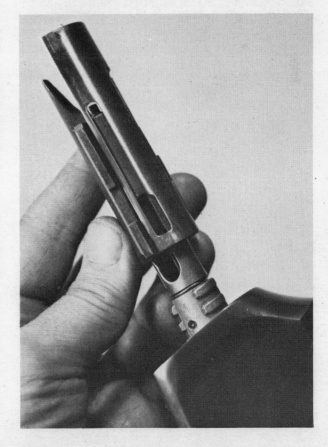

23. Move the bolt cover to the rear of the bolt, and push upward on the right lower edge, tipping it over toward the left, and snapping its guide flange out of the groove on the bolt.

24. Drift out the cross-pin in the rear tail of the bolt, and take out the firing pin and its return spring toward the rear. The ends of the cross-pin are contoured with the bolt tail, and care should be taken not to deform the ends.

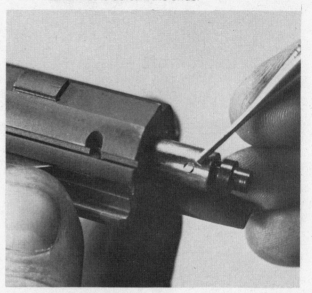

25. Push the cam pin upward out of the bolt sleeve, and remove it.

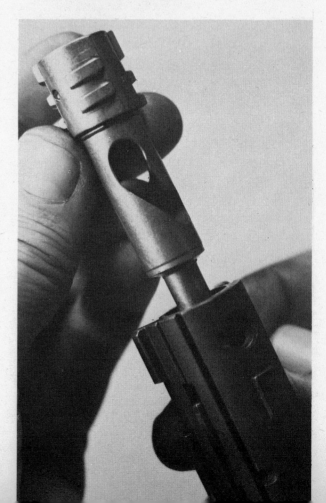

26. Move the bolt forward out of the bolt sleeve.

27. Drifting out the vertical pin on the left side of the bolt carrier will allow removal of the timing latch toward the left. The pin must be removed upward.

28. The ejector is retained at the front of the bolt by a vertical pin. **Caution:** *Restrain the ejector, and ease it out after removal of the pin, as the ejector spring is compressed.*

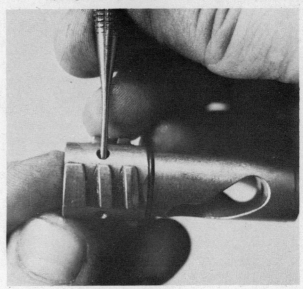

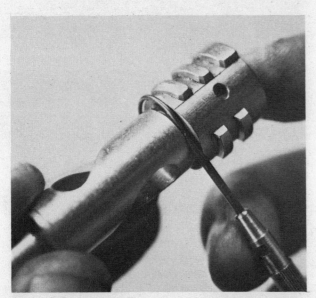

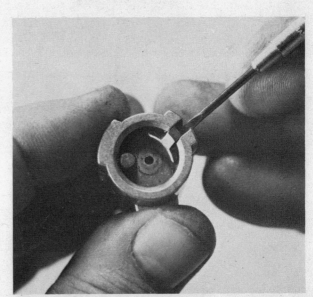

29. Use a small screwdriver to push the extractor spring up out of its groove, and remove the spring toward the rear.

30. After the spring is removed, the extractor can be moved downward, into the bolt face recess, and is taken out toward the front.

Reassembly Tips:

1. When replacing the bolt in the bolt carrier, be sure the flat between the bolt lugs is on *top,* and the extractor and ejector at upper left and lower right (front view).

2. When replacing the cam pin in the bolt and sleeve, the small hole at the center of the cam pin must be oriented properly for passage of the firing pin.

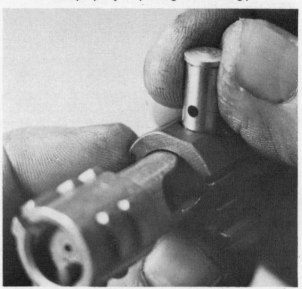

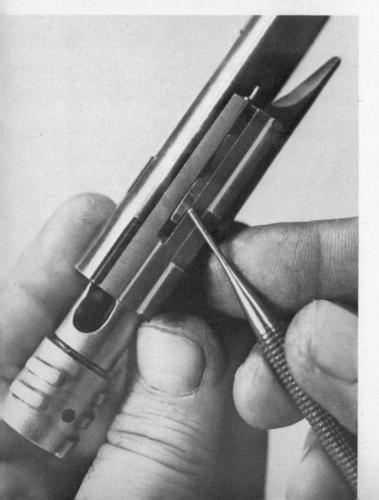

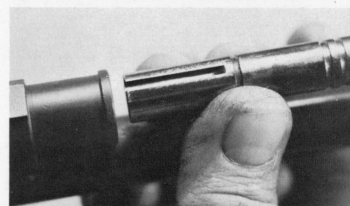

4. When replacing the gas piston, note that there is a guide pin at the lower rear of the gas cylinder, and the piston must be oriented so its rear groove will mate with the pin.

3. When replacing the bolt in the receiver, the bolt must be at its forward position in the sleeve, to allow the timing latch to be retracted.

Browning
Automatic Rifle

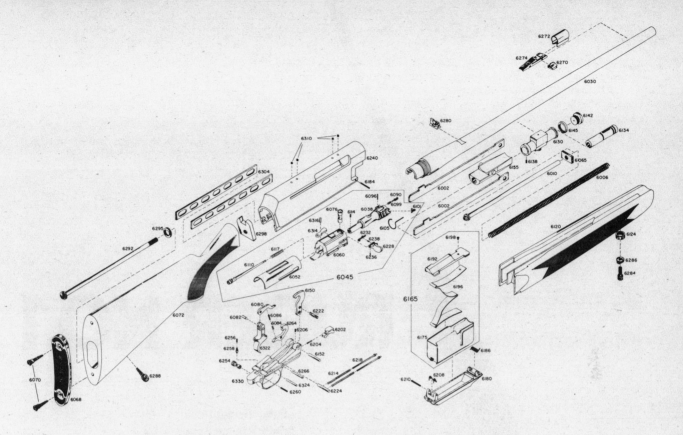

6002	Action Rod—Right or Left	6196	Magazine Follower Spring
6006	Action Spring	6198	Magazine Follower Spring Rivet
6010	Action Spring Guide	6202	Magazine Latch
6030	Barrel	6204	Magazine Latch Spring
6038	Bolt	6206	Magazine Latch Stop Pin
6045	Bolt Assembly	6208	Magazine Retaining Spring
6052	Bolt Cover	6210	Magazine Retaining Spring Pin
6060	Bolt Sleeve	6214	Mainspring—Right or Left
6065	Buffer Assembly	6218	Mainspring Guide—Right or Left
6068	Buttplate	6222	Mainspring Pin—Hammer
6070	Buttplate Screws (2)	6224	Mainspring Pin—Trigger Guard
6072	Buttstock	6228	Operating Handle
6076	Cam Pin	6232	Operating Handle Lock
6080	Disconnector	6236	Operating Handle Lock Pin
6082	Disconnector Pin	6238	Operating Handle Lock Spring
6084	Disconnector Spring	6240	Receiver
6086	Disconnector Spring Plunger	6254	Safety Cross Bolt
6090	Ejector	6256	Safety Spring
6096	Ejector Retaining Pin	6258	Safety Spring Plunger
6099	Ejector Spring	6260	Safety Spring Retaining Pin
6101	Extractor	6264	Sear
6105	Extractor Spring	6266	Sear Pin
6110	Firing Pin	6270	Sight Bead Front
6114	Firing Pin Retaining Pin	6272	Sight Hood Front
6117	Firing Pin Spring	6274	Sight Ramp Front
6120	Fore-end	6280	Sight Assembly Folding Leaf
6124	Fore-end Escutcheon		Rear
6130	Gas Cylinder	6284	Sling Eyelet Front
6134	Gas Piston	6286	Sling Eyelet Washer
6138	Gas Piston Stop Pin	6288	Sling Eyelet Rear
6142	Gas Regulator	6292	Stock Bolt
6145	Gas Regulator Gasket	6295	Stock Bolt Washer
6150	Hammer	6298	Stock Bolt Plate
6152	Hammer Pin	6304	Support Rail—Right or Left
6155	Inertia Piece	6310	Telescope Mount Filler
6165	Magazine Complete		Screws (4)
6175	Magazine Body	6314	Timing Latch
6180	Magazine Floor Plate	6316	Timing Latch Retaining Pin
6184	Magazine Floor Plate Pivot Pin	6322	Trigger
6186	Magazine Floor Plate Spring	6324	Trigger Pin
6192	Magazine Follower	6330	Trigger Guard

RUGER NO.1

Data:	Ruger No. 1
Origin:	United States
Manufacturer:	Sturm, Ruger & Company Southport, Connecticut
Cartridges:	Most popular calibers from 22-250 to 458
Over-all length:	42 inches
Barrel lengths:	22, 24 and 26 inches
Weight:	8 pounds

In 1967, Bill Ruger re-created the classic single-shot rifle, and over the past thirteen years it has proved to be an outstanding success. The action and some other features of the gun have some relationship to the old Fraser and Farquharson rifles from England, but the mechanism is pure Ruger, and superior to any other gun of this type, before or since. Also, in contrast to the older guns of this type, the takedown and reassembly operations are not difficult.

Disassembly:

1. Remove the angled screw on the underside of the fore-end and take off the fore-end forward and downward.

2. Remove the fore-end takedown nut, and set it aside to prevent loss.

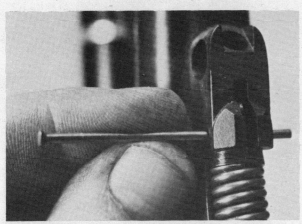

3. Cycle the action to cock the hammer, and insert a small piece of rod through the transverse hole in the front tip of the hammer spring strut. Pull the trigger to release the hammer.

4. Move the hammer spring assembly slightly toward the rear, tip the front of the assembly downward, and remove it toward the front. If the assembly is to be taken apart, proceed with caution, as the spring is compressed.

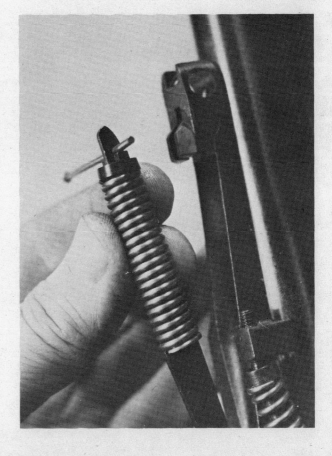

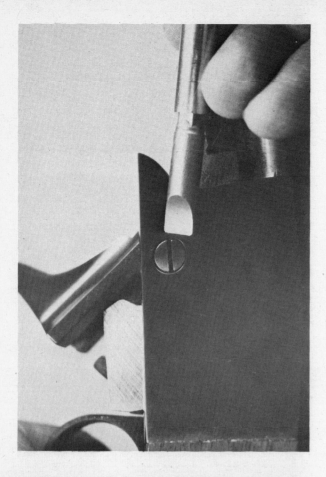

5. Remove the cap screw on the lever pivot, and push out the pivot toward the opposite side. The action should be opened while this is done. If the screw is very tight, the lever pivot head has a screw slot, and it can be held with another screwdriver.

6. Remove the hammer downward.

7. Push the breechblock back upward, close the lever, then open the lever about half way, and remove the lever and breechblock assembly downward out of the receiver as a unit.

8. Detach the breechblock from the lever arm, and remove the ejector roller from the left side of the breechblock.

9. Holding the breechblock with its left side downward, reach into the underside of the block and work the hammer transfer block back and forth until its pivot pin protrudes from the left side enough to be caught with a fingernail or small screwdriver and pulled out. The pin has a cannelure at its left tip for this purpose.

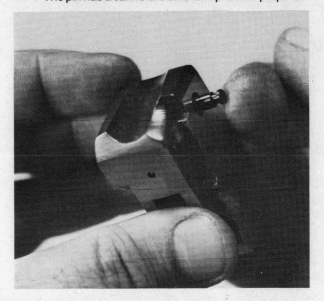

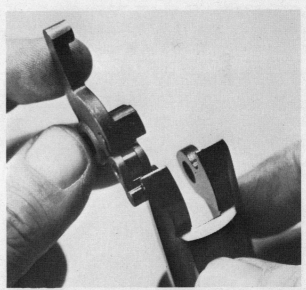

10. Remove the hammer transfer block from the bottom of the breechblock. The firing pin and its return spring can now be taken out from inside the breechblock.

11. The breechblock arm and the lever links are easily separated from each other. Note that the links are joined by a roll pin, and this should be left in place unless removal is necessary for repair.

12. Backing out the cross-screw in the tail of the lever will allow removal of the lever latch and its spring.

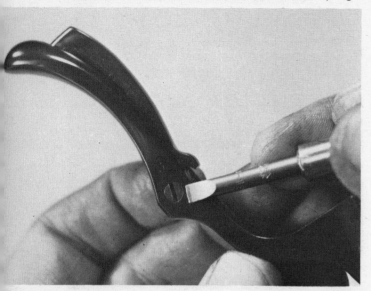

13. Remove the ejector downard, and take care not to lose the plunger and spring mounted in its side.

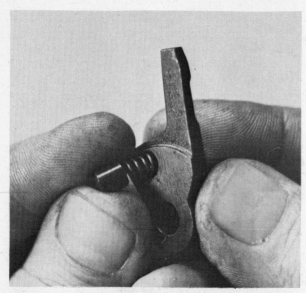

14. The plunger and spring are easily removed from the side of the ejector.

15. Tip the ejector lever (ejector cam) downward, and take off its spring and guide assembly downward. Note that the guide is two separate parts.

16. Drifting out its pivot pin will allow removal of the ejector cam lever toward the front.

17. The buttstock is retained by a through-bolt from the rear. Take off the buttplate, and use a B-square stock tool or a large screwdriver to back out the stock bolt. Remove the stock toward the rear. If it is very tight, bump the front of the comb with the heel of the hand to start it.

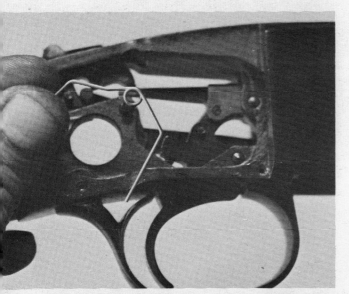

18. Unhook the upper arm of the safety positioning spring from its stud on the safety, and remove the spring from its mounting post toward the right.

19. Removal of the safety button requires the drifting out of two roll pins in its underlug, just below the upper tang.

20. Drifting out this post from the opposite side (from right to left) will release the safety arm and safety bar as a unit to be moved toward the rear and taken out toward the side. This is the same post that is the mounting stud for the safety positioning spring.

21. The trigger guard is retained by two roll pins at the front and rear, crossing the lower tang of the receiver. When these are drifted out, the guard is removed downward.

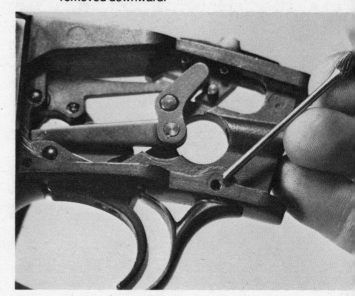

22. The trigger and sear are retained by cross-pins, and are joined by a link. After the pins are removed, the trigger and sear are moved slightly toward the rear, then are taken out downward, with their attendant springs.

Reassembly Tips:

1. This view of the right side of the receiver with the stock removed shows the internal parts in their proper order. The safety is shown in the on-safe position.

2. This view of the left side of the receiver shows the safety in the off-safe position.

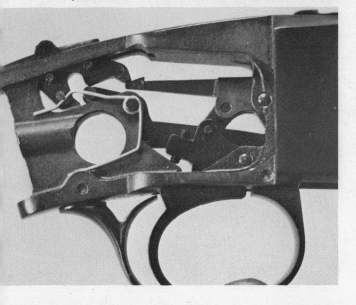

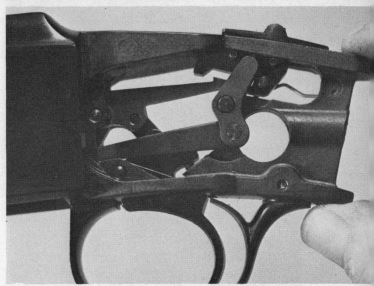

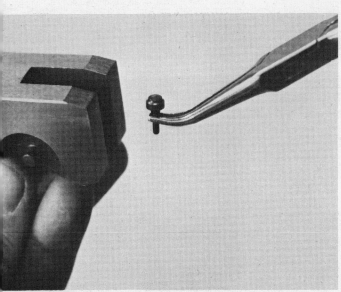

3. After the firing pin spring is in place inside the breechblock, grip the firing pin with forceps or very slim pliers, and set the firing pin point into the spring.

4. When replacing the hammer transfer block, note that the concave area in its lower extension goes toward the rear.

5. When replacing the hammer spring assembly, note that the down-turned neck at the rear of the strut goes in that position—downward.

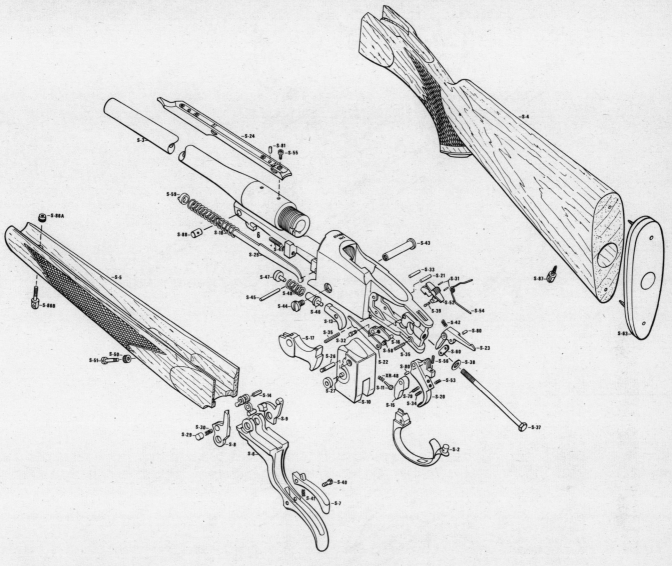

S-3	Barrel	S-15	Hammer Transfer Block	S-52	Safety
S-55	Barrel Rib Screws (4)	S-18	Hammer Spring	S-16	Safety Arm
S-81	Barrel Rib Dowels (2)	S-59	Hammer Spring Retaining	S-32	Safety Arm Pivot Pin
S-9	Breech Block Arm		Washer	S-22	Safety Bar
S-10	Breech Block	S-26	Hammer Transfer Block	S-58	Safety Bar Pivot Pin
S-8	Ejector		Pivot Pin	S-54	Safety Detent Spring
S-13	Ejector Cam	S-25	Hammer Strut	S-39	Safety Detent Spring Pin
S-45	Ejector Cam Pivot Pin	S-6	Lever	S-23	Sear
S-29	Ejector Plunger	S-7	Lever Latch	S-56	Sear Adjustment Screw
S-30	Ejector Plunger Spring	S-40	Lever Latch Pivot Pin	S-60	Sear Link
S-27	Ejector Roller	S-41	Lever Latch Spring	S-80	Sear Link Pins (2)
S-46	Ejector Strut	S-14	Lever Link and Pin	S-33	Sear Pivot Pin
S-49	Ejector Strut Adj. Screw		Assemblies (2)	S-42	Sear Spring
S-48	Ejector Strut Spring	S-43	Lever Pivot Pin	S-62	Sling Swivel Bank
S-47	Ejector Strut Swivel	S-83	Lever Pilot Groove Pin	S-66	Sling Swivel Band Set Screw
S-11	Firing Pin	S-44	Lever Pivot Screw	S-4	Buttstock
XR-48	Firing Pin Spring	S-97	Pistol Grip Cap (Not Numbered)	S-37	Stock Bolt
S-50	Fore-end Escutcheon	S-61	Pistol Grip Cap Medallion	S-38	Stock Bolt Washer
S-51	Fore-end Takedown Screw		(Not Shown)	S-20	Trigger
S-65	Front Sight Base (Not Shown)	S-36	Pistol Grip Cap Screw	S-53	Trigger Adjustment Spring
S-70	Front Sight Base Set		(Not Shown)	S-2	Trigger Guard
	Screw (Not Shown)	S-77	Rear Sight (Optional)	S-35	Trigger Guard Retaining Pins (2)
S-67	Front Sight Blade (Not Shown)	S-63	Recoil Pad	S-21	Trigger Pivot Pin
S-69	Front Sight Plunger	S-84	Recoil Pad Screws (2)	S-34	Trigger Spring Adj. Screw
	Spring (Not Shown)	S-24	Rib (Scope)	S-79	Trigger Stop Screw
S-68	Front Sight Retaining	S-31	Roll Pins for Safety Thumb	S-88	Fore-end Takedown Nut
	Plunger (Not Shown)		Piece (2)		
S-17	Hammer				

Ruger
M-77 Bolt Action Rifle

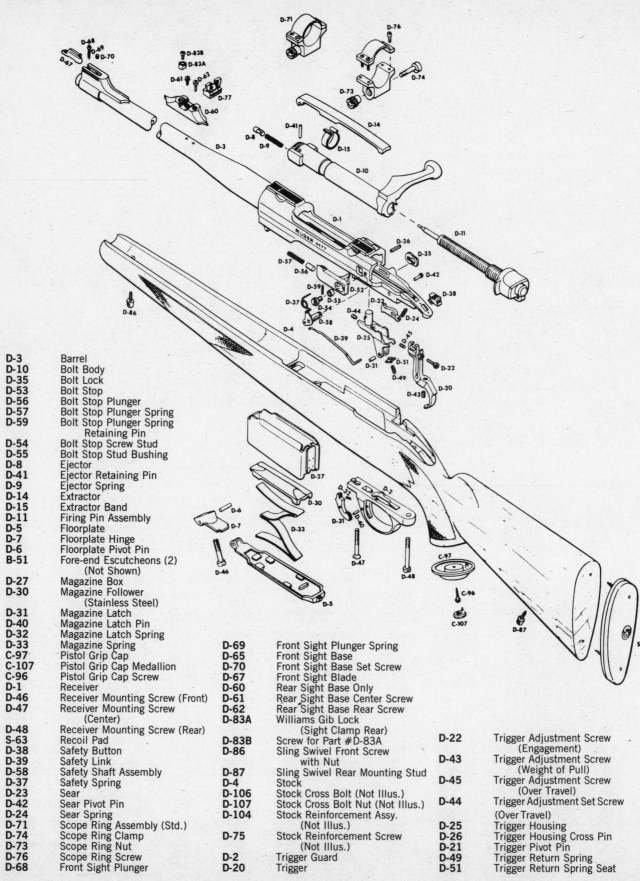

D-3	Barrel
D-10	Bolt Body
D-35	Bolt Lock
D-53	Bolt Stop
D-56	Bolt Stop Plunger
D-57	Bolt Stop Plunger Spring
D-59	Bolt Stop Plunger Spring Retaining Pin
D-54	Bolt Stop Screw Stud
D-55	Bolt Stop Stud Bushing
D-8	Ejector
D-41	Ejector Retaining Pin
D-9	Ejector Spring
D-14	Extractor
D-15	Extractor Band
D-11	Firing Pin Assembly
D-5	Floorplate
D-7	Floorplate Hinge
D-6	Floorplate Pivot Pin
B-51	Fore-end Escutcheons (2) (Not Shown)
D-27	Magazine Box
D-30	Magazine Follower (Stainless Steel)
D-31	Magazine Latch
D-40	Magazine Latch Pin
D-32	Magazine Latch Spring
D-33	Magazine Spring
C-97	Pistol Grip Cap
C-107	Pistol Grip Cap Medallion
C-96	Pistol Grip Cap Screw
D-1	Receiver
D-46	Receiver Mounting Screw (Front)
D-47	Receiver Mounting Screw (Center)
D-48	Receiver Mounting Screw (Rear)
S-63	Recoil Pad
D-38	Safety Button
D-39	Safety Link
D-58	Safety Shaft Assembly
D-37	Safety Spring
D-23	Sear
D-42	Sear Pivot Pin
D-24	Sear Spring
D-71	Scope Ring Assembly (Std.)
D-74	Scope Ring Clamp
D-73	Scope Ring Nut
D-76	Scope Ring Screw
D-68	Front Sight Plunger

D-69	Front Sight Plunger Spring
D-65	Front Sight Base
D-70	Front Sight Base Set Screw
D-67	Front Sight Blade
D-60	Rear Sight Base Only
D-61	Rear Sight Base Center Screw
D-62	Rear Sight Base Rear Screw
D-83A	Williams Gib Lock (Sight Clamp Rear)
D-83B	Screw for Part #D-83A
D-86	Sling Swivel Front Screw with Nut
D-87	Sling Swivel Rear Mounting Stud
D-4	Stock
D-106	Stock Cross Bolt (Not Illus.)
D-107	Stock Cross Bolt Nut (Not Illus.)
D-104	Stock Reinforcement Assy. (Not Illus.)
D-75	Stock Reinforcement Screw (Not Illus.)
D-2	Trigger Guard
D-20	Trigger

D-22	Trigger Adjustment Screw (Engagement)
D-43	Trigger Adjustment Screw (Weight of Pull)
D-45	Trigger Adjustment Screw (Over Travel)
D-44	Trigger Adjustment Set Screw (Over Travel)
D-25	Trigger Housing
D-26	Trigger Housing Cross Pin
D-21	Trigger Pivot Pin
D-49	Trigger Return Spring
D-51	Trigger Return Spring Seat

RUGER MODEL 77

Data: Ruger Model 77
Origin: United States
Manufacturer: Sturm, Ruger & Company
Southport, Connecticut
Cartridges: Most popular calibers from 22-250 to 458
Magazine capacity: 3 to 5 rounds
Over-all length: 42 to 44 inches
Barrel length: 22 to 26 inches
Weight: 6¾ pounds (Standard)

With some elements of the classic Mauser/Springfield rifle, in 1968 Bill Ruger created a gun that includes the best points of the old and new. Internally, the Model 77 is all modern, with several Ruger innovations, such as the angled front action mounting screw which pulls the action not only down in the stock, but also back, snugging the recoil lug against the interior of the stock. The firing mechanism is uncomplicated, and takedown and reassembly are not difficult.

Disassembly:

1. Open the bolt and move it to the rear, while holding the bolt stop pulled out toward the left. Remove the bolt from the rear of the receiver.

2. Insert a small piece of rod (or a drift punch) at the lower rear of the cocking piece, into the hole provided. This will lock the striker in rear position. Unscrew the striker assembly counter-clockwise (rear view).

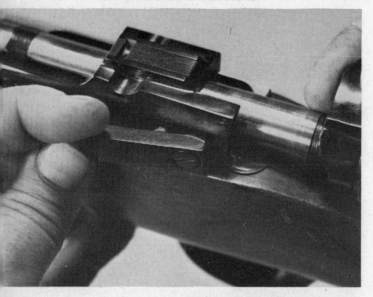

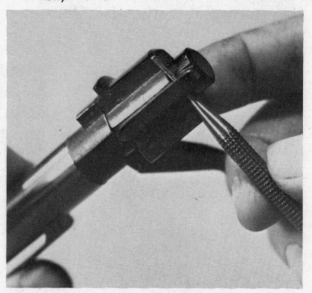

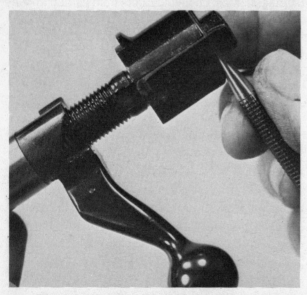

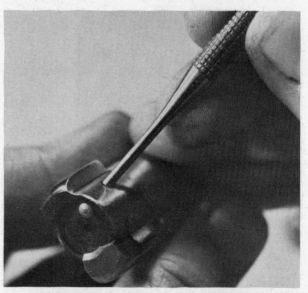

3. Remove the striker assembly from the rear of the bolt. It is possible to grip the front of the striker in a vise and push the bolt endpiece forward to expose a cross-pin in the cocking piece, and drifting out this pin would release the parts of the striker assembly. There is, however, no reasonably easy way to do this without special tools, and the factory cautions against taking this assembly apart.

4. Drifting out the vertical pin at the front of the bolt will release the ejector and its spring toward the front. **Caution:** *The spring is compressed, so restrain the ejector and ease it out.*

5. Turn the extractor counter-clockwise (rear view) until it is aligned with the base of the bolt handle, then use the Brownells extractor pliers or a small screwdriver blade to lift the front underlug of the extractor out of its groove at the front of the bolt, and push the extractor off the flanges of the mounting ring toward the front.

6. Open the magazine floorplate, and slide the magazine spring out of its slots. The follower can be removed from the spring in the same way.

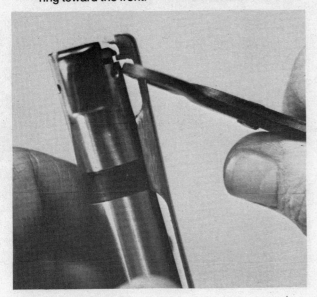

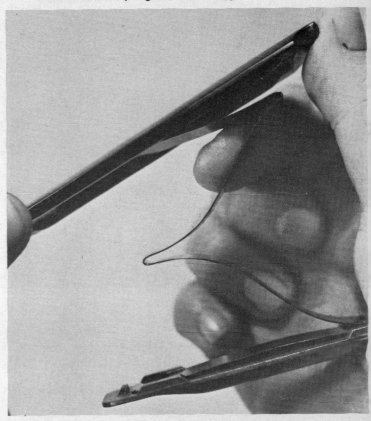

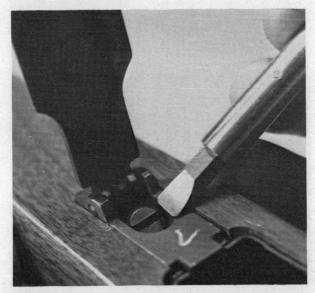

7. Remove the large angled screw inside the front of the magazine floorplate base.

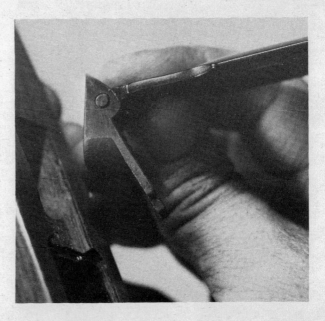

8. Remove the magazine floorplate and its base downward. Pushing out the hinge pin will allow separation of the floorplate and its base.

9. Remove the vertical screw at the front of the trigger guard. Remove the vertical screw at the rear of the trigger guard, and take off the trigger guard downward. Separate the action from the stock.

10. Drifting out the cross-pin in the front of the trigger guard will allow removal of the magazine floorplate latch and its spring.

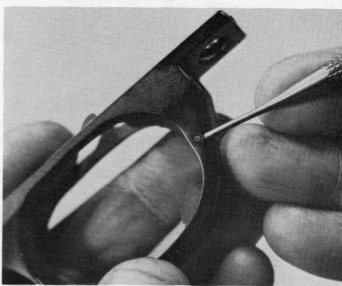

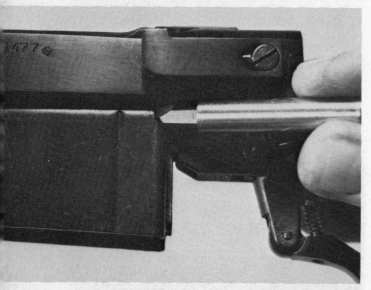

11. The magazine box is a press fit in its recess in the bottom of the receiver. Insert a tool in the openings on each side at the upper rear of the box, and gently pry it away from the receiver.

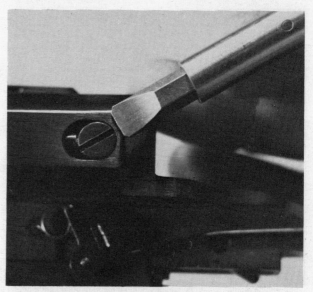

12. The bolt stop is removed by backing out its mounting screw toward the left.

13. As the screw is backed out, the bolt stop plunger will drop from the edge of the screw head to the internal bushing, and the stud screw is then easily removed.

14. Drifting out the vertical roll pin at the front of the bolt stop will allow removal of the spring and plunger toward the front, and the bushing from the rear opening.

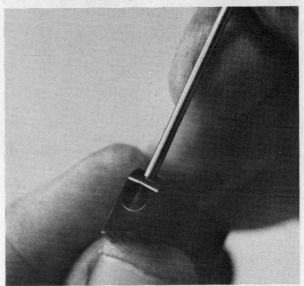

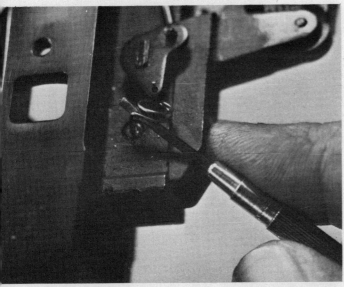

15. With the safety in the on-safe position, use a small screwdriver to lift the front arm of the safety positioning spring out of the center of the trigger housing roll pin. When it is clear, swing it downward, and unhook it from the hole in the edge of the safety shaft plate.

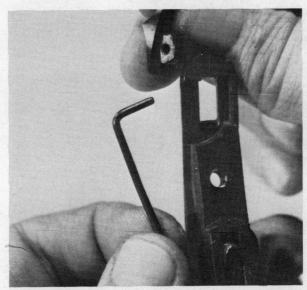

16. Move the rear tip of the safety link out of its cross-hole in the underside of the safety button, and unhook its forward end from the safety plate. The safety button can now be removed.

17. After the link rod is removed, push the safety plate toward the right, moving the right tip of its shaft slightly out of the right side of the housing. The safety bolt lock can then be slid off the shaft downward, then removed toward the right.

18. Remove the safety shaft and and its attached plate toward the left.

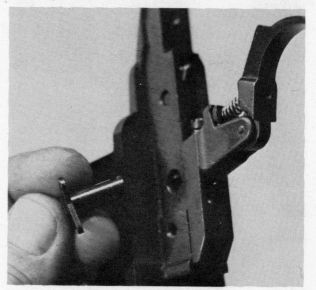

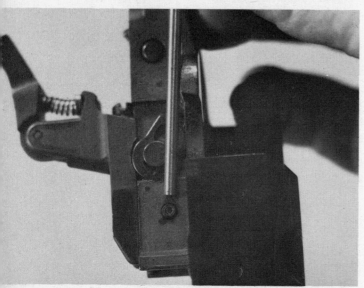

19. Drift out the trigger housing cross-pin toward the left, using a roll pin punch. It is important that the ends of this pin are not deformed, as the safety positioning spring must be remounted inside the pin.

20. Remove the trigger housing downward.

21. Move the trigger spring base out of its seat at the rear of the housing, and remove the spring toward the rear. **Caution:** *The spring is under tension.*

22. Pushing out the trigger pin will release the trigger from the housing. The trigger adjustment screws should not be disturbed.

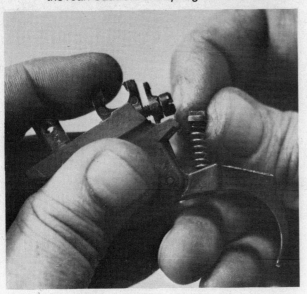

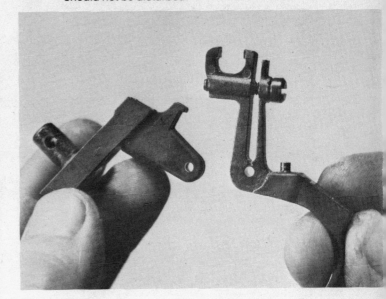

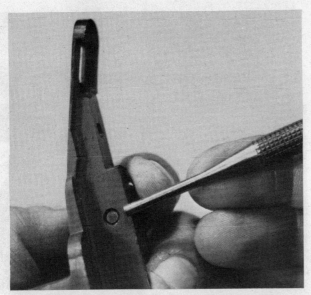

23. Restrain the sear against its spring tension, and push out the sear pin toward the right side. Remove the sear and its spring downward.

Reassembly Tips:

1. When replacing the safety shaft, the trigger must be pulled to clear the shaft tunnel for insertion.

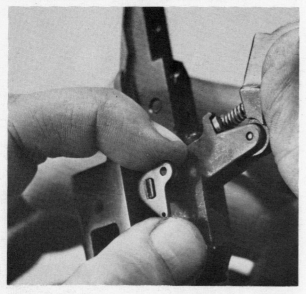

2. When replacing the safety button, note that its longer slope goes toward the front.

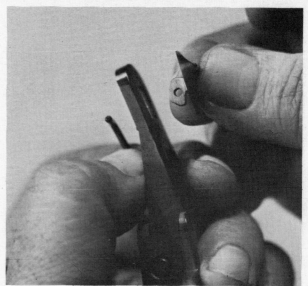

3. Before replacing the bolt stop on the receiver, insert a small screwdriver to jump the plunger back onto the edge of the post screw. During installation, take care that the plunger doesn't slip off the edge.

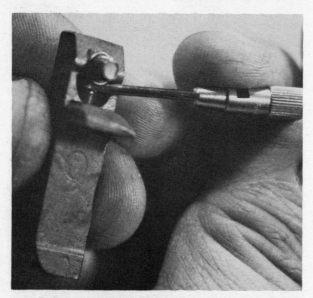

4. When replacing the extractor on the bolt, use the Brownells extractor pliers to compress the mounting ring flanges while sliding the extractor onto them. After it is well started into the flanges, use the pliers to lift the underlug at the front of the extractor onto the front edge of the bolt. Take care to lift the front of the extractor no more than is absolutely necessary for clearance.

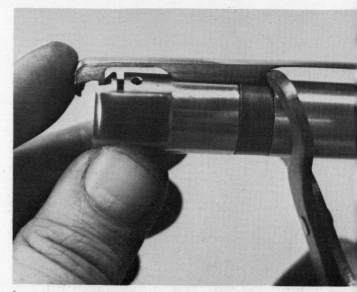

RUGER 44 CARBINE

Data: Ruger 44 Carbine
Origin: United States
Manufacturer: Sturm, Ruger & Company
Southport, Connecticut
Cartridge: 44 Magnum
Magazine capacity: 4 rounds
Over-all length: 36¾ inches
Barrel length: 18½ inches
Weight: 5¾ pounds

When the Ruger 44 Autoloading Carbine arrived in 1961, it was the first rifle chambered for this round, and is still the only semi-auto regularly available in this chambering. It has gained much popularity as a close-range gun for medium game, and the ballistics of its cartridge are comparable to the old 30-30. Like all of Bill Ruger's creations, it is an engineering masterpiece. It is not unnecessarily complicated, but an inter-dependency of certain parts makes takedown and reassembly an endeavor best left to the professional.

Disassembly:

1. Pull back the operating handle to lock the bolt open. Remove the cross-screw at the bottom of the barrel band, and take off the band toward the front.

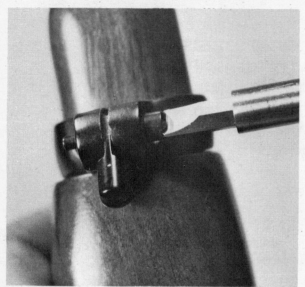

2. Lift the action at the front, and disengage its rear hook from the recoil block in the stock. Take out the action upward and toward the front.

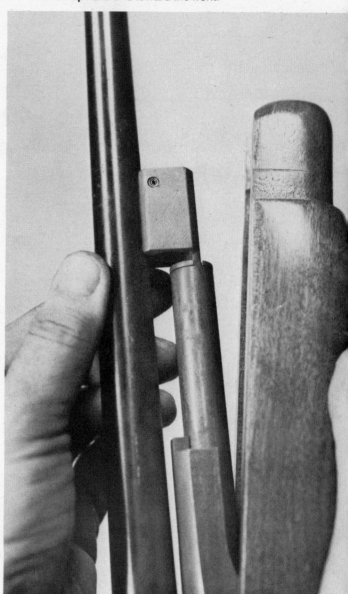

3. If necessary, the recoil block can be removed by taking off the buttplate and backing out the through-bolt which enters the block from the rear. The block is then removed forward and upward.

4. Push the lifter latch, and ease the bolt to closed position. Drift out the cross-pin at the rear of the receiver.

5. Move the trigger housing toward the rear, and take it off downward.

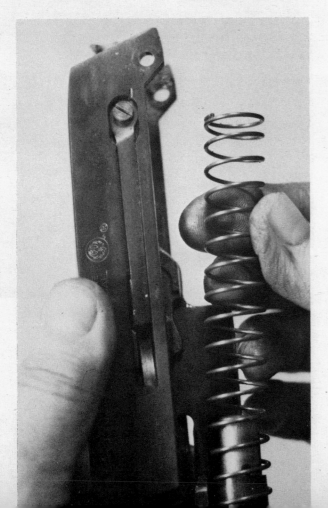

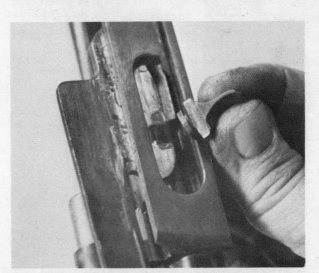

7. Remove the bolt handle from its slot in the action slide, and take it off toward the right.

6. With the gun inverted, grip the rear of the recoil spring firmly, and lift the action slide away from the bottom of the receiver. As soon as the rear end of the spring has cleared the edge of the receiver, slowly release the spring and remove it toward the rear.

8. Remove the action slide and magazine tube together from the bottom of the receiver. Separate the magazine tube from the action slide.

9. Drifting out the roll pin at the front of the magazine tube will allow removal of the tube endpiece, magazine spring, and follower. **Caution:** *The spring is under tension, so control the endpiece and ease it out.*

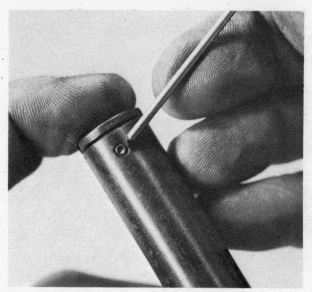

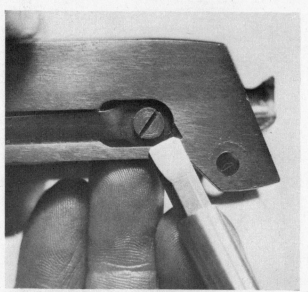

10. Remove the screw at the left rear of the receiver, and take off the ejector toward the left.

11. Insert a finger through the ejection port to turn the bolt and free its locking lugs, then move it toward the rear about half-way. Lift the bolt out of the underside of the receiver.

12. The gas piston is usually easy to remove from the rear of the gas cylinder. If it is tight because of powder residue, tap the rear flange of the cylinder with a plastic hammer to nudge it out.

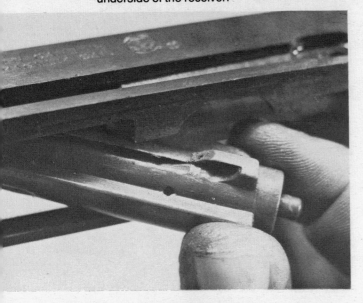

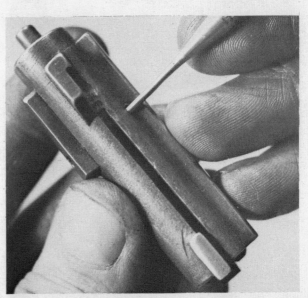

13. The piston block plug at the front of the gas cylinder is retained by two concentric roll pins, and is removed toward the front. In normal takedown, it is best left in place.

14. The firing pin is retained in the bolt by a pin at the rear, and the firing pin and its return spring are taken out toward the rear.

15. The extractor is retained by a vertcial pin at the front of the bolt, and this pin must be driven out upward. The extractor and its coil spring are then removed toward the right.

16. Restrain the hammer, pull the trigger, and ease the hammer down to the fired position. Unhook the outer arms of the hammer spring, on each side of the housing, from the grooved ends of the hammer pivot pin, partially relieving the tension of the springs. **Caution:** *Use pliers to disengage the springs, as they are under heavy tension.*

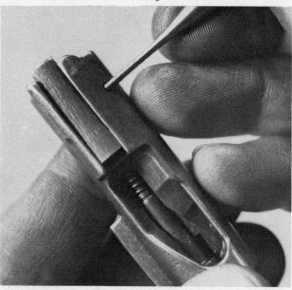

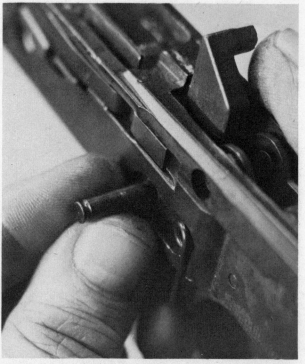

17. When the spring arms are turned downward, the hammer spring pin can be pushed out and removed. After removal of the pin the springs will be loose, but they are not taken out at this time.

18. Push out the hammer pivot pin toward either side.

19. Remove the hammer upward.

20. Drift out the cross-pin that retains the lifter latch.

21. Raise the lifter at the front, and take out the lifter latch downward. The plunger and spring are easily detached from the rear of the lifter latch.

22. Move the front of the lifter back to its lowered position to relieve tension on the cam spring, and push out the lifter cam pin toward the left.

23. Insert an angled drift punch through the lifter cam pin hole, and lever the lifter cam slightly toward the rear. Raise the front of the lifter, and remove the cam and its spring upward and toward the front.

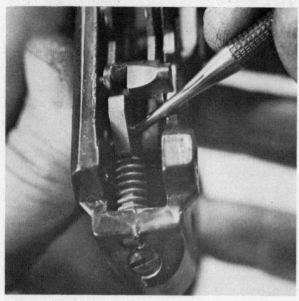

24. Insert a small screwdriver on the left side at the rear tip of the carrier, and push the lifter dog pin out toward the right until it can be grasped with pliers and pulled out. Remove the lifter dog upward.

25. Squeeze the rear arms of the carrier (lifter) together, to move the side studs from their holes in the sides of the housing, and remove it upward and toward the rear.

26. Push out the trigger pin, and move the twin hammer springs out to each side to clear the trigger and sear assembly.

27. Remove the trigger, sear, and disconnector assembly upward, and remove the sear spring from its well in the housing.

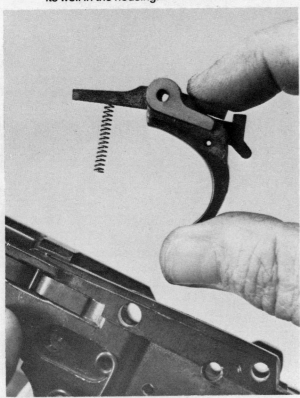

28. Remove the trigger plunger and spring from its hole at the rear of the trigger guard.

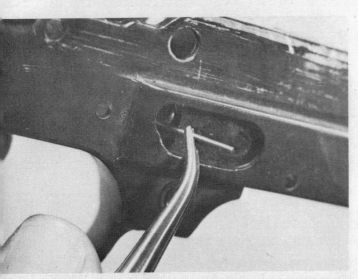

29. Move the hammer springs inward, one at a time, tip the outer arms outward, and push the springs into the interior of the trigger housing for removal.

30. Grip the safety with smooth-jawed parallel pliers, and give it one-quarter turn clockwise (right side view). Remove the safety toward the left. **Caution:** *The safety plunger and spring will be released as the safety clears, so insert a screwdriver into the housing to restrain them.*

31. The flat cartridge stop spring is retained on the left side of the trigger housing by a vertical pin which is in a blind hole. Use a small screwdriver to nudge it upward until it can be grasped with pliers and taken out. The flat spring is then removed toward the left.

32. After the flat spring is removed, take out the rear-most of the two coil springs from its hole in the trigger housing.

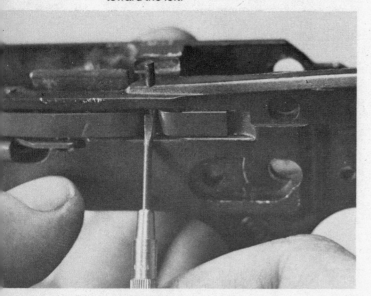

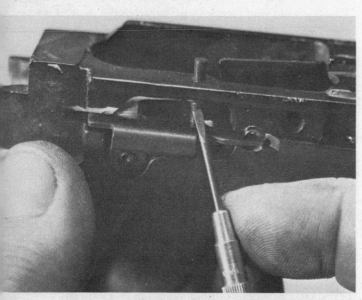

33. The cartridge stop and flapper pivot pin is also in a blind hole, and is removed in the same way as the previous one. Note that the cartridge stop spring will be released when the pin is out, so control it.

Reassembly Tips:

34. Remove the cartridge stop and its spring toward the left, and move the flapper inward and take it out toward the top of the housing.

1. When replacing the cartridge stop system, note that the cartridge stop spring and the flapper spring are of unequal length. Remember that the shorter spring goes at the front, under the tail of the cartridge stop.

2. When replacing the flat cartridge stop spring, it is necessary to lay the housing on its right side on a firm surface, and use a small drift punch to depress the spring at its pin dip to allow passage of the pin.

3. It is possible to install the sear/trigger/disconnector system by just holding them in place, but the use of a slave pin to hold the parts together will make it much easier. Be sure the lower end of the sear spring enters its hole inside of the trigger housing, and be sure the rear tail of the disconnector goes in front of the trigger spring plunger at the rear.

4. When replacing the hammer springs, they must be reinserted from inside the trigger group. When the long arm of the spring is protruding to the outside, insert a drift punch into the center of the spring, and tilt the drift toward the front of the housing, levering the spring into its hole.

5. Installing the hammer is perhaps the most difficult of reassembly operations. Be sure the short inner arms of both hammer springs engage the underside of the small roller at the lower rear of the hammer. Push the hammer straight downward, and insert a drift punch through the hammer pivot hole to hold it in place for insertion of the cross-pin. Be sure the spring ends are not allowed to slip from beneath the roller during installation of the pin. Remember to replace the spring cross-pin, and re-hook the spring arms onto the hammer pivot pin.

6. When replacing the magazine tube, note that the slot in the tube endpiece of offset, and must fit onto the flange at the rear of the gas piston housing. The larger area of the endpiece goes toward the barrel, as shown.

7. When replacing the magazine tube and recoil spring assembly, note that at the rear the spring must bear against the receiver, and must not extend into the recess for the rear tip of the magazine tube, as shown.

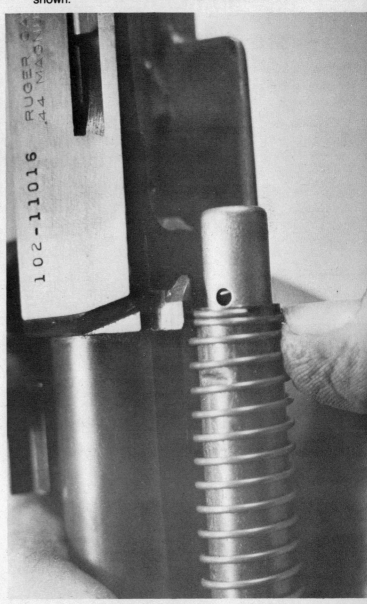

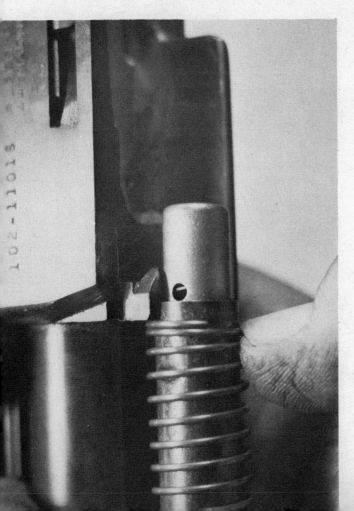

8. When properly assembled, the spring and tube will be as shown.

RUGER 44 MAGNUM CARBINE

Disassembly—Pull slide handle (27) back and press up on lifter latch (59) to release slide and bolt. Loosen barrel band screw (14) and remove barrel band (13). Pull barrel and receiver assembly up and disengage flange at rear of receiver from recoil block (15) in stock. Push receiver cross pin (18) out of receiver and pull trigger guard assembly from bottom of receiver. Disassembly of lock mechanism is not recommended. Invert receiver and pull slide (26) back and upward while holding compressed slide spring (28); remove slide, release spring (28) and draw it out rear of slide. Disengage slide handle (27) from slot in slide and disengage slot in face of magazine plug (32) from lip at rear of piston block on underside of barrel. Withdraw slide with magazine assembly from barrel and receiver assembly. Magazine may be taken down by drifting out magazine plug cross pin (33) and removing plug, spring and follower from magazine tube. Bolt (19) can be removed by rotating bolt slightly in receiver from its forward locked position and drawing it rearward to position where bolt lugs will clear cuts in receiver. Press in cartridge guide plate (7) from inside receiver and lift bolt out. Reassemble in reverse order.

Parts List

1. Barrel
2. Rear Sight
3. Scope Mount Filler Screws
4. Ejector Screws
5. Scope Mount Filler Screws
6. Ejector
7. Cartridge Guide Plate
8. Cartridge Guide Plate Screw
9. Piston
10. Piston Block Plug
11. Piston Block Plug Retaining Pin
12. Front Sight
13. Barrel Band
14. Barrel Band Screw
15. Recoil Block
16. Recoil Block Bolt Washer
17. Recoil Block Bolt
18. Receiver Cross Pin
19. Bolt
20. Extractor
21. Extractor Pivot Pin
22. Extractor Pivot Pin
23. Firing Pin Retaining Pin
24. Firing Pin Retaining Spring
25. Firing Pin
26. Slide
27. Slide Handle
28. Slide Spring
29. Magazine Tube
30. Magazine Follower
31. Magazine Spring
32. Magazine Plug
33. Magazine Plug Cross Pin
34. Butt Plate (Not shown)
35. Butt Plate Screws (Not shown)
36. Receiver
37. Disconnector Plunger
38. Disconnector Plunger Spring
39. Disconnector Plunger Spring Screw
40. Lifter Cam
41. Lifter Cam Spring
42. Lifter Cam Pin
43. Hammer Spring, Left Hand
44. Hammer Spring, Right Hand
45. Hammer Spring Retaining Pin
46. Safety
47. Safety Detent Plunger
48. Safety Detent Plunger Spring
49. Trigger
50. Trigger Cross Pin
51. Sear
52. Sear Spring
53. Disconnector
54. Trigger Pivot Pin
55. Hammer Pivot Pin
56. Hammer
57. Hammer Roller
58. Hammer Roller Pivot Pin
59. Lifter Latch
60. Lifter Latch Pivot Pin
61. Lifter Latch Spring
62. Lifter Latch Plunger
63. Lifter Dog
64. Lifter Dog Pivot Pin
65. Lifter Assembly
66. Cartridge Stop Flat Spring
67. Retaining Pin
68. Cartridge Stop
69. Cartridge Stop Coil Spring
71. Flapper Spring
72. Cartridge Stop Pivot Pin
73. Trigger Guard and Housing

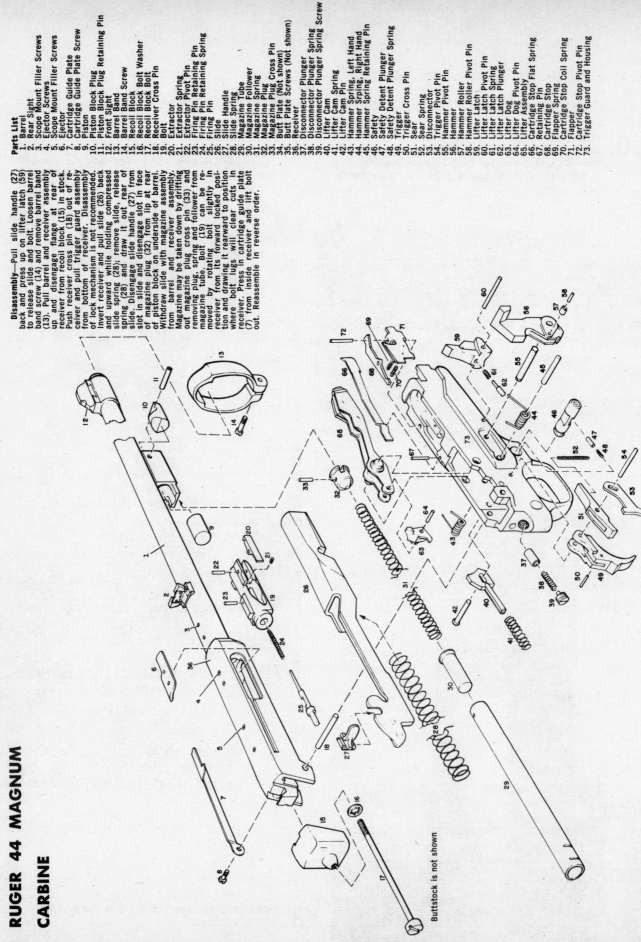

Buttstock is not shown

MARLIN MODEL 336

Data: Marlin Model 336
Origin: United States
Manufacturer: Marlin Firearms Company
North Haven, Connecticut
Cartridge: 30-30 Winchester, 35 Remington
Magazine capacity: 6 rounds
Over-all length: 38½ inches
Barrel length: 20 inches
Weight: 7 pounds

An extensive re-design of the Marlin Model 36 (1936) rifle, the Model 336 was first offered in 1948. It was initially available in several calibers, but in recent years only the 30-30 and 35 chamberings have been in production. Although most lever action guns are generally more complicated than other manually-operated actions, the Model 336 has a relatively easy takedown, with no really difficult points. Several sub-models of this gun were made, and the instructions will apply to any of these.

Disassembly:

1. Partially open the lever, and take out the lever pivot cross-screw. Remove the lever downward.

2. Remove the bolt toward the rear.

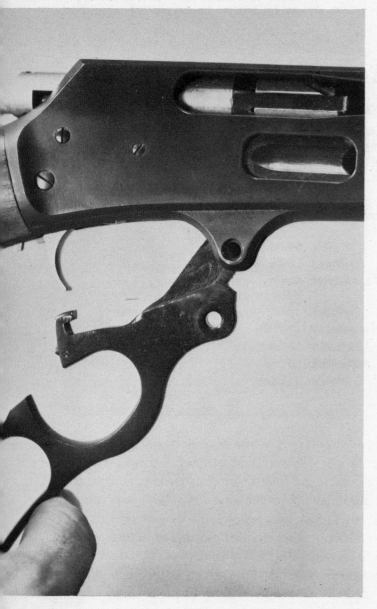

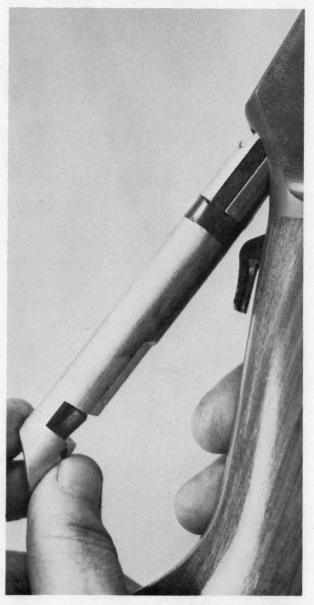

3. Push the ejector mounting stud inward, and remove the ejector from inside the receiver. The ejector spring is staked in place, and removal in normal disassembly is not advisable, except for repair.

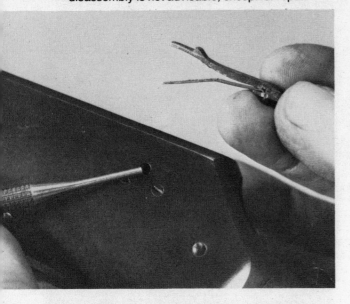

4. Drifting out the vertical roll pin at the rear of the bolt will release the rear firing pin and its spring for removal toward the rear.

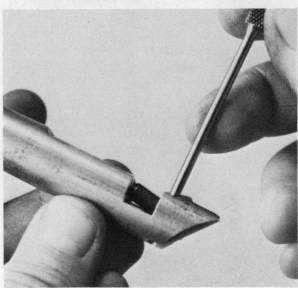

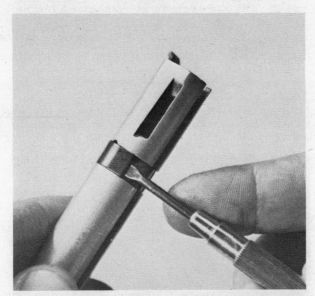

5. Use a small screwdriver to pry the extractor clip off its recess on the front of the bolt, using a finger-tip to lift the front of the extractor out of its channel. Removal of the extractor will give access to the vertical pin that retains the front firing pin. After the pin is drifted out, the firing pin is removed toward the rear.

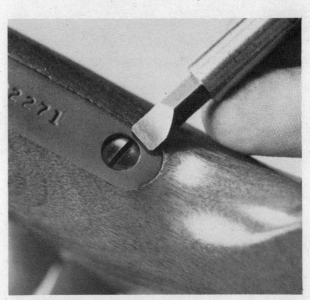

6. Remove the vertical screw at the rear of the upper tang, and take off the stock toward the rear. If the stock is tight, bump the front of the comb with the heel of the hand to start it off.

7. Depress the trigger block (arrow), on the underside behind the trigger, and gently lower the hammer to the fired position. With smooth-jawed pliers or strong fingers, grip the upper portion of the hammer spring base plate, tilt it forward, and slide it toward the side, moving its lower end out of its groove in the lower tang. Keep a firm grip on the plate, as the spring is under some tension, even when at rest. Remove the plate, and the hammer spring, toward the rear.

8. Remove the hammer pivot screw, and take out the hammer upward. Drifting out the cross-pin at the rear of the hammer will release the hammer spring strut, but in normal takedown it is best left in place.

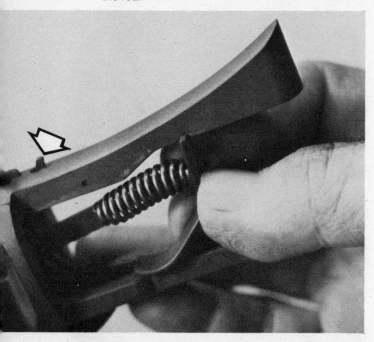

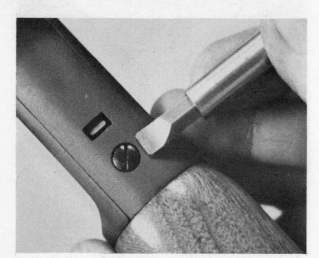

9. Remove the vertical screw on the underside at the forward end of the trigger housing.

10. Remove the screw on the left side of the receiver at lower center.

11. Remove the trigger housing downward and toward the rear. If it is very tight, it may be necessary to tap it with a plastic hammer to start it out.

12. Drifting out the trigger cross-pin will allow the trigger and sear to be removed downward. The small pin just forward of the trigger is the contact for the lever latch, and does not have to be removed.

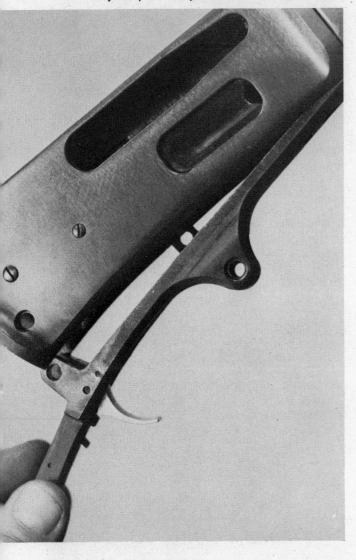

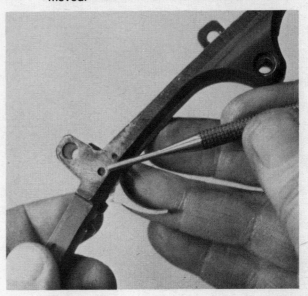

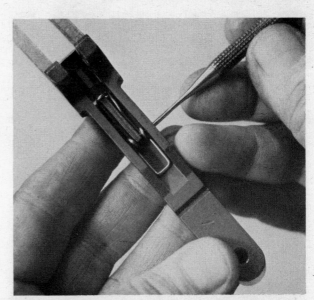

13. A small cross-pin in the lower tang portion of the trigger housing retains the trigger safety block and the combination spring that powers the block and the trigger/sear system. After the pin is drifted out, the block and spring are removed upward. **Note:** The spring is under tension. Control it, and ease it out.

14. The lever latch plunger and its spring are retained in the lever by a cross-pin, and are removed toward the rear. The short coil spring is quite strong, so control it and ease it out.

15. After the trigger housing plate is taken off, the bolt locking block can be moved downward out of the receiver.

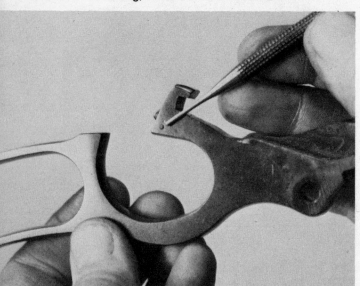

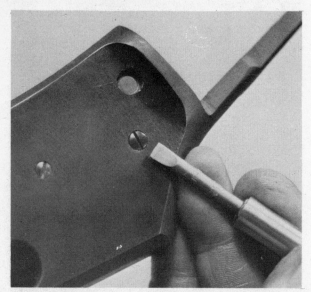

16. Remove the carrier pivot screw, located on the right side of the receiver at center rear.

17. Remove the carrier downward. The carrier rocker and its spring are retained on the left side of the carrier by a vertical pin.

18. Remove the small screw on the right side of the receiver to the rear of the loading port, and take out the loading gate from inside the receiver.

19. Remove the screw on the underside of the magazine tube at its forward end, and take out the tube endpiece, magazine spring, and follower. **Caution:** *Some magazine springs are more powerful than others, and all are under some tension. Ease the endpiece out, and control the spring.*

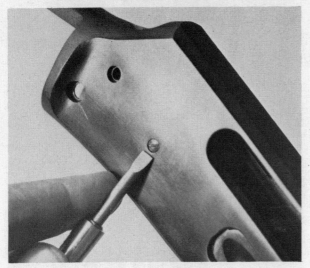

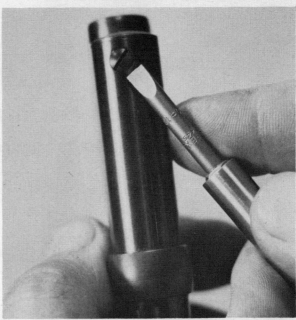

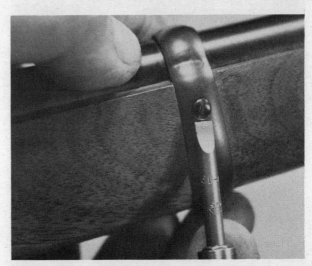

20. Slide the front sight hood off toward the front, remove the two vertical screws in the front sight base, and take off the front sight upward.

21. Take out the cross-screw in the front barrel band. Take out the cross-screw in the rear barrel band, and slide the barrel band off toward the front.

22. Move the fore-end wood forward to free the magazine tube, then slide the magazine tube, fore-end wood, and front barrel band off toward the front.

Reassembly Tips:

1. When replacing the magazine tube, be sure its rear tip enters the well in the front of the receiver. Be sure it is oriented at the front so its screw groove will align with the hole in the front barrel band.

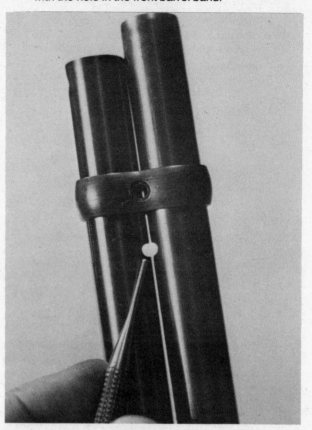

2. When replacing the hammer spring system, hook the lower end of the spring plate in its groove in the lower tang, tip the top of the plate forward, beneath the upper tang, and slide the plate across into place.

Parts List

1. Receiver
2. Dummy Screws (6)
3. Breech Bolt
4. Extractor
5. Rear Firing Pin Retaining Pin (long)
5A. Front Firing Pin Retaining Pin (short)
6. Front Firing Pin
7. Rear Firing Pin
8. Firing Pin Spring
9. Hammer
10. Hammer Rod
11. Hammer Rod Pin
12. Mainspring
13. Mainspring Adjusting Plate
14. Hammer Screw
15. Tang Screw
16. Trigger Guard Plate
17. Trigger Guard Plate Screw
18. Trigger Guard Plate Support Screw
19. Carrier Rocker
20. Carrier Rocker Spring
21. Carrier Rocker Rivet
22. Carrier
23. Carrier Screw
24. Locking Bolt
25. Ejector (with spring)
26. Loading Spring
27. Loading Spring Screw
28. Trigger
29. Trigger Pin
30. Sear.
31. Trigger Safety Block
32. Trigger Safety Block Spring
33. Trigger Safety Block Pin
34. Finger Lever
35. Finger Lever Plunger
36. Finger Lever Plunger Spring
37. Finger Lever Plunger Pin
38. Finger Lever Screw
39. Barrel
40. Rear Sight
41. Rear Sight Elevator
42. Front Sight
43. Front Band
44. Front Band Screw
45. Magazine Tube
46. Magazine Tube Follower
47. Magazine Spring
48. Magazine Tube Plug
49. Magazine Tube Plug Screw
50. Rear Band
51. Rear Band Screw

Disassembly—Open finger lever (34) halfway and remove finger lever screw (38). Pull finger lever down and out of receiver. Pull breech bolt (3) out of receiver and remove ejector (25) from slot in left side of receiver. Remove tang screw (15) and pull buttstock off to rear. Mainspring (12) and adjusting plate (13) are removed by lowering hammer (9) and tipping top of adjusting plate forward and sideward from under top tang portion of receiver. Remove hammer screw (14). Press trigger and remove hammer (9) from top of receiver. Remove trigger guard plate screw (17) and trigger guard plate support screw (18) and drop trigger guard plate (16) from bottom of receiver. Trigger (28) and sear (30) are removed from trigger guard plate by drifting out trigger pin (29). Trigger safety block (31) and spring (32) are removed by drifting out trigger safety block pin (33). Remove carrier screw (23) at right of receiver and drop carrier (22) out of bottom of receiver. Loading spring (26) is removed by unscrewing loading spring screw (27) from right of receiver. Remove magazine tube plug screw (49) and draw magazine tube plug (48) out of magazine tube (45). Magazine spring (47) and follower (46) are drawn out of tube to the front. Remove front band screw (44) and slide band (43) off to front. Remove rear band screw (51) and loosen rear band (50). Slide wooden fore-end (not shown in drawing) up on barrel slightly and draw magazine tube from receiver. Fore-end is removed by sliding off rear band. Reassemble in reverse order.

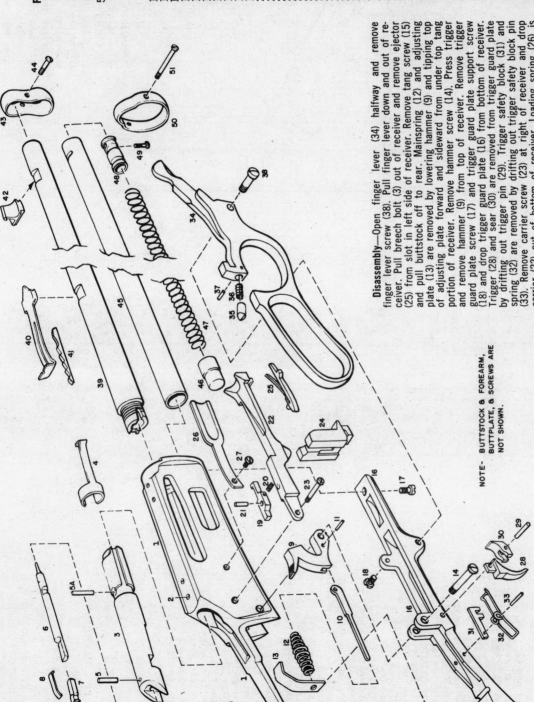

NOTE— BUTTSTOCK & FOREARM, BUTTPLATE, & SCREWS ARE NOT SHOWN.

MARLIN MODEL 336

MARLIN MODEL 39A

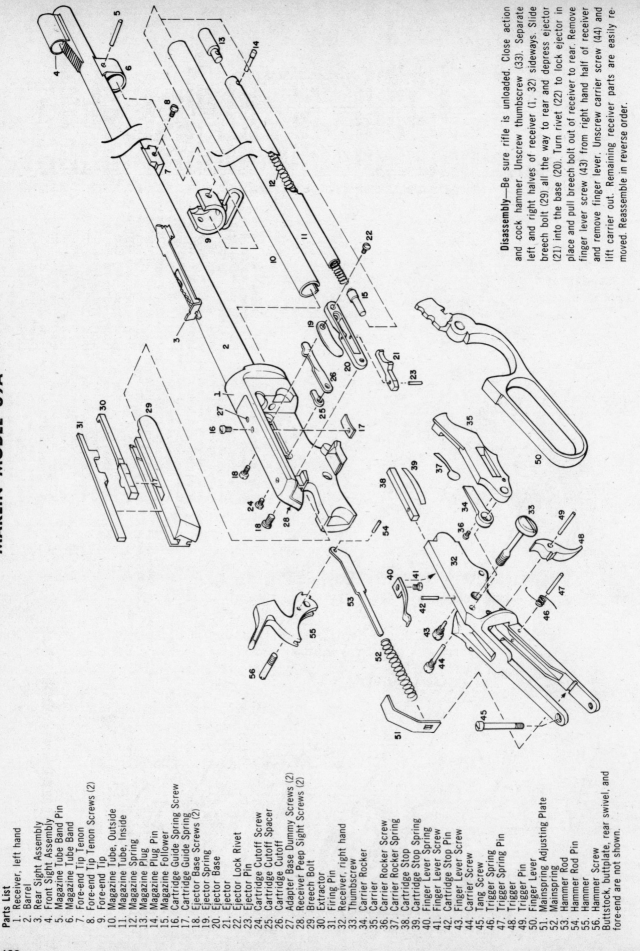

Disassembly—Be sure rifle is unloaded. Close action and cock hammer. Unscrew thumbscrew (33). Separate left and right halves of receiver (1, 32) sideways. Slide breech bolt (29) all the way to rear and depress ejector (21) into the base (20). Turn rivet (22) to lock ejector in place and pull breech bolt out of receiver to rear. Remove finger lever screw (43) from right hand half of receiver and remove finger lever. Unscrew carrier screw (44) and lift carrier out. Remaining receiver parts are easily removed. Reassemble in reverse order.

Parts List

1. Receiver, left hand
2. Barrel
3. Rear Sight Assembly
4. Front Sight Assembly
5. Magazine Tube Band Pin
6. Magazine Tube Band
7. Fore-end Tip Tenon
8. Fore-end Tip Tenon Screws (2)
9. Fore-end Tip
10. Magazine Tube, Outside
11. Magazine Tube, Inside
12. Magazine Spring
13. Magazine Plug
14. Magazine Plug Pin
15. Magazine Follower
16. Cartridge Guide Spring Screw
17. Cartridge Guide Spring
18. Ejector Base Screws (2)
19. Ejector Spring
20. Ejector Base
21. Ejector
22. Ejector Lock Rivet
23. Ejector Pin
24. Cartridge Cutoff Screw
25. Cartridge Cutoff Spacer
26. Cartridge Cutoff
27. Adapter Base Dummy Screws (2)
28. Receiver Peep Sight Screws (2)
29. Breech Bolt
30. Extractor
31. Firing Pin
32. Receiver, right hand
33. Thumbscrew
34. Carrier Rocker
35. Carrier Rocker
36. Carrier
37. Carrier Rocker Screw
38. Carrier Rocker Spring
39. Cartridge Stop
40. Cartridge Stop Spring
41. Finger Lever Spring
42. Finger Lever Screw
43. Cartridge Stop Pin
44. Finger Lever Screw
45. Carrier Screw
46. Tang Screw
47. Trigger Spring
48. Trigger Spring Pin
49. Trigger Pin
50. Finger Lever
51. Mainspring Adjusting Plate
52. Mainspring
53. Hammer Rod
54. Hammer Rod Pin
55. Hammer
56. Hammer Screw
    Buttstock, buttplate, rear swivel, and
    fore-end are not shown.

190

MARLIN MODEL 39A

Data: Marlin Model 39A
Origin: United States
Manufacturer: Marlin Firearms
North Haven, Connecticut
Cartridge: 22 Short, Long or Long Rifle
Magazine capacity: 26 Short, 21 Long, 19 Long Rifle
Over-all length: 40 Inches
Barrel length: 24 inches
Weight: 6½ pounds

When the Marlin company introduced the first lever-action, repeating 22 rimfire rifle in 1891, it had one particularly notable feature: It was the first repeating 22 rifle that would feed Short, Long, and Long Rifle cartridges interchangeably. The basic gun was slightly redesigned in 1897, 1922, and 1938, finally arriving at the excellent Model 39A that is so popular today. Except for slight manufacturing changes—such as the use of modern round-wire springs—the internal mechanism is basically unchanged from the original 1891 version. With the exception of a shorter barrel and carbine-style, straight-gripped stock, the Mountie model is mechanically identical.

Disassembly:

1. Use a coin to start the large knurled takedown screw on the right side of the receiver, then use the fingers to back it out until its threads are free. An internal shoulder will keep the screw from coming completely out.

2. Set the hammer on the safety step, and bump the left side of the stock with the heel of the hand to force the stock and receiver plate toward the right. Separate the stock and its attached parts from the front portion of the gun.

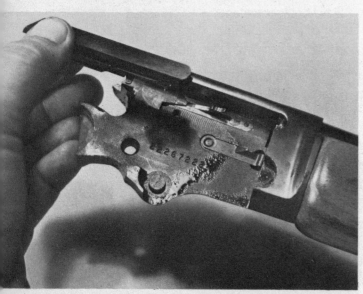

3. Slide the breechblock (bolt) toward the rear until its lower projection stops against the shoulder of the receiver, then remove the bolt toward the right side of the frame.

4. The firing pin is easily lifted from the top of the breechblock.

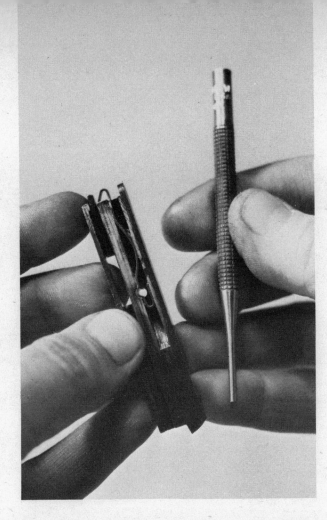

5. Insert a drift punch of the proper size through the small hole in the underside of the breech-block, and push the extractor upward and out of its recess in the top of the bolt.

6. The ejector housing is retained on the inside of the receiver by two screws which enter from the outside left of the receiver, near the top. Back out the two screws, and remove the ejector assembly toward the right. The ejector spring will be released by removal of the housing, and drifting out a vertical pin will free the ejector for removal. In normal takedown, the ejector lock rivet is not removed. The cartridge stop (arrow), located below the ejector and toward the front, is retained by a single screw which also enters from the outside left of the receiver. Back out this screw, and remove the stop and its spacer block toward the right.

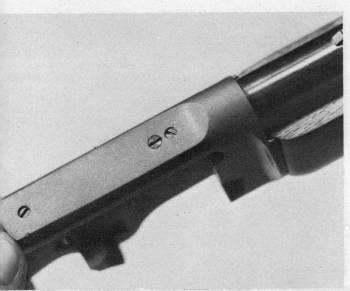

7. The cartridge guide spring, located just above the chamber, is retained by a screw which enters from the top of the receiver. This is the larger screw near the front scope mount screw. The cartridge guide spring is removed downward.

8. Drifting out the small cross-pin in the magazine tube hanger will allow removal of the outer magazine tube toward the front. If the inner magazine tube is to be taken apart, drifting out the cross-pin which also locks the tube in place will allow removal of the knurled endpiece, spring, and follower. There is some risk of damage to the thin tube, and in normal takedown the inner tube should be left assembled.

9. Removal of the two screws in the fore-end cap will allow it to be taken off forward, and the fore-end cap base can then be driven out of its dovetail toward the right side. When doing this, take care not to damage the screw holes. The fore-end can now be moved slightly forward and taken off downward.

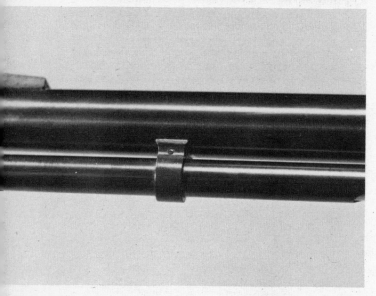

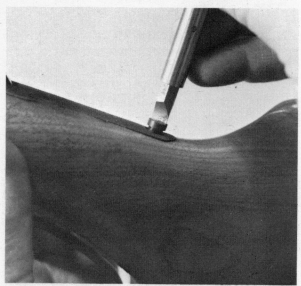

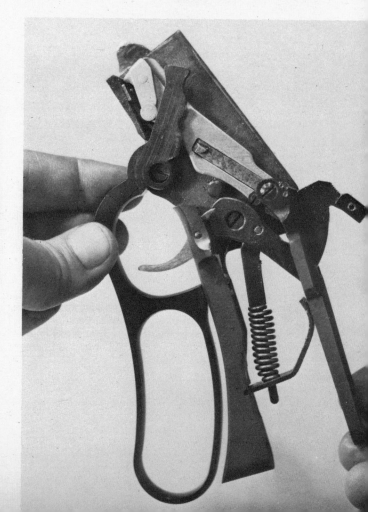

10. Take out the stock mounting bolt, the large screw at the rear tip of the upper tang. The stock can now be removed toward the rear. If the fitting is very tight, it may be necessary to bump the front of the comb with the heel of the hand or a soft rubber hammer.

11. The firing mechanism is shown in proper order, prior to disassembly. Note the relationship of all parts, to aid in reassembly.

12. Grip the upper part of the hammer spring base with pliers and slide it out toward either side, moving its lower end out of its slot in the lower tang. The hammer, of course, must be at rest (in fired position). Remove the base and the spring toward the rear.

13. Take out the hammer pivot screw, and remove the hammer from the top of the frame. During this operation, it will be necessary to tilt the attached hammer strut slightly to one side or the other to clear. Proceed carefully, and use no force.

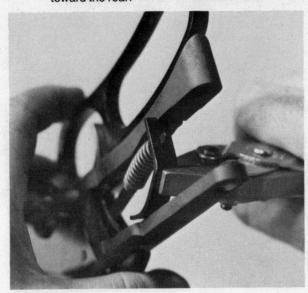

14. Move the takedown screw over until its threads engage the threads in the right side of the receiver, and unscrew it toward the right side for removal.

15. Remove the small screw on the underside of the frame, just forward of the lever, and take out the lever spring from inside the frame.

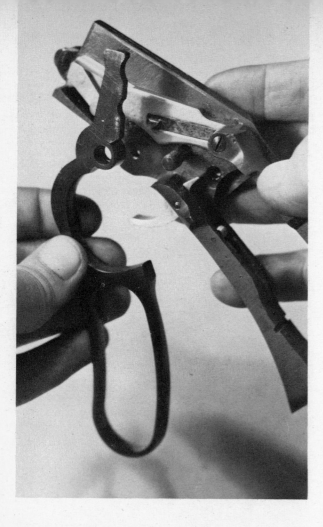

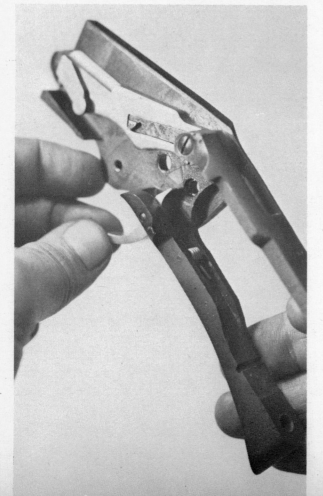

16. Take out the lever pivot screw, and remove the lever toward the left.

17. Take out the carrier pivot screw, and remove the carrier assembly toward the front. Taking out the carrier rocker screw will allow removal of the rocker and its spring from the carrier.

18. Drift out the trigger pin toward the right, and remove the trigger downward. Drift out the trigger spring pin, and remove the trigger spring from inside the frame.

Reassembly Tips:

1. When replacing the hammer spring and its base, be sure the hammer is at rest, and insert a lower corner of the base into its slot in the lower tang, then tip the upper part downward and slip it under the upper tang, moving it inward into place.

2. When rejoining the front and rear parts of the gun, be sure the breechblock is all the way forward, the hammer at full cock or on the safety step, and take care that the front tongue of the sideplate (arrow) is properly engaged with its mating recess in the main frame.

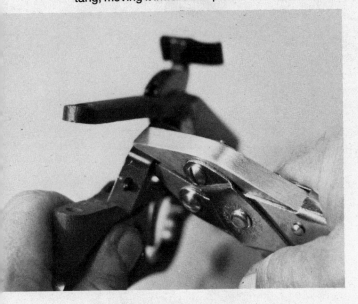

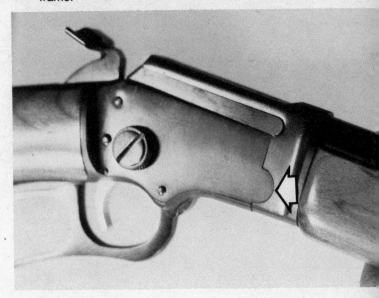

Avoid over-tightening of the small screw which holds the cartridge guide spring above the chamber, or the spring may crack. This advice also applies to the cartridge stop screw. Both should be firm and snug, but use no excessive force.

When replacing the extractor in the top of the breechblock, start its rear portion into the recess, then flex the front portion slightly for proper alignment and push it into place.

Ruger
Model 10/22 Rifle

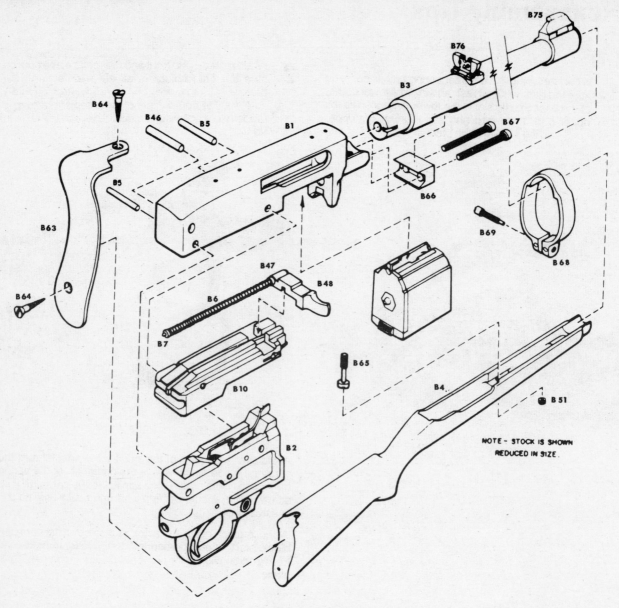

NOTE - STOCK IS SHOWN
REDUCED IN SIZE

B-3	Barrel					
B-68	Barrel Band	B-17	Hammer			
B-69	Barrel Band Screw	B-18	Hammer Strut			
B-66	Barrel Retainer (V-Block)	B-19	Hammer Pivot Pin			
B-67	Barrel Retainer Screws (2)	B-43	Hammer Bushings (2)	B-83	Receiver Filler Screws (4)
B-10	Bolt Assembly	B-44	Hammer Spring		(Top of Receiver) (Not Shown)
B-7	Bolt Handle, Guide Rod and	B-45	Hammer Strut Washer	B-7	Recoil Spring, Guide Rod and
	Recoil Spring Assembly	BX-1	Magazine Assembly		Bolt Handle Assembly
B-41	Bolt Lock		(Not Numbered)	B-22	Rebound Spring Stop Pin (Not Shown)
B-42	Bolt Lock Spring	B-29	Magazine Cap	B-4	Stock
B-46	Bolt Stop Pin	B-28	Magazine Cap Nut	B-23	Sear
B-63	Buttplate (Carbine or Sporter)	B-34	Magazine Latch	B-24	Sear Spring
B-64	Buttplate Screws (2)	B-35	Magazine Latch Pivot Pin &	B-52	Safety
B-25	Disconnector		Ejector Pin (2)	B-53	Safety Detent Plunger
B-26	Disconnector Pivot Pin	B-36	Magazine Latch Plunger	B-54	Safety Detent Plunger Spring
B-8	Ejector	B-37	Magazine Latch Plunger Spring	B-75	Front Sight (Bead)
B-14	Extractor	B-32	Magazine Rotor	B-76	Rear Sight (Open)
B-16	Extractor Plunger	B-33	Magazine Rotor Spring	B-2	Trigger Guard Assembly
B-51	Stock Escutcheon	B-30	Magazine Screw	B-20	Trigger
B-15	Extractor Spring	B-27	Magazine Shell	B-21	Trigger Pivot Pin
B-11	Firing Pin	B-31	Magazine Throat (Steel)	B-39	Trigger Plunger
B-12	Firing Pin Rebound Spring	B-1	Receiver	B-40	Trigger Plunger Spring
B-13	Firing Pin Stop Pin	B-5	Receiver Cross Pins (2)	B-65	Takedown Screw

RUGER 10/22

Data:	Ruger 10/22
Origin:	United States
Manufacturer:	Sturm, Ruger & Company Southport, Connecticut
Cartridge:	22 Long Rifle
Magazine capacity:	10 rounds
Over-all length:	36¾ inches
Barrel length:	18½ inches
Weight:	5¾ pounds

Since its introduction in 1964, the Model 10/22 has established an enviable record of reliability. Over the past fifteen years, I have repaired only one of these guns, and that one had been altered by its owner. Originally offered in Carbine, Sporter, and International models, the latter having a full Mannlicher-style stock, the gun is now available in only Carbine and Sporter styles, with the only differences being in the stock and barrel band. The instructions will generally apply to any of the 10/22 guns.

Disassembly:

1. Loosen or remove the cross-screw at the lower end of the barrel band, and take off the barrel band toward the front. If the band is tight, applying slight downward pressure on the barrel will make it move off more easily.

2. Remove the magazine, and cycle the action to cock the internal hammer. Back out the main stock screw, located on the underside just forward of the magazine well.

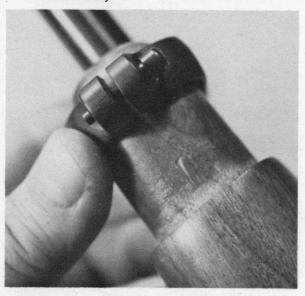

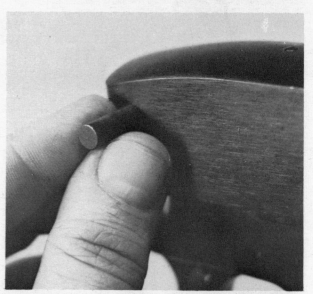

3. Center the safety, halfway between its right and left positions, so it will clear the stock on each side, and move the action upward out of the stock.

4. When the action is removed from the stock, the bolt stop pin, the large cross-pin at the rear of the receiver, will probably be loose and can be easily taken out at this time.

6. If the bolt stop pin was not taken out earlier, it must be removed now. With the gun inverted, move the bolt all the way to the rear, and tip the front of the bolt outward, away from the inside roof of the receiver. **Caution:** *Keep a firm grip on the bolt handle, as the bolt spring is fully compressed.* Ease the bolt handle forward, slowly relieving the spring tension, and remove the bolt from the underside of the receiver. Remove the bolt handle and its attached spring and guide rod from the ejection port.

5. Drift out the front and rear cross-pins (arrows) that hold the trigger group on the receiver. Then remove the trigger group downward.

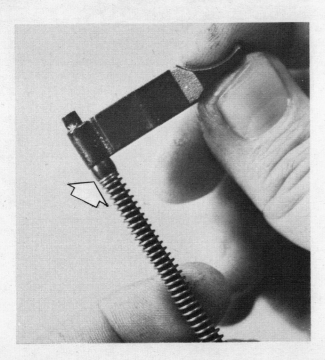

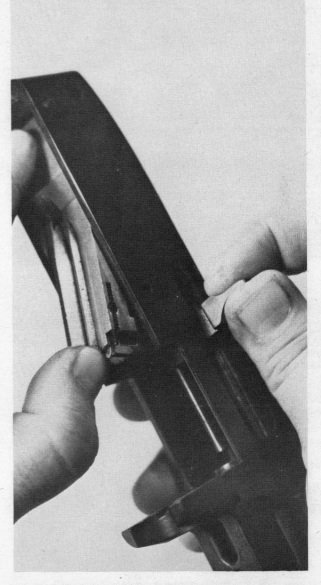

7. The bolt spring guide rod is staked at the forward end, ahead of the bolt handle, and if the stake lumps are filed off for disassembly, a new guide rod may be required. In normal disassembly, this unit is best left intact. If it is taken apart, be careful not to lose the small spacer (arrow) between the spring and the handle at the forward end.

8. The firing pin is retained by a roll cross-pin at the upper rear of the bolt. Use a roll-pin punch to drift out the cross-pin, and remove the firing pin and its return spring toward the rear.

9. To remove the extractor, insert a small screwdriver to depress the extractor spring plunger, and hold it in while the extractor is lifted out of its recess. **Caution:** *Take care that the screwdriver doesn't slip, as the plunger and spring can travel far if suddenly released.* Ease them out slowly, and remove them from the bolt.

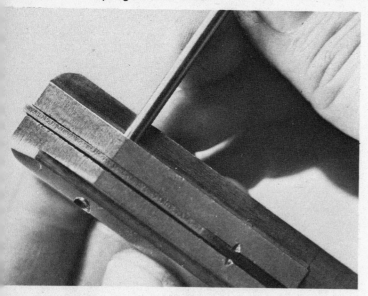

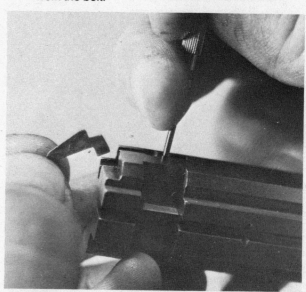

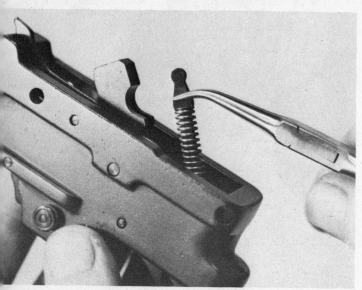

10. Restrain the hammer against the tension of its spring, pull the trigger, and ease the hammer forward, beyond its normal fired position. The hammer spring assembly can now be moved forward and upward, out of the trigger group. The hammer spring assembly can be taken apart by compressing the spring and sliding the slotted washer off the lower end of the guide. Proceed with caution, as the spring is under tension.

11. Before going any further with disassembly of the trigger group, carefully note the relationship of all parts and springs, to aid in reassembly. Tip the front of the ejector out of its slot in the front of the trigger group, push out the cross-pin at the rear of the ejector, and remove the ejector upward. Note that removal of the cross-pin will also release the upper arm of the bolt latch spring.

12. A cross-pin at the lower front of the trigger group pivots and retains the bolt latch and the magazine catch lever. The bolt latch is removed upward. Restrain the magazine catch plunger with a fingertip, remove the catch lever downward, and ease the plunger and its spring out toward the front.

13. Hold the trigger back to remove sear tension from the hammer, and push out the hammer pivot cross-pin. Remove the hammer assembly upward. The bolt latch spring encircles the hammer bushing on the right side, and the two hammer pivot bushings are easily removed from the hammer.

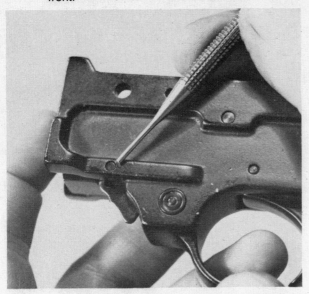

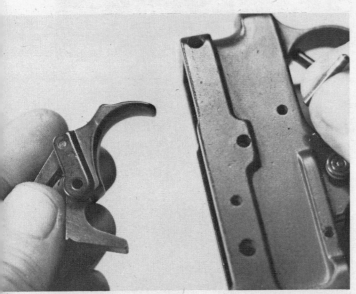

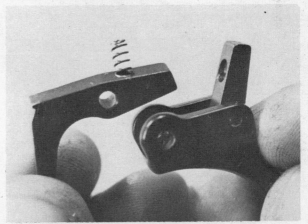

14. Note the position of the sear and disconnector in the top of the trigger before disassembly. Push out the trigger pivot cross-pin, and remove the trigger/sear/disconnector assembly upward. As the trigger is moved upward, the trigger spring and plunger will be released at the rear of the trigger guard. Ease them out, and remove them downward and toward the front.

15. The sear is removed from the trigger toward the front, along with the combination sear and disconnector spring. Drifting out the cross-pin at the upper rear of the trigger will release the disconnector for removal.

16. Grip the safety firmly with a thumb and finger at each end, and give it one-quarter turn toward the front, then push it out toward the left. **Caution:** *Insert a fingertip inside the trigger group, above the safety, to arrest the safety plunger and spring, as they will be released as the safety is moved out.*

17. In normal takedown, removal of the barrel is not advisable. If necessary, however, use an Allen wrench to back out the two large screws that secure the barrel retainer block, and take out the barrel toward the front. If the barrel is tight, grip the barrel in a padded vise and use a nylon hammer to tap the receiver off toward the rear.

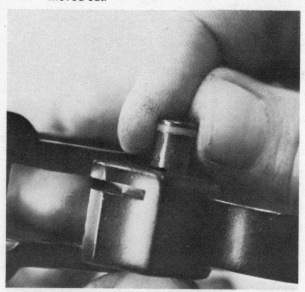

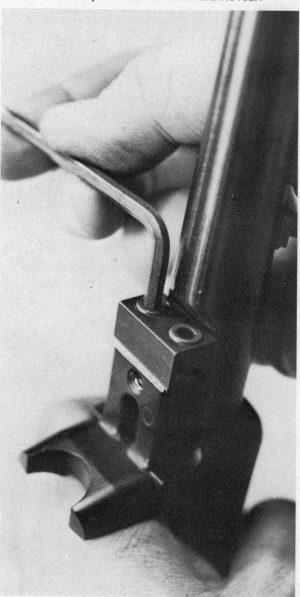

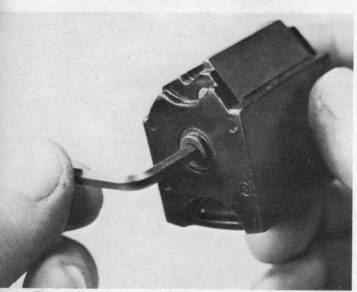

18. Magazine disassembly is not recommended in normal takedown. If it becomes necessary, removal of the screw at the front of the magazine will allow the back plate to be taken off, and the internal parts can then be taken out toward the rear. A word of caution—*don't remove the spring from the rotor.* Carefully note the relationship of all parts to aid in reassembly.

Reassembly Tips:

1. When replacing the trigger/sear/disconnector assembly in the trigger group, use a slave pin to hold the three parts and the spring in position for re-insertion. The photo shows the parts in place, and the slave pin in the pivot-hole.

2. When replacing the hammer, its pivot-bushings, and the bolt latch spring, note that the spring must be on the right side of the hammer, as shown. Be sure the lower arm of the spring engages its notch in the cross-piece of the bolt latch. The upper arm of the spring goes below the cross-pin that retains the ejector.

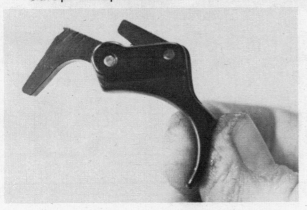

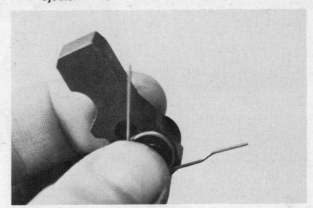

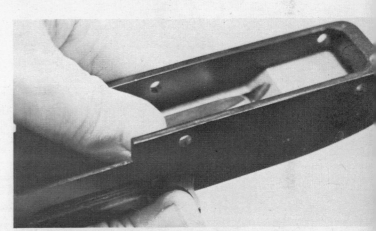

4. When replacing the bolt in the receiver, remember that the bolt handle must be fully to the rear, with the spring compressed, before the bolt can be tipped back into engagement with the handle at the front.

When replacing the action in the stock, be sure the safety is again set between its right and left positions to clear the interior as the action is moved into place.

If the magazine has been disassembled, insert the screw in the magazine body, and place the rotor and spring on the screw, with the longer hub of the rotor toward the front. Replace the feed throat, being sure the larger end stud enters its recess at the front. Put the backplate back on the magazine body, and hold it in place. Insert the front of the hexagonal-headed magazine nut into the rear of the spring, and be sure the hooked tip of the spring engages the hole in the nut. Turn the nut clockwise (rear view) until the rotor stops turning, then give it an additional 1¼ turns to properly tension the spring. Move the nut into its recess, and tighten the magazine screw, taking care not to over-tighten it.

3. When replacing the magazine catch system, remember that the bolt latch must be in place before the catch lever, plunger, and spring are installed. Insert the magazine catch plunger and spring first, then put in the catch lever from below, and the upper arm of the lever will hold the plunger and spring in place while the cross-pin is inserted. Be sure the cross-pin passes through the bolt latch and the magazine catch.

SAVAGE / ANSCHUTZ MODEL 54

Data:	Savage/Anschutz Model 54
Origin:	Germany
Manufacturer:	J.G. Anschutz Gmbh, Ulm/Donau (Imported by Savage Arms, Westfield, Massachusetts)
Cartridge:	22 Long Rifle
Magazine capacity:	5 rounds
Over-all length:	41⅞ inches
Barrel length:	22½ inches
Weight:	6¾ pounds

The Anschutz family has been making fine guns in Germany since 1793, and the J. G. Anschutz firm was established in Zella-Mehlis about 1922. In the postwar years, the factory was relocated to Ulm/Donau. In 1966 Savage Arms began importing an elegant little Anschutz rifle, the Model 54, and the gun is still available. In recent times, the U.S. dollar has suffered in comparison with the German Mark, making the Savage/Anschutz Model 54 quite expensive. Many discriminating shooters, though, feel that the quality is worth the price.

Disassembly:

1. Remove the magazine, and back out the screw on the underside, at the rear of the trigger guard. When the screw is out, flex the trigger guard very slightly to free it from its recess in the stock at the rear, and swing the guard out to the side, to give access to the rear vertical screw in the trigger plate. Back out the rear trigger plate screw.

2. Remove the main action screw, located at the center of the trigger plate, just forward of the guard, and separate the action from the stock. The smaller screw at the front of the trigger plate is a wood screw that retains the trigger plate on the stock. With the plate removed, it is possible to take off the guard, if necessary, by turning off its nut on the inside of the plate.

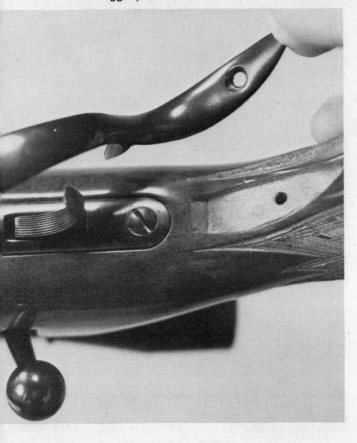

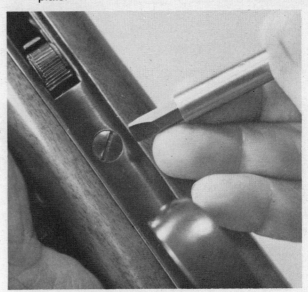

3. To remove the bolt, open it and move it toward the rear while depressing the bolt stop, located on the left side of the receiver, and withdraw the bolt toward the rear. Note that the safety must be in the horizontal off-safe position before the bolt can be opened.

4. Grip the front section of the bolt, and turn the safety lever counter-clockwise (rear view) until the striker drops to the fired position. Continue turning the safety until it stops, and it can then be taken off toward the rear.

5. The cocking indicator and its spring are held inside the safety dome by an enlarged coil at the rear end of the indicator spring, and the indicator and spring are easily removed by pushing them out toward the front.

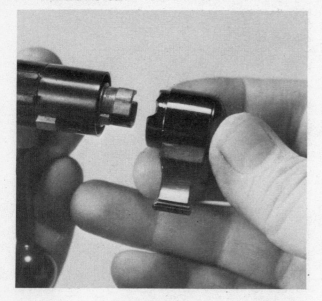

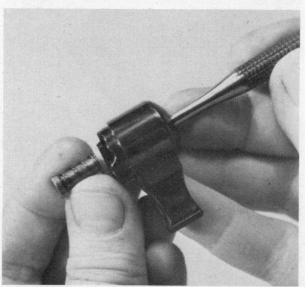

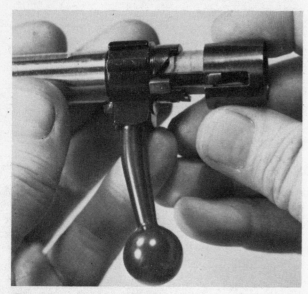

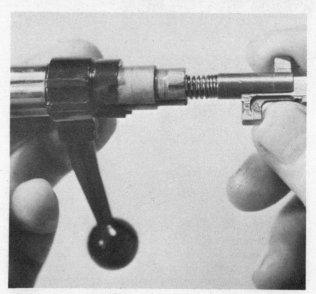

6. Remove the safety sleeve toward the rear.

7. Remove the striker assembly toward the rear.

8. To disassemble the striker assembly, grip the rear of the striker in a strong hand or a padded vise, and push the ridged collar at the front of the spring very slightly toward the rear, give it a half turn, and ease it off toward the front, slowly releasing the tension of the spring. **Caution:** *Control the striker spring.* Remove the collar, spring, and rear spring guide from the striker/firing pin toward the front.

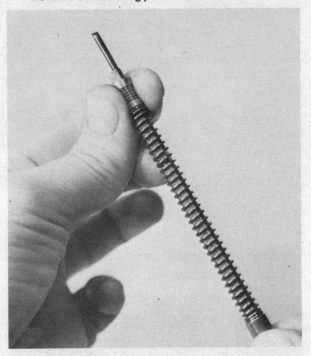

9. After the striker assembly is removed, take off the bolt handle toward the rear.

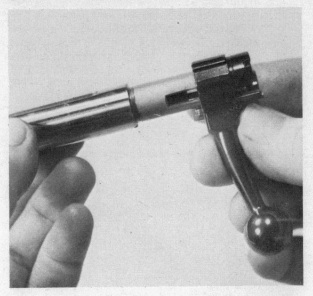

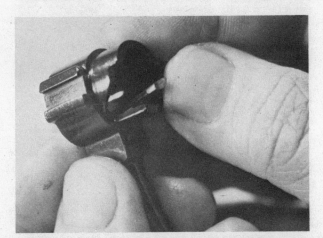

10. To remove the bolt handle positioning plunger and its spring, push the plunger toward the rear, and tip its flat rear end inward, then move the part out toward the front of the handle sleeve. Take care not to lose the small coil spring.

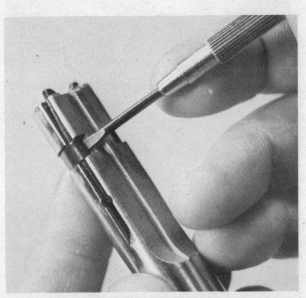

11. The extractors are retained on the front of the bolt by a semi-circular spring clip. Use a small screwdriver to pry either end of the clip outward, and ease it off the top of the bolt. The extractors are then easily removed toward each side. Take care to pry the clip only enough to clear the bolt body during removal, as it also is the spring for the extractors, and must not be weakened.

12. The trigger mount is secured at the rear of the receiver by a single vertical screw, and access to the screw head is limited by a rear projection of the mount. An offset or angle-tip screwdriver must be used. Take care not to lose the lock-washer under the screw head. Note that it is possible to remove the entire trigger assembly without disturbing the adjustment settings of the trigger spring screw and sear engagement screw. If necessary, these are also easily removed. The nut must be loosened to take out the sear engagement screw at the front. The cross-pin can also be driven out, separating the trigger from the mount, but this is usually staked at the ends, so take care not to deform the upper arms of the trigger during removal of the pin. In normal take-down, the assembly is best left intact.

13. The sear is retained on the underside of the receiver by a cross-pin, and is removed downward, along with its spring, after the pin is drifted out.

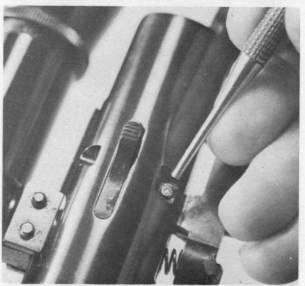

14. The bolt stop is retained on the left side of the receiver by a vertical pin. After the pin is drifted out, the bolt stop and its coil spring are removed toward the left.

15. The magazine housing and catch assembly is retained on the underside of the receiver by two large screws at its front and rear. The rear screw is a limited access type, and will require the use of an angled-tip screwdriver for removal. The rear screw also secures the internal rear magazine guide and the bolt guide within the receiver. After removal of the screws, the magazine housing and guide are taken off downward, and the bolt guide can be removed from inside the receiver.

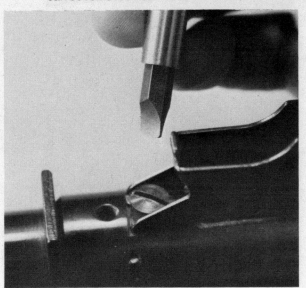

Reassembly Tips:

1. Before the reassembled bolt can be put back into the receiver, it must be re-cocked. Grip the forward portion of the bolt in a padded vise, and move the bolt handle counter-clockwise (rear view) until the striker lug on the underside is in the position shown, and the striker indicator is protruding from the rear of the safety dome. Note that the safety lever must be in its off-safe position before the bolt handle can be moved.

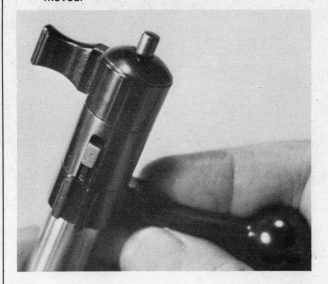

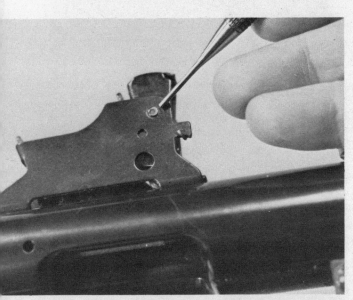

16. The magazine catch and its spring are mounted on a cross-pin in the rear of the magazine housing, and the cross-pin is usually semi-riveted at the ends. Care must be taken when drifting it out, to avoid deformation of the magazine housing and the catch. If the catch and spring don't need repair, they are best left on the housing.

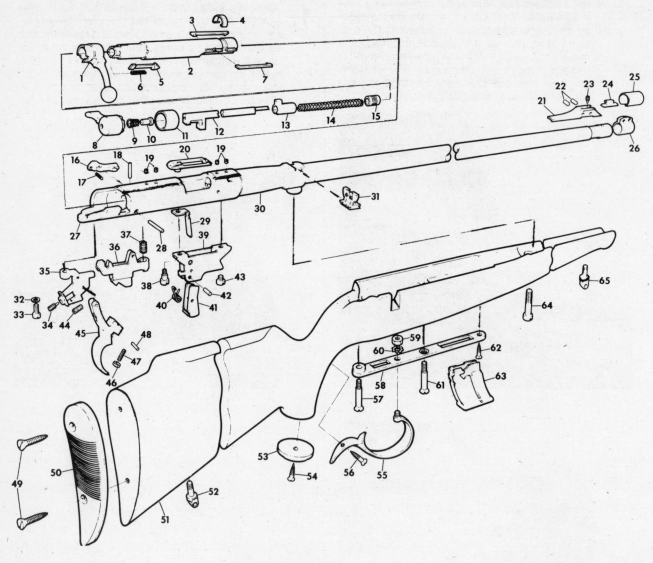

1	Bolt Handle	23	Front Sight Base Screw	45	Trigger
2	Bolt Case (Only)	24	Front Sight	46	Trigger Adjusting Screw
3	Extractor (Left)	25	Front Sight Hood		Safety Knob
4	Extractor Lock Ring	26	Front Sight Band	47	Trigger Adjusting Screw
5	Bolt Handle Locking Pin	27	Receiver	48	Trigger Pin
6	Bolt Handle Locking Pin	28	Trigger Plate Pin	49	Buttplate Screws (2)
	Spring	29	Magazine Guide (Rear)	50	Buttplate
7	Extractor (Right)	30	Barrel	51	Stock
8	Safety	31	Rear Sight	52	Swivel Stud (Rear)
9	Cocking Indicator Spring	32	Trigger Bracket Screw	53	Pistol Grip Cap
10	Cocking Indicator		Lock Washer	54	Pistol Grip Cap Screw
11	Safety Jacket	33	Trigger Bracket Screw	55	Trigger Guard
12	Firing Pin	34	Trigger Spring Adjusting	56	Trigger Guard Screw
13	Firing Pin Spring Guide (Rear)		Screw	57	Rear Assembly Screw
14	Mainspring	35	Trigger Bracket	58	Floorplate
15	Firing Pin Spring Guide (Front)	36	Trigger Plate	59	Trigger Guard Nut
16	Bolt Stop	37	Trigger Plate Spring	60	Trigger Guard Nut Lock
17	Bolt Stop Spring	38	Magazine Guide Screw (Rear)		Washer
18	Bolt Stop Hinge Pin	39	Magazine Guide	61	Front Assembly Screw
19	Dummy Screws (4)	40	Magazine Retainer Spring	62	Floorplate Screw
20	Bolt Guide	41	Magazine Retainer	63	Magazine Assembly
21	Front Sight Base	42	Magazine Retainer Pin	64	Barrel Assembly Screw
22	Front Sight Base Retaining	43	Magazine Guide Screw Front	65	Swivel Stud (Front)
	Screws (2)	44	Trigger Spring		

U.S. 1903 SPRINGFIELD

Data:	U.S. 1903 Springfield
Origin:	United States
Manufacturer:	Springfield Arsenal and Rock Island Armory
Cartridge:	30-06 Springfield
Magazine capacity:	5 rounds
Over-all length:	43.2 inches
Barrel length:	24 inches
Weight:	8.6 pounds

Adopted by the U.S. as military standard in 1903, this rifle replaced the Krag-Jorgensen, and was used until the adoption of the M1 Garand in 1936. Although officially replaced, the Springfield saw quite a bit of use during World War II. In 1942, the Remington Arms Company did a slight re-design of the gun, mostly to make it easier to manufacture, and this rifle was designated the Model 1903A3. The main differences were in the use of stamped-steel parts to replace several of the machined parts of the original gun, such as the magazine floorplate, and the rear sight was moved to the rear of the receiver. Mechanically, they are essentially the same.

Disassembly:

1. Cycle the bolt to cock the striker, and set the safety lever in the vertical position. Set the magazine cutoff lever, located at the left rear of the receiver, at its mid-position, angled slightly upward from the horizontal. Remove the bolt toward the rear.

2. Depress the bolt sleeve lock (arrow), located on the left side, and unscrew the sleeve and striker assembly counter-clockwise (rear view). Remove the sleeve and striker assembly toward the rear, taking care not to trip the safety lever.

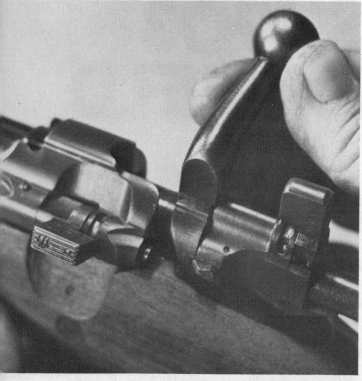

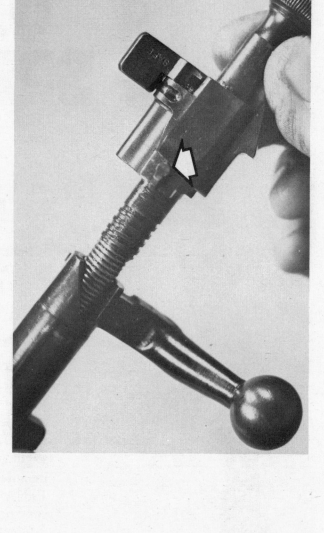

3. Holding firmly to the sleeve and striker knob, turn the safety back to the off-safe position and allow the striker to move forward in the sleeve. Grip the serrated area on the retaining sleeve, just to the rear of the firing pin, and pull the sleeve toward the rear until it clears the back of the firing pin. Remove the firing pin toward the side. **Caution:** *Rest the striker knob on a firm surface during this operation, and keep a firm grip on the firing pin retaining sleeve, as the striker spring is quite strong.*

4. Slowly release the spring tension, and remove the retaining sleeve and the spring toward the front.

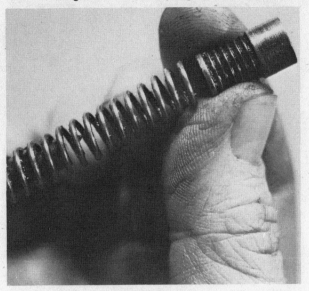

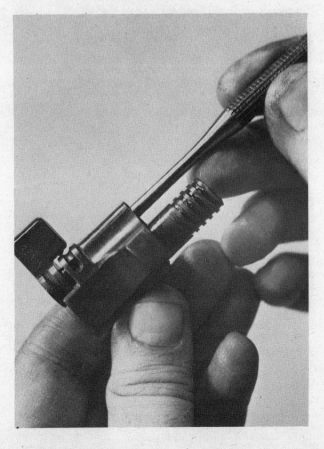

5. Slide the bolt sleeve off the striker rod toward the front.

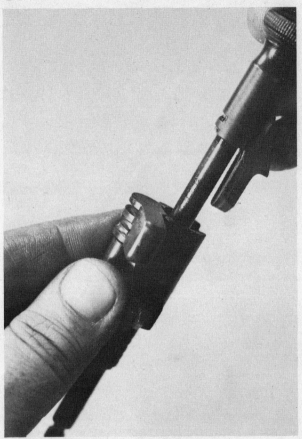

6. Turn the safety lever back to its mid-position and rest the lower rear edge of the bolt sleeve on a firm surface. Use a drift punch against the front tip of the safety shaft to drive it out toward the rear. Note that the safety plunger and spring will be released as the safety clears the rear of the bolt sleeve, so ease them out and take care that they are not lost.

7. Turn the extractor clockwise (rear view) until its front underlug is out of the groove at the front of the bolt, and is aligned with the un-grooved area on the bolt. Push the extractor forward and off its T-mount on the bolt ring.

8. Insert a drift punch in the hole on the underside, just forward of the trigger guard, and depress the magazine floorplate latch. Move the floorplate toward the rear. Remove the floorplate and the attached spring and follower downward. The spring is easily detached from the floorplate and follower.

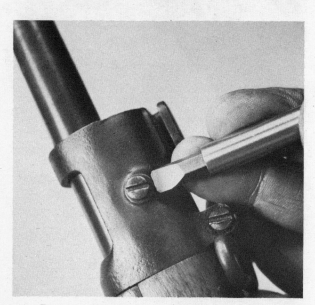

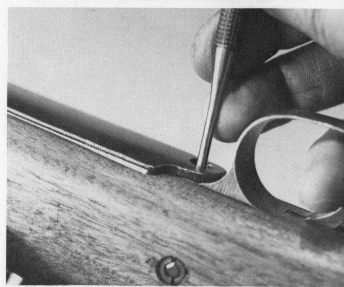

9. Remove the cross-screw in the front barrel band, and slide the barrel band forward.

10. Depress the lock spring on the right side, in front of the rear barrel band (after the band screw and sling loop are removed), and slide the band off toward the front. Move the upper handguard wood forward, and take it off.

11. Remove the large vertical screws on the under-side at the front and rear of the magazine/trigger guard unit. Remove the action from the stock, and take off the trigger guard unit downward.

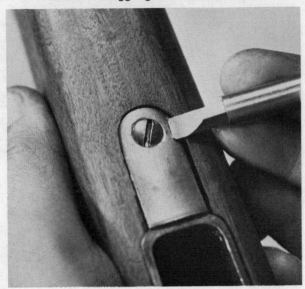

12. The ejector is retained on the left side of the receiver by a vertical pin with a slotted screw-type head at its lower end. If the pin is unusually tight, using a screwdriver to turn it will help to loosen it, but for removal it is driven out downward. The ejector is taken out toward the inside of the re-ceiver.

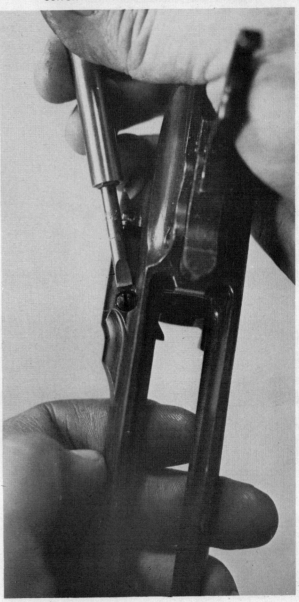

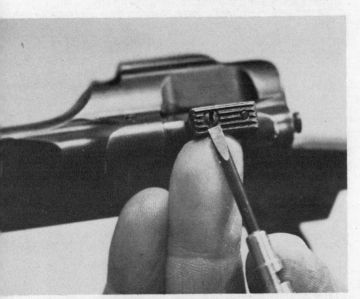

13. Remove the small screw in the serrated end of the bolt stop/magazine cutoff lever.

14. The bolt stop pivot has a cannelure at its rear tip, allowing it to be pulled out with a fingernail or a screwdriver blade. When removing the pivot pin, keep slight inward pressure on the bolt stop, to relieve spring pressure on the pin.

15. Remove the bolt stop/magazine cutoff toward the left, taking care not to lose the positioning plunger and its spring.

16. Push out the sear pivot pin toward the left. As soon as its large head clears its recess in the underside of the receiver, exert slight pressure on the front of the sear to compress the spring and assist withdrawal of the pin.

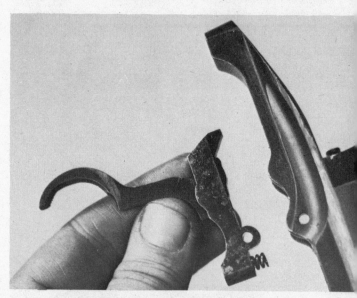

17. Remove the trigger, sear, and sear spring assembly downward. Drifting out the trigger cross-pin will allow separation of the trigger from the sear.

18. To take the front barrel band completely off, the front sight must be drifted out of its dovetail to allow the band to pass. The front sight blade is retained in the dovetailed base by a cross-pin.

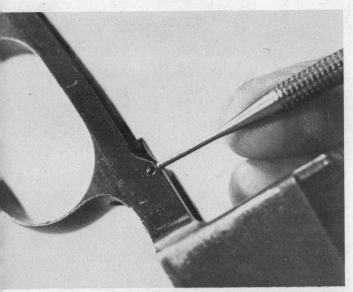

19. Drifting out the cross-pin in the trigger guard unit will allow removal of the magazine floorplate latch and its spring upward. The spring is quite strong, so control it and ease it out.

Reassembly Tips:

1. When replacing the safety lever in the bolt sleeve, insert a small screwdriver to depress the positioning plunger and spring, and note that the lever should be in its midway (vertical) position for installation.

Before the bolt is replaced in the receiver, the striker must be in the cocked position, with the bolt handle raised. Since the Springfield has a cocking knob, this is easily done.

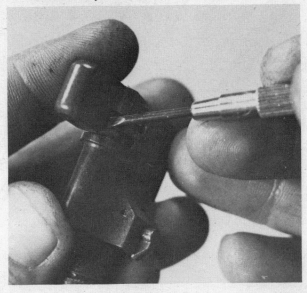

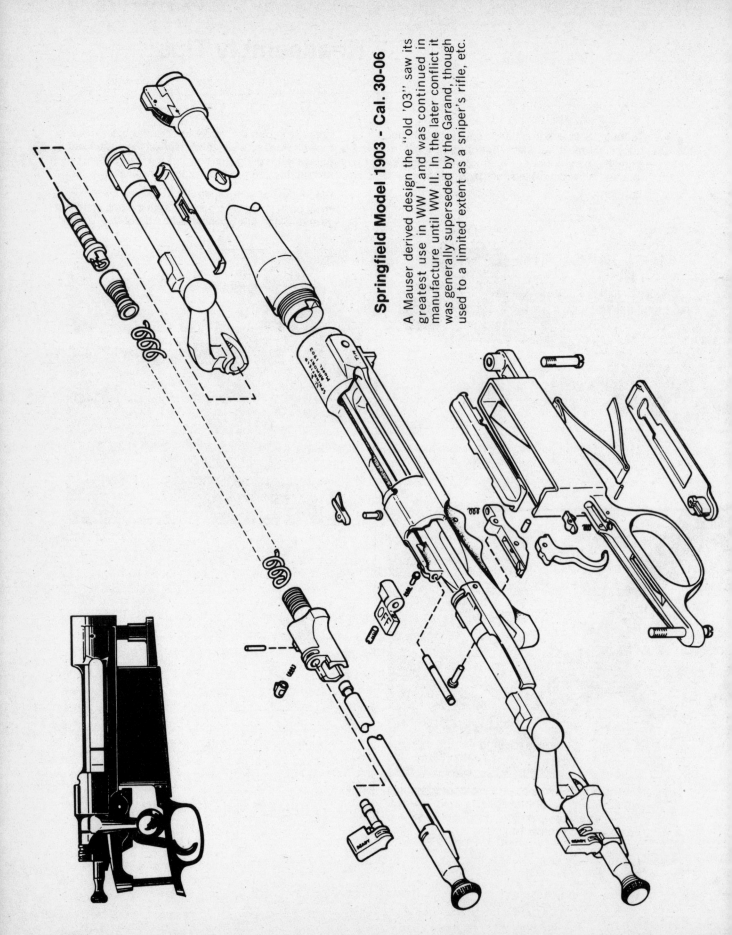

Springfield Model 1903 - Cal. 30-06

A Mauser derived design the "old '03" saw its greatest use in WW I and was continued in manufacture until WW II. In the later conflict it was generally superseded by the Garand, though used to a limited extent as a sniper's rifle, etc.

MAUSER MODEL 1898

Data: Mauser Model 1898 (Karabiner 98k)
Origin: Germany
Manufacturer: Various government arsenals
Cartridge: 7.92mm Mauser (8×57mm Mauser)
Magazine capacity: 5 rounds
Over-all length: 43.6 inches
Barrel length: 23.62 inches
Weight: 9 pounds

The classic Model 1898 Mauser rifle was made in both military and sporting versions from 1898 to 1935, when the military rifle was redesigned to become the Model 98k, the famous Karabiner of World War II. After the war, countless numbers of 98k guns were brought into the U.S. as war souvenirs, and later a large quantity of stored guns were sold on the surplus market. The actions were popular as the basis for sporting rifles, while the full military guns in top condition were a prize for collectors. Many of today's finest commercial sporting rifles have action designs based on the original Mauser 98 system.

Disassembly:

1. Cycle the bolt to cock the striker, and turn the safety lever up to the vertical position. Open the bolt, and move it toward the rear while holding the bolt stop pulled out toward the left. Remove the bolt from the rear of the receiver.

2. Depress the bolt sleeve lock plunger, located on the left side, and unscrew the bolt sleeve counter-clockwise (rear view), taking care not to trip the safety lever from its vertical position. Remove the bolt sleeve and striker assembly toward the rear.

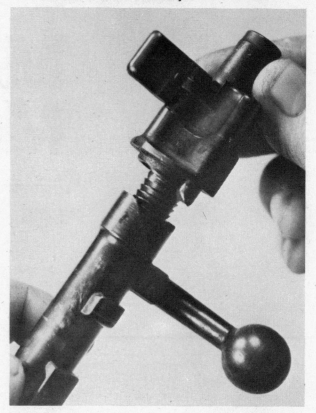

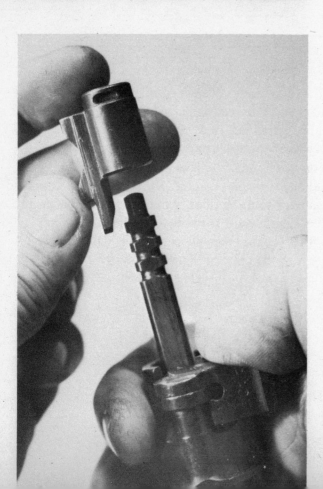

3. If the round takedown bushing is still in the side of the buttstock, insert the firing pin section of the striker shaft into the hole in the center of the bushing to hold the assembly for takedown. If the gun does not have the original stock and bushing, grip the front of the striker in a vise. Either way, take care to exert no side pressure. Holding the bolt sleeve against the tension of the striker spring, turn the safety lever back to off-safe position, and push the bolt sleeve toward the front until the rear edge of the sleeve clears the front of the cocking piece underlug. Turn the cocking piece a quarter-turn in either direction, and remove it from the rear end of the striker shaft. **Caution:** *Keep a firm grip on the bolt sleeve, holding the compressed striker spring.*

4. Slowly release the spring tension, moving the bolt sleeve off the rear of the striker shaft, and removing the spring toward the rear.

5. Turn the safety lever over to the right side (clockwise, rear view), and remove it toward the rear.

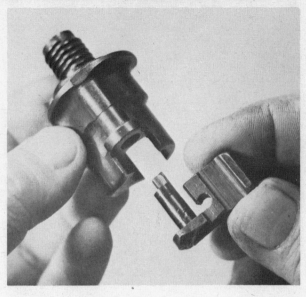

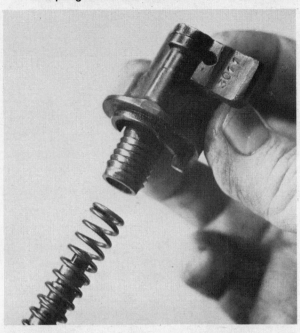

6. To remove the bolt sleeve lock plunger and its spring, push the plunger inward, and turn it to bring its retaining stud into the exit track. Remove the plunger and spring toward the front.

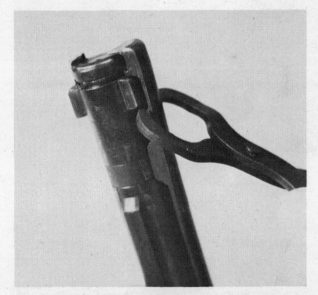

7. If you have the Brownells extractor pliers, use them to raise the front of the extractor just enough to clear the groove at the front of the bolt. A screwdriver inserted beneath the extractor can also do this. With the extractor lifted, turn it clockwise (rear view) until it is aligned with the grooveless area at the front of the bolt.

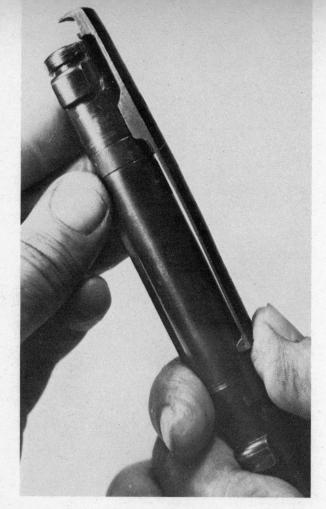

8. Push the extractor straight off toward the front. The mounting ring is not removed from the bolt in normal disassembly.

9. Insert a medium-sized drift punch in the hole at the rear of the magazine floorplate, and depress the floorplate latch. Move the floorplate toward the rear.

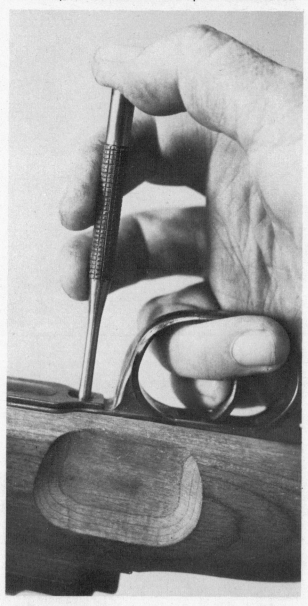

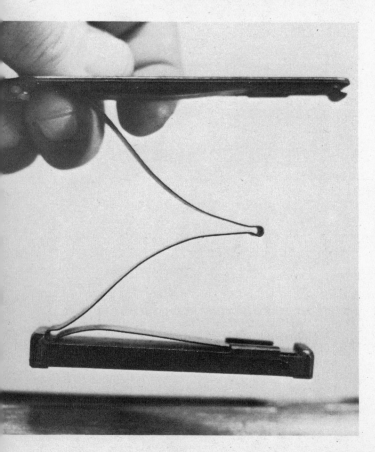

10. Remove the magazine floorplate, spring, and follower downward. The spring is easily detached from the plate and follower.

11. If the end section of cleaning rod is present in the front of the stock, unscrew it and remove it. Depress the front barrel band latch and slide the barrel band off toward the front.

12. The spring latch is now free to be removed from its recess in the stock, and the rear barrel band can be slid off forward and removed. The upper handguard wood can also be taken off at this time.

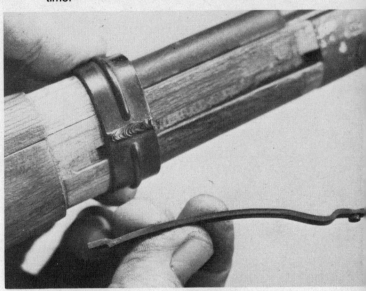

13. Remove the lock screws, and take out the larger vertical screws on the underside of the stock at the front and rear of the trigger/magazine housing.

14. Remove the trigger/magazine housing downward, and separate the action from the stock.

15. The magazine floorplate latch is retained by a cross-pin in the trigger/magazine housing, and is removed downward. **Caution:** *This is a very strong spring, so control the plunger and ease it out.*

16. Remove the small vertical screw at the left rear of the receiver, the pivot for the bolt stop. Then remove the bolt latch/ejector assembly toward the left side.

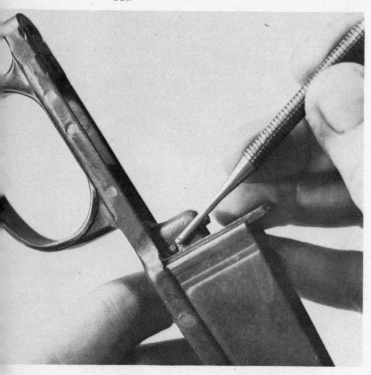

17. Remove the ejector toward the front.

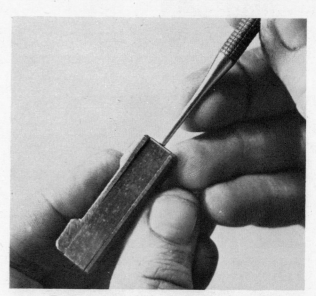

18. To remove the combination bolt latch and ejector spring, set a drift punch against its rear edge, and drive it out toward the front. When the rear tip has cleared the cross-piece at the rear of the bolt latch, the tip of the spring will move inward, and can then be levered out toward the front with a screwdriver blade.

Reassembly Tips:

19. Drifting out the cross-pin that retains the sear will allow removal of the sear, sear spring, and the attached trigger downward. The trigger cross-pin can be drifted out to separate the trigger from the sear.

1. When replacing the combination bolt stop and ejector spring, it will be necessary to insert a screwdriver or some other tool to lift its rear tip onto the cross-piece at the rear of the bolt stop, as the spring is driven into place.

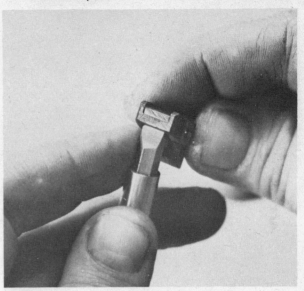

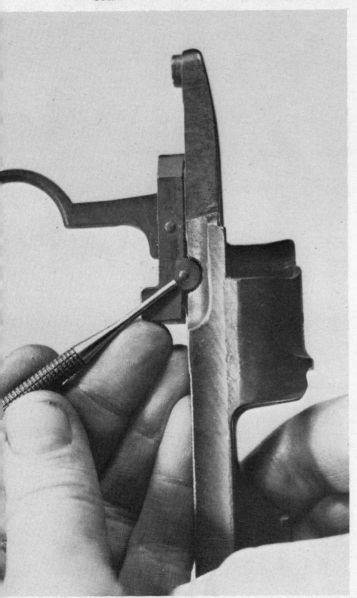

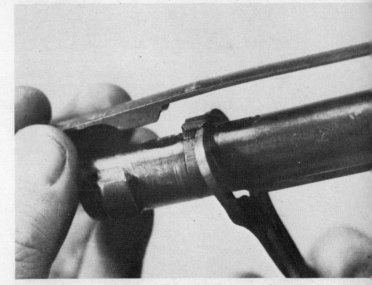

2. When replacing the extractor on the bolt, be sure the mounting ring flanges are aligned with the ungrooved area at the front of the bolt. Use the Brownells pliers or some other tool to compress the ring flanges, and slide the extractor onto the ring.

228 : Mauser 1898

3. With the extractor pliers or a screwdriver blade, lift the front of the extractor while depressing the center of its tail, to lift the underlug at the front over the edge of the bolt face. When the underlug is aligned with the groove, turn the extractor back toward the left (counter-clockwise, rear view), until it covers the right lug of the bolt.

4. Before the bolt sleeve and striker assembly can be put back into the bolt, the striker must be moved to the rear and the safety turned into the vertical on-safe position. As the assembly is turned into place, the sleeve latch plunger must be pushed in twice—once to clear the bolt handle, and again as it enters its locking notch.

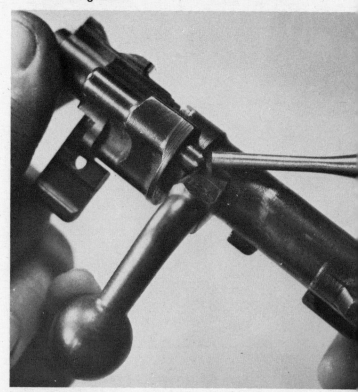

MAUSER 98

Although developed earlier, the adoption of this world famous action by Germany in 1898 gave it the name it retains to this day. Basically, the action remained the same until about 1943 when manufacturing "short cuts" began to appear.

The "caliber" was changed, however, about 1904. As introduced, the weapon was chambered for the Model 88 cartridge (bullet diameter .318—groove diameter .320). About 1904-1905 the Spitzer bullet was adopted and, as this bullet is .323 in diameter, the groove diameter was changed to .325. Both barrels have the same land diameter—.311. With the introduction of the new bullet, barrels were "free-bored" for about 23 m/m. (98 Mausers barreled before 1905 should be carefully checked as modern 7.9 ammo will create dangerous pressure peaks.) Originally, military barrels chambered for the new cartridge had an "S" stamped over the chamber.

Commercial actions were, in the main, identical to the military with the following variations: Rifles intended for factory-fitted telescopic sights had a flat top rear bridge. Some actions were a trifle longer (Magnum Mausers) and some were smaller (Baby Mausers). The strengths of these were supposedly no different from the original but varied approximately ³⁄₈" larger and smaller.

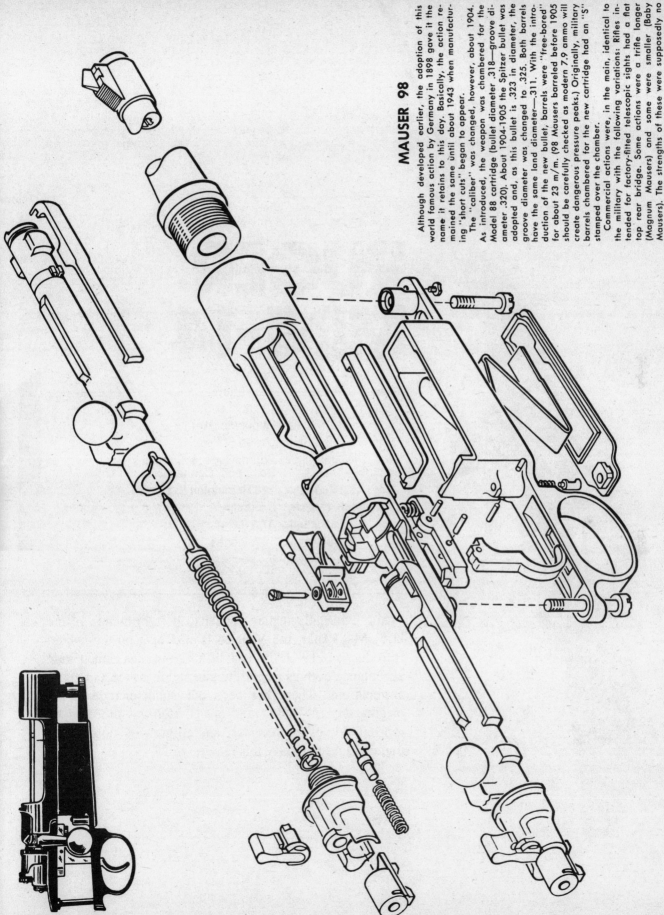

229

RUGER MINI-14

Data:	Ruger Mini-14
Origin:	United States
Manufacturer:	Sturm, Ruger & Company
	Southport, Connecticut
Cartridge:	223 Remington (5.56mm)
Magazine capacity:	5 rounds
Over-all length:	37¼ inches
Barrel length:	18½ inches
Weight:	6.4 pounds

While externally it may appear to be a miniature of the U.S. M-14 rifle, the Mini-14 is all Ruger on the inside. Introduced in 1973, this neat little carbine has gained wide acceptance both as a sporting gun and in police and guard applications. There has been one small change in the original design—a bolt hold-open button was added on the top left side of the receiver, and all guns of more recent manufacture will have this feature.

Disassembly:

1. Remove the magazine, and cycle the action to cock the internal hammer. Push the safety back to the on-safe position, and insert a non-marring tool through the hole at the rear of the trigger guard to spring the guard downward at the rear. Swing the guard toward the front until it stops.

2. Remove the trigger housing downward.

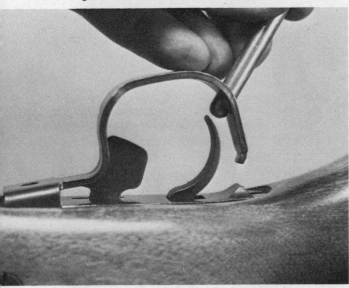

3. Tip the rear of the action upward out of the stock, and remove it toward the front.

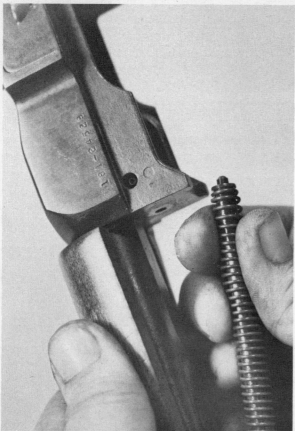

4. Grasp the recoil spring firmly at the rear, where it joins the receiver, and lift the tip of the guide out of its hole in the front of the receiver. **Caution:** *This is a strong spring, so keep it under control.* Tilt the spring and guide upward, slowly release the tension, and remove the spring and guide toward the rear.

5. Move the slide assembly toward the rear until its rear lug aligns with the exit cut in the slide track, and move the operating handle upward and toward the right. Remove the slide assembly.

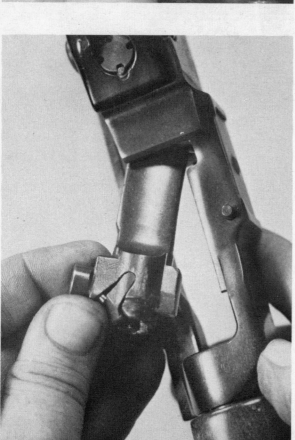

6. Move the bolt forward to the position shown, and remove it upward and toward the right. The bolt must be turned to align the underlug of the firing pin with the exit cut in the bottom of the bolt track.

7. In normal takedown, the gas block assembly should not be removed. If it is necessary, use an Allen wrench to remove the four vertical screws, separating the upper and lower sections of the gas block. The gas port bushing will be freed with removal of the lower block, so take care that it isn't lost.

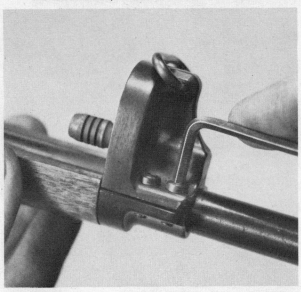

8. Slide the bolt hold-open cover downward out of its slots in the receiver and remove it.

9. Depress the bolt latch plunger on top of the left receiver rail, and lift the bolt lock out of its recess toward the left. **Caution:** *The bolt latch retains the plunger, so control the plunger and ease it out upward, along with its spring.*

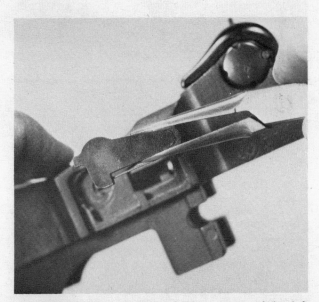

10. The front magazine catch, located in the front of the receiver below the barrel, is retained by a roll cross-pin, accessible through holes on each side. Drift out the cross-pin, and remove the catch toward the front.

11. Insert a small screwdriver beside the extractor plunger, and turn and tip the screwdriver to depress the plunger. Move the extractor upward out of its recess. **Caution:** *As the extractor post clears the ejector, it will be released, so restrain the ejector and ease it out toward the front. Also, take care to keep the extractor plunger under control, and ease it out.* Removal of the extractor will also free the firing pin to be taken out toward the rear.

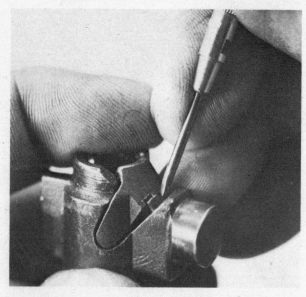

12. Close and latch the trigger guard, and insert a piece of rod or a drift punch through the hole in the rear tip of the hammer spring guide.

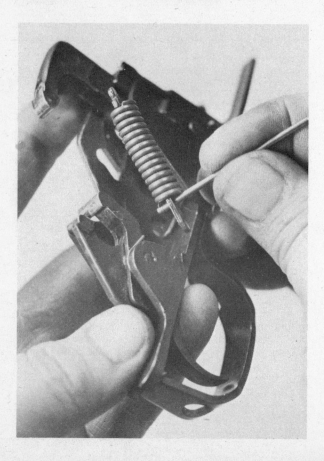

13. Restrain the hammer, move the safety to the off-safe position, and pull the trigger to release the hammer. The rod will trap the hammer spring on the guide. Tip the front of the guide upward, out of its recess at the rear of the hammer, and remove the guide assembly toward the right. If the spring is to be taken off the guide, proceed with care, as the spring is fully compressed.

14. Push out the hammer pivot, and remove the hammer upward and toward the right.

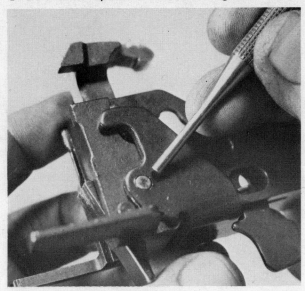

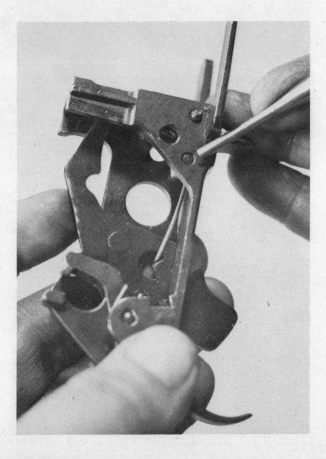

15. Move the safety back to the on-safe position, and take off the trigger guard downward and toward the rear.

16. Drift out the safety spring pin toward the left, ease the spring tension slowly, and move the spring toward the rear, unhooking it from the safety. Remove the spring toward the right rear.

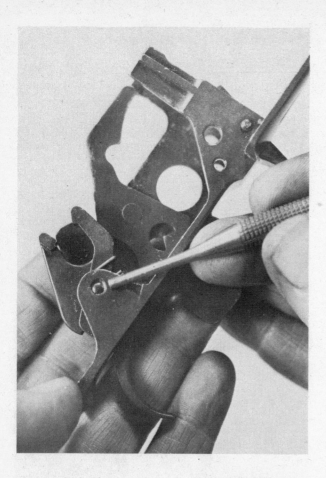

17. Restrain the trigger and sear assembly, and drift out the trigger cross-pin.

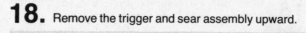

18. Remove the trigger and sear assembly upward.

19. The trigger spring is easily detached from the trigger, and the pivot bushing can be drifted out to free the secondary sear and its coil spring from the top of the trigger. **Caution:** *Use a roll-pin punch to avoid damaging the bushing, and take care to restrain the sear against the tension of its spring.*

20. Tip the upper portion of the safety catch toward the right, moving is pivot stud out of its hole in the trigger housing, and remove the safety upward.

21. The main magazine catch is retained by a cross-pin at the front of the trigger housing, and the pin must be drifted out toward the left. **Caution:** *The strong magazine catch spring will also be released when the pin is removed, so insert a shop cloth into the housing behind the spring to catch it. This spring is rather difficult to re-install, so if removal is not necessary for repair, the catch is best left in place.*

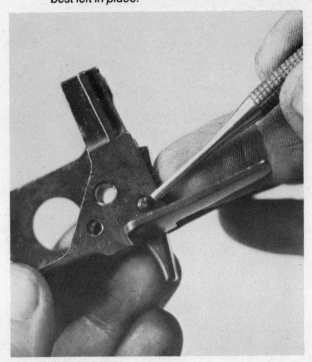

Reassembly Tips:

1. When installing the trigger and sear assembly, tilt the assembly forward, and be sure the front hooks of the trigger spring engage the top of the cross-piece in the housing. Push the assembly downward and toward the rear until the cross-pin can be inserted.

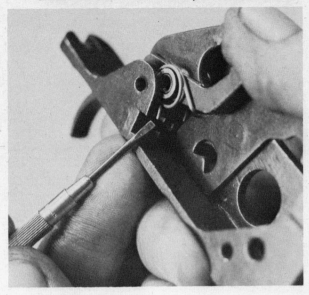

When replacing the safety spring, be sure that its front arm goes on the right side of the rear arm of the magazine catch spring. Otherwise, the safety spring pin cannot be fully inserted.

Ruger
Mini-14 Rifle

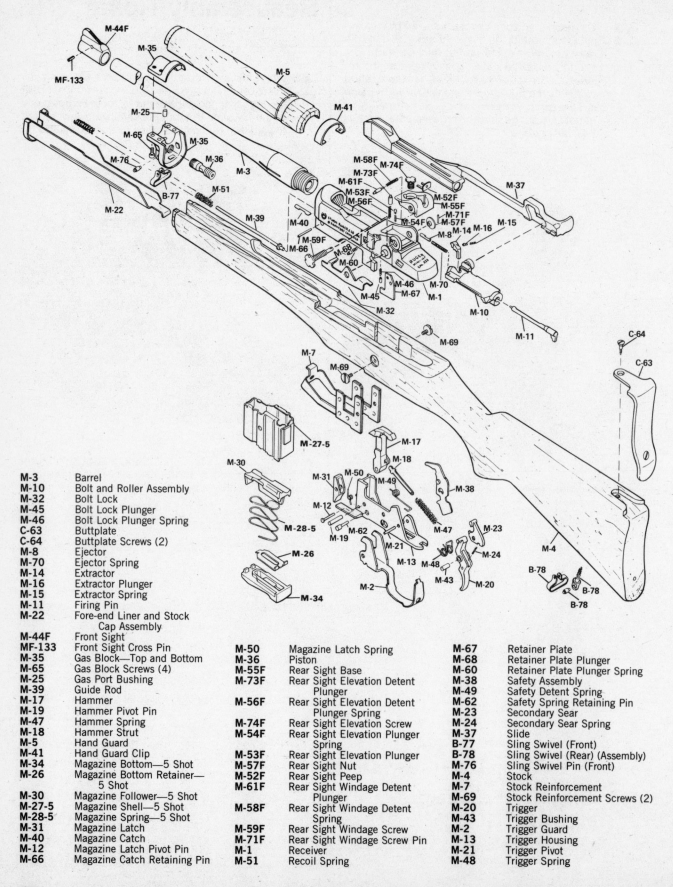

M-3	Barrel		
M-10	Bolt and Roller Assembly		
M-32	Bolt Lock		
M-45	Bolt Lock Plunger		
M-46	Bolt Lock Plunger Spring		
C-63	Buttplate		
C-64	Buttplate Screws (2)		
M-8	Ejector		
M-70	Ejector Spring		
M-14	Extractor		
M-16	Extractor Plunger		
M-15	Extractor Spring		
M-11	Firing Pin		
M-22	Fore-end Liner and Stock Cap Assembly		
M-44F	Front Sight		
MF-133	Front Sight Cross Pin		
M-35	Gas Block—Top and Bottom	M-50	Magazine Latch Spring
M-65	Gas Block Screws (4)	M-36	Piston
M-25	Gas Port Bushing	M-55F	Rear Sight Base
M-39	Guide Rod	M-73F	Rear Sight Elevation Detent Plunger
M-17	Hammer		
M-19	Hammer Pivot Pin	M-56F	Rear Sight Elevation Detent Plunger Spring
M-47	Hammer Spring		
M-18	Hammer Strut	M-74F	Rear Sight Elevation Screw
M-5	Hand Guard	M-54F	Rear Sight Elevation Plunger Spring
M-41	Hand Guard Clip		
M-34	Magazine Bottom—5 Shot	M-53F	Rear Sight Elevation Plunger
M-26	Magazine Bottom Retainer— 5 Shot	M-57F	Rear Sight Nut
		M-52F	Rear Sight Peep
M-30	Magazine Follower—5 Shot	M-61F	Rear Sight Windage Detent Plunger
M-27-5	Magazine Shell—5 Shot		
M-28-5	Magazine Spring—5 Shot	M-58F	Rear Sight Windage Detent Spring
M-31	Magazine Latch		
M-40	Magazine Catch	M-59F	Rear Sight Windage Screw
M-12	Magazine Latch Pivot Pin	M-71F	Rear Sight Windage Screw Pin
M-66	Magazine Catch Retaining Pin	M-1	Receiver
		M-51	Recoil Spring

M-67	Retainer Plate
M-68	Retainer Plate Plunger
M-60	Retainer Plate Plunger Spring
M-38	Safety Assembly
M-49	Safety Detent Spring
M-62	Safety Spring Retaining Pin
M-23	Secondary Sear
M-24	Secondary Sear Spring
M-37	Slide
B-77	Sling Swivel (Front)
B-78	Sling Swivel (Rear) (Assembly)
M-76	Sling Swivel Pin (Front)
M-4	Stock
M-7	Stock Reinforcement
M-69	Stock Reinforcement Screws (2)
M-20	Trigger
M-43	Trigger Bushing
M-2	Trigger Guard
M-13	Trigger Housing
M-21	Trigger Pivot
M-48	Trigger Spring

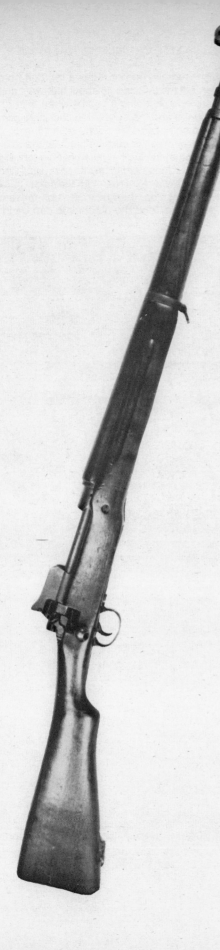

U.S. MODEL 1917 ENFIELD

Data: U.S. P-17 Enfield
Origin: United States
Manufacturers: Remington Arms Company, at Ilion, New York, and Eddystone, Pennsylvania, and Winchester in New Haven, Connecticut
Cartridge: 30-06
Magazine capacity: 5 rounds
Over-all length: 46.3 inches
Barrel length: 26 inches
Weight: 9 pounds

This rifle was originally developed by the British between 1910 and 1913, and was chambered for an experimental 276-cal. rimless round. When issued as a substitute standard gun for the British forces, the chambering was for the regular 303 British round, and the rifle was called the P-14 Enfield. When the U.S. entered World War I, the supply of 1903 Springfield rifles on hand was small, and a number of P-14 Enfields, left over from British contracts, were converted to 30-06, and designated as the U.S. Model 1917, or P-17 Enfield.

Disassembly:

1. Open the bolt, and pull the bolt stop outward, holding it out while removing the bolt toward the rear.

2. For bolt disassembly, do not remove the bolt from the receiver. Lift the bolt handle about half-way, and push forward on it, opening a gap between the rear of the bolt sleeve and the front of the cocking piece. Insert a thin piece of steel (a penny works fine, too) into the gap, trapping the cocking piece at the rear. In some guns, pushing the half-lifted handle forward will not open an adequate gap. In this case, open the bolt and move it toward the rear, turn the safety back to the on-safe position, then push the bolt forward until the gap opens and the steel plate can be inserted.

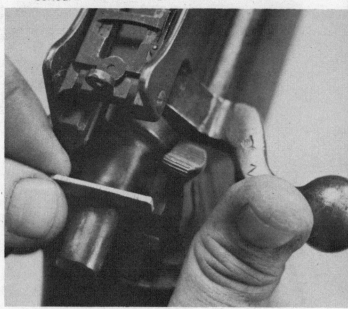

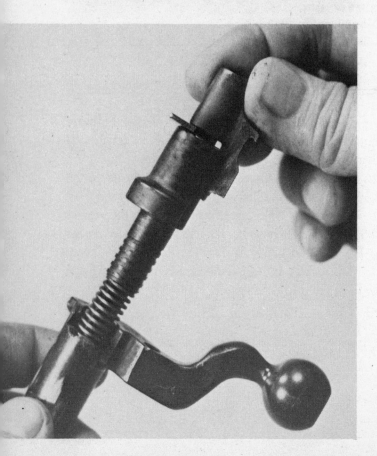

3. Taking care not to dislodge the steel plate, remove the bolt from the receiver as described in step #1, and unscrew the bolt sleeve and striker assembly from the rear of the bolt.

4. With the front of the striker gripped firmly in a vise, push the bolt sleeve toward the front, and remove the steel plate inserted earlier. Push the sleeve forward until the rear edge clears the front of the cocking lug, and rotate the cocking piece one quarter turn in either direction. Remove the cocking piece from the rear of the striker shaft. **Caution:** *Keep the bolt sleeve under control, as the powerful striker spring is compressed.*

5. Release the spring tension slowly, and remove the bolt sleeve and striker spring toward the rear.

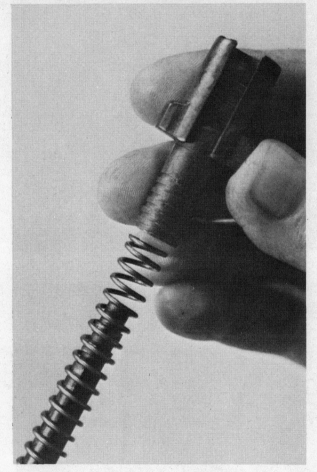

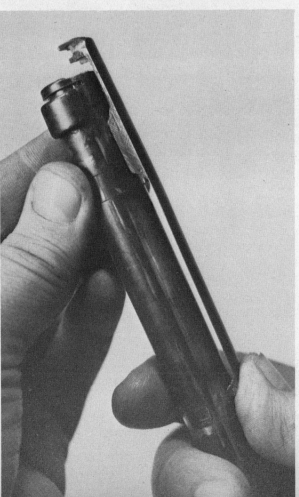

6. Turn the extractor clockwise (rear view) until it is aligned with the gas port, and its front underlug is out of the groove at the front, and push it off its mount toward the front.

7. Insert a drift punch in the hole at the rear of the magazine floorplate, and depress the floorplate latch. Slide the plate slightly toward the rear, and remove it downward, along with the magazine spring and follower. The spring is easily detached from the floorplate and follower by sliding it out of its mounting slots.

8. Remove the cross-screw in the front barrel band, slide it toward the front, and take off the front upper handguard wood.

9. Drift out the cross-pin in front of the rear barrel band, and move it forward off the stock. It may be necessary to also loosen the sling loop cross-screw at the bottom of the band. The rear upper handguard can now be moved forward, and taken off upward.

10. Remove the screw on the underside, in the front tab of the trigger and magazine housing. Remove the screw on the underside at the rear of the trigger guard, and separate the action from the stock. The magazine box can be removed from the stock, and the guard and magazine housing can be taken off downward.

11. Drifting out the cross-pin in the guard will allow removal of the magazine floorplate latch and its spring upward.

12. Drifting out the cross-pin in the front sight will allow removal of the front sight assembly toward the front. This unit is usually tight, and may have to be nudged off with a hammer and nylon drift. Take care not to lose the front sight key, which will be released as the sight is removed. The front band, rear band, and the rear upper handguard ring can now be taken off toward the front.

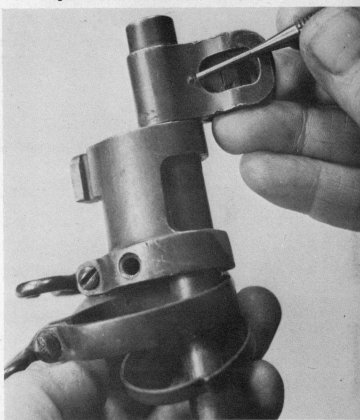

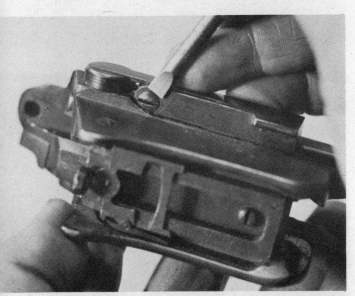

13. Remove the vertical screw that retains the bolt stop, at the left rear of the receiver, and take off the bolt stop and ejector assembly toward the left. The spring rest plug can also be taken out toward the left.

14. Tip the rear tail of the bolt stop spring inward, to lift its front hooks from inside the stop, and remove the spring and ejector toward the rear.

15. Remove the small cross-screw at the right rear of the receiver, and take off the safety lever retainer toward the rear.

16. With the safety lever in the on-safe position (toward the rear), insert a small-diameter drift punch to depress the safety plunger and spring, and remove the safety toward the right. Restrain the plunger and spring, and ease them out. As the safety is moved toward the right, the drift must be removed to allow the cross-piece to pass, then is re-inserted to restrain the plunger and spring.

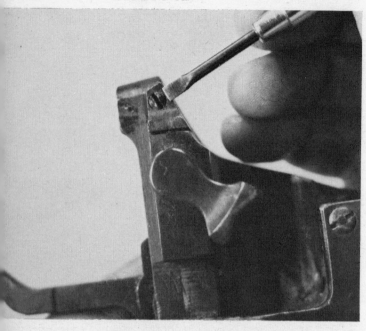

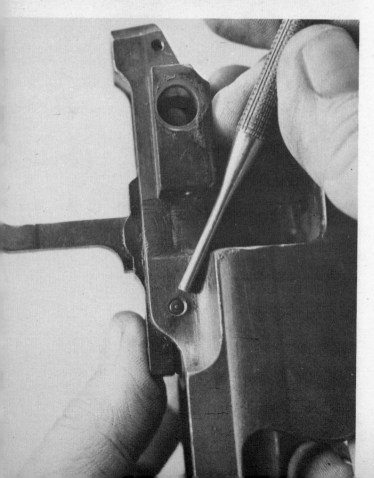

17. Drift out the sear cross-pin toward the left. Exert upward pressure on the front of the sear, and the cross-pin can be pushed out more easily.

Reassembly Tips:

18. Remove the sear, trigger, and sear spring downward. Drifting out the trigger cross-pin will allow separation of the trigger from the sear.

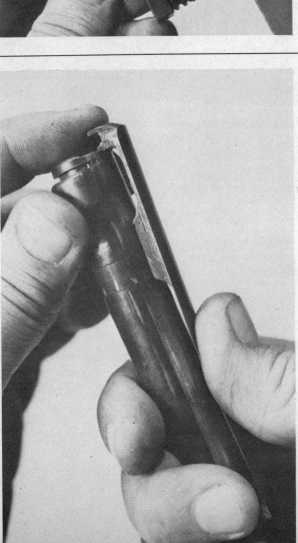

1. When replacing the safety lever, insert a slim tool from the rear to depress the safety plunger and spring while the safety is inserted.

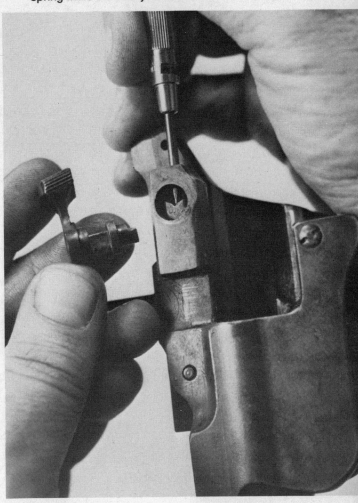

2. When replacing the extractor, after it is started back onto its flanges on the mounting ring, depress the tail of the extractor while lifting the beak at the front, to clear its underlug over the front edge of the bolt. Lift it only enough to clear.

ENFIELD (Model 1917) Cal. 30-06

Developed from British Service Rifles which were being produced in the U.S.A. during World War I, as enough 1903 Springfields could not be made fast enough. The 1917 Enfield has a 26" bbl. and is 46¼" overall. The D.C.M. disposed of thousands of these between the wars, and many were converted to sporters.

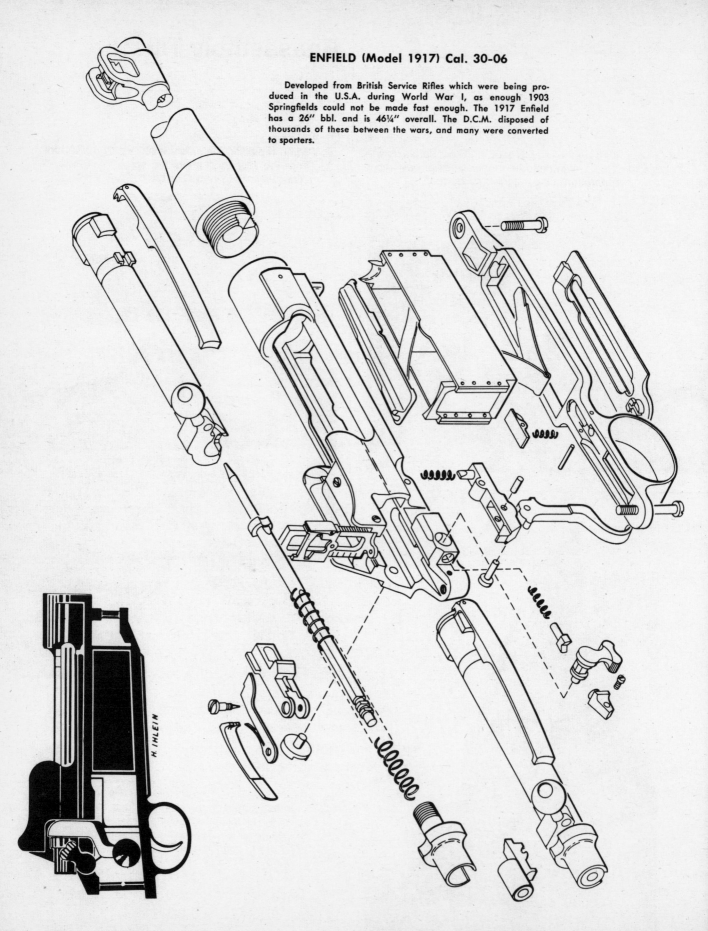

H. IHLEIN

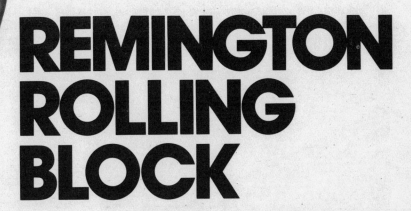

REMINGTON ROLLING BLOCK

Data: Remington Rolling Block

Origin: United States

Manufacturer: Remington Arms Company, Ilion, New York, Springfield Armory, and armories in several foreign countries

Cartridges: 50 U.S., 45 Danish, 43 Spanish, 7×57, many others

Over-all length: 46 inches (Carbine, 35⅝ inches)

Barrel length: 30 inches (Carbine, 20½ inches)

Weight: 8½ pounds (Carbine, 7 pounds)

Note: Weights and measurements are for the 7mm model of 1897-1902, used mainly in Central and South America

In 1866, Joseph Rider re-designed the Remington-Geiger action, and the Rolling Block was born. In the years between 1870 and 1900, this gun became the official military arm of a large number of countries, and was also used by the U.S. Navy. Its ingenious "rolling" breech-block made the action a very strong one, and its simplicity made it ideal for military use. The era of the bolt action repeater ended its military career, but Remington made it as a sporting rifle up to 1933.

Disassembly:

1. Back out the vertical screw at the rear of the upper tang, and remove the buttstock toward the rear. If the stock is very tight, bump the front of the comb with the heel of the hand to start it.

2. If the gun is equipped with a saddle ring, back out the ring bar screw, and swing the bar upward. Remove the ring. The bar is threaded into the side of the receiver, and is not removed at this time.

3. Remove the screw at the center of the lock plate, located between the two large pins on the left side of the receiver (Note: Remington called the lock plate the "button"). Take off the lock plate toward the left.

4. Cock the hammer, and push out the breechblock pivot pin toward the left. If the pin is tight, use a non-marring nylon or brass drift punch to start it.

5. Remove the small screw on the left side of the receiver, just below the breechblock pivot hole.

6. Remove the breechblock assembly, including the ejector, upward and toward the rear.

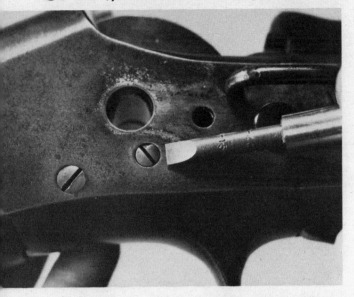

7. The ejector is easily detached from the left side of the breechblock.

8. Drifting out the lower cross-pin in the breechblock will allow the firing pin retractor to be taken out downward, and removal of the upper cross-pin will free the firing pin, which is taken out toward the rear.

9. Restrain the hammer, pull the trigger, and ease the hammer down beyond its normal full forward position. Push out the hammer pivot toward the left.

10. Remove the hammer upward.

11. If the gun has a saddle ring bar, it can now be unscrewed from the left side of the receiver and taken off. When unscrewing it, lift its free end slightly during the first few turns, to avoid marring the receiver.

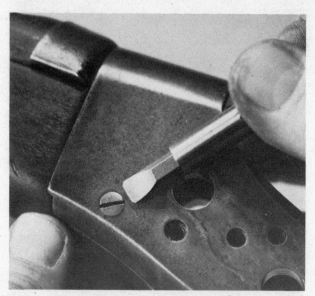

12. Remove the cross-screw at the lower front of the receiver.

13. Remove the cross-screw at the lower rear of the receiver.

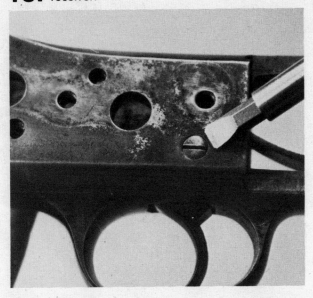

14. Remove the trigger guard assembly downward and toward the rear.

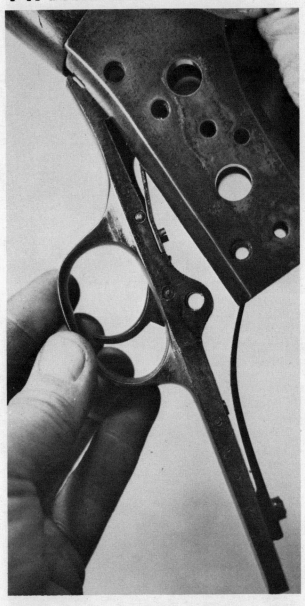

15. Remove the hammer spring screw, and take off the hammer spring upward.

16. Remove the trigger spring screw, and take out the trigger spring upward.

17. Drift out the trigger cross-pin, and remove the trigger upward.

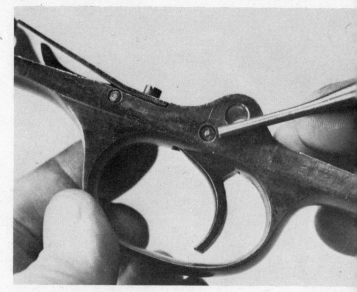

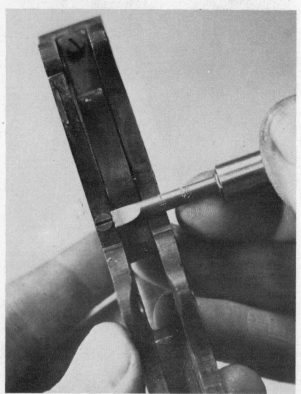

18. Remove the ejector spring screw, and take off the ejector spring upward.

19. Drift out the cross-pin at the front of the guard, and remove the breechblock locking lever upward. **Caution:** *This pin is very near the upper edge of the guard frame, so take care that the edge is not broken during removal.*

20. Remove the vertical screw at the front of the guard unit, and take out the locking lever spring upward.

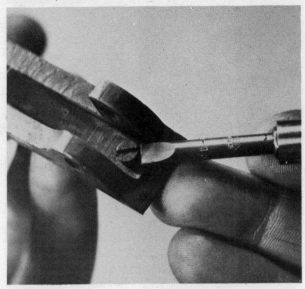

21. If the gun is a full-length rifle, there will be three barrel bands to be removed. On the carbine, as shown, remove the single band by depressing its spring latch and sliding it off toward the front. The fore-end wood can now be taken off downward.

22. Before the upper handguard wood can be removed, the rear sight must be taken off by backing out its two screws, at the front and rear of the sight base.

Reassembly Tips:

1. After the hammer is installed on its pivot in the receiver, insert a tool from the rear to depress the front of the hammer spring, to insure that the tip of the spring engages the spring lobe on the rear of the hammer.

2. When replacing the breechblock assembly in the receiver, you must exert downward pressure on the assembly while inserting the pivot pin, to slightly compress the lock lever and the ejector spring.

Disassembly—Check action to be sure rifle is unloaded. Unscrew button screw (21) and remove button (20) from left wall of receiver (1). Cock hammer (10) and drift out breechblock pin (18). Lift breechblock (11) up out of receiver with extractor parts and firing pin intact. Release hammer and drift out hammer pin (19). Lift hammer out of receiver. Withdraw ramrod (40) and slide barrel bands (35,37,38) off barrel and fore-end to front. Remove fore-end. To remove buttstock, remove tang screw (7) and pull buttstock off tang to rear. Unscrew front and rear guard plate screws (8,9) from side of receiver and drop guard plate assembly intact out bottom of receiver. Guard plate parts (springs, trigger, locking lever) are all easily removed from guard plate (22). Reassemble in reverse order.

Variations in the Navy Model 1869 Remington rifle are shown in the box. The extractor A fits into slot at rear of the barrel. B is extractor retaining screw. C, ramrod stop, is contained in fore-end. Other variations not shown are a firing pin spring, a retaining screw and an anti-friction roller at the tip of the mainspring.

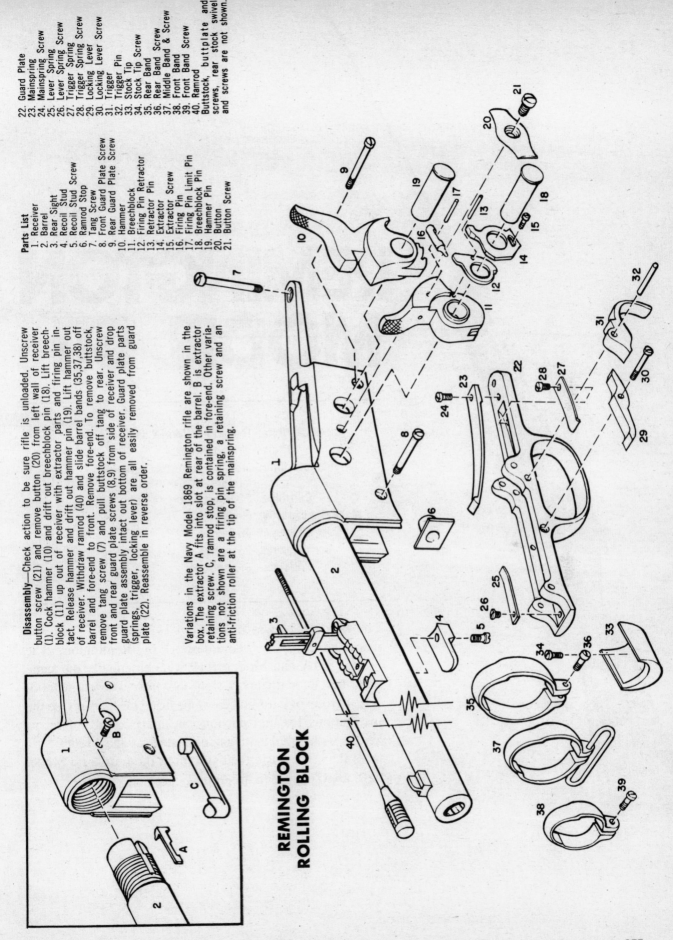

REMINGTON ROLLING BLOCK

REMINGTON MODEL 511

Data: Remington Model 511
Origin: United States
Manufacturer: Remington Arms Company
Bridgeport, Connecticut
Cartridge: 22 Short, Long, or Long Rifle
Magazine capacity: 6 rounds
Over-all length: 43 inches
Barrel length: 25 inches
Weight: 5½ pounds

The Model 511 was made from 1939 to 1962, and was marketed as the "Scoremaster" by Remington. The Model 511A and Model 511P were essentially the same gun, but with different sight systems. The entire 500-series group of guns had the same firing mechanism, so the instructions for that portion can apply to any of them. Those with tubular magazines, such as the Model 512, have the same basic feed system as the semi-auto Model 550, also covered in this book.

Disassembly:

1. Remove the magazine, and back out the main stock mounting screw, located at the forward end of the magazine plate on the underside. This is a coin-slotted screw, and a U.S. nickel fits it best. Remove the action from the stock. The magazine plate can be removed from the stock by taking out the small wood screw at the rear of the plate.

2. To remove the bolt, hold the trigger back, open the bolt, and withdraw it from the receiver toward the rear. Note that the safety must be in off-safe position (forward) during this operation.

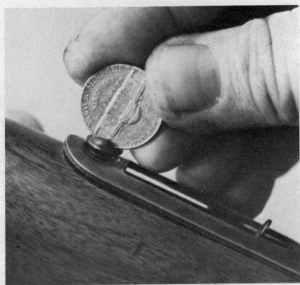

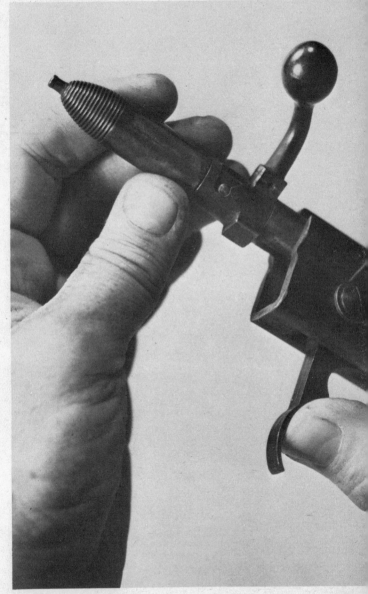

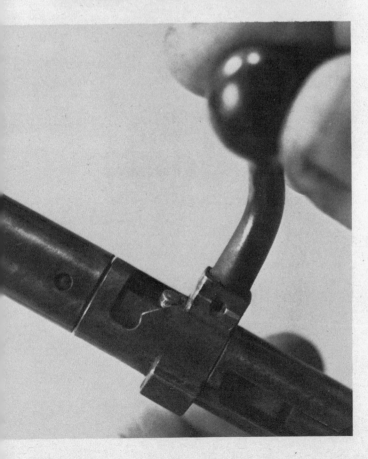

3. With the front portion of the bolt gripped in a padded bench vise, turn the bolt handle to allow the striker to move forward to fired position, partially relieving the tension of its spring. The photo shows the handle already turned, and the striker in the forward position.

4. With a drift punch of the proper size, drift out the cross-pin at the forward edge of the domed end-piece at the rear of the bolt. **Caution:** *Be sure the drift punch is of proper size, and that it has enough reach before its taper, to avoid any stress on the holes in the endpiece.* The endpiece is case-hardened, and if strained it will break at the forward edge. Also, the striker spring is under tension, so control the endpiece and ease it off.

5. Remove the endpiece toward the rear, and take out the striker spring and guide.

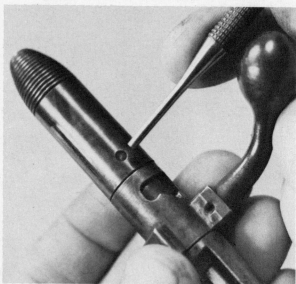

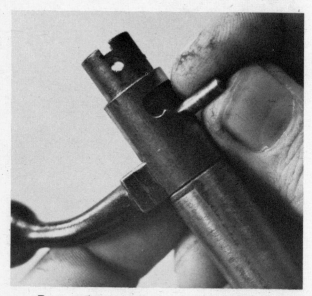

6. Remove the cross-pin that is the cocking lug for the striker toward either side. With the striker spring tension removed, the pin is easily pushed out.

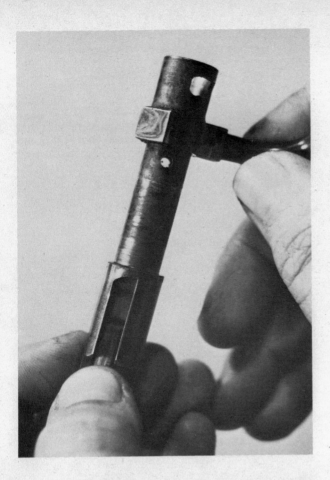

7. Remove the bolt handle and sleeve toward the rear.

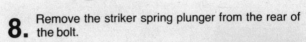

8. Remove the striker spring plunger from the rear of the bolt.

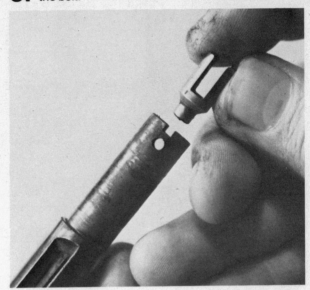

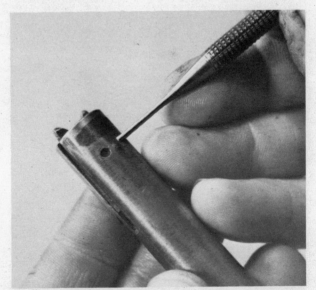

10. The extractors are retained by two vertical pins at the front of the bolt. Drift out the pins, and remove the extractors and their small coil springs from each side.

9. At the opening on the underside of the bolt near the front, nudge the striker toward the rear until it emerges, and remove it.

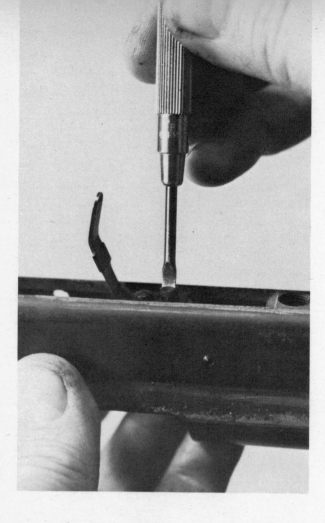

11. The magazine catch is tempered to be its own spring, and is secured to the receiver insert on the underside by two screws. The catch is removed downward.

12. The safety lever is retained on the right side of the receiver by a large flat screw. Removal of the screw will allow the safety lever to be taken off toward the right.

14. Drift out the large cross-pin at the rear that serves as the trigger pivot. This will release the trigger within the receiver, but not for removal at this time.

13. The safety tumbler can now be pushed inward and removed from the rear of the receiver. Note that the trigger spring and plunger are bearing on the safety, and will be released as the tumbler is taken out. The spring and plunger can also be removed at this time.

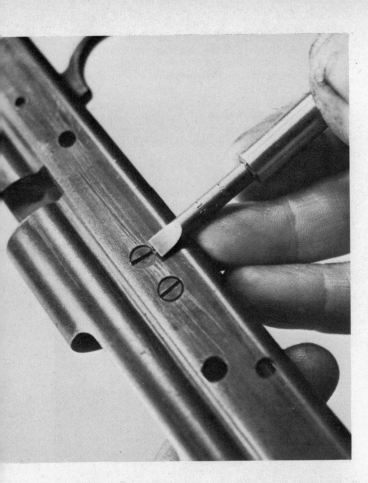

15. There are two screws on the left side of the receiver. Removal of the rear screw will release the sear within the receiver. The sear is attached to the front of the trigger, and is not removed at this time.

16. Remove the other screw, the one toward the front. This will release the receiver insert, the small block inside the receiver which is the base for the ejector and magazine catch. The ejector can now be removed upward, and the insert is slid forward inside the receiver until it meets the front insert.

17. With the insert block moved forward out of the way, the trigger/sear assembly can now be moved forward inside the receiver and removed from the bottom, through the larger opening cleared by the moving of the insert. The sear pivot on the front of the trigger is riveted in place, and in normal disassembly should not be removed.

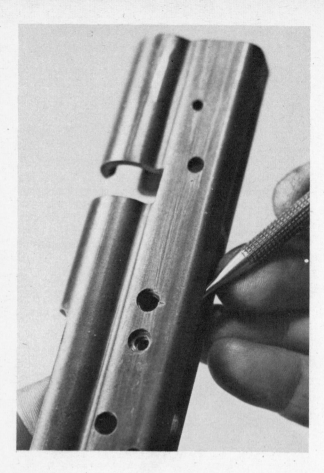

2. When replacing the ejector and insert block, place the insert block in the front portion of the receiver, align the ejector with the holes in the left side of the receiver and hold it in position with a tool, then move the insert block back beside the ejector until it is also aligned with the holes. The front screw can then be put in. **Note:** Remember that the sear/trigger assembly must be placed inside the receiver (but not installed) before the insert and ejector are replaced.

3. When replacing the safety tumbler, leave the trigger pin out until the tumbler is installed. Remember that the toothed flange on the tumbler must be installed downward, to engage the trigger spring plunger. After the safety lever is secured to the tumbler by its screw, the trigger is easily pushed upward against the tension of its spring and aligned with its cross-pin.

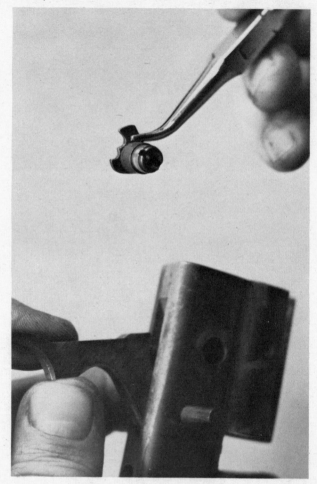

4. When replacing the bolt endpiece, grip the front portion of the bolt in a padded vise, and be sure the striker is in the forward (fired) position. Push downward on the endpiece until its holes align with the holes in the bolt, and insert a drift punch of appropriate size to hold the endpiece in place while starting the original cross-pin. Be sure the striker spring plunger is turned so the cross-pin will pass between its rear arms. Be sure the cross-pin is in alignment as its tip reaches the other side, and avoid any extreme force or stress on the endpiece.

18. After the trigger/sear assembly is removed, the insert block can be taken out of the receiver toward the rear.

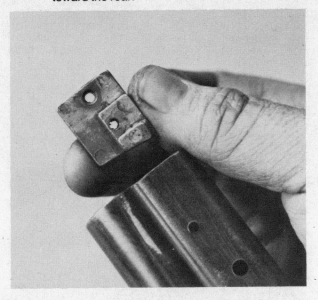

19. The barrel is retained in the receiver by two cross-pins, and removal of these will also release the front insert block. In normal disassembly, these parts should not be disturbed. The rear sight is retained by two small screws on top of the barrel.

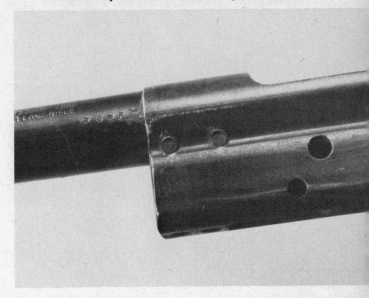

Reassembly Tips:

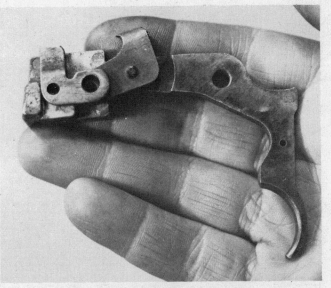

1. To aid in re-installing the insert block, ejector, and trigger/sear assembly, this photo shows the proper relationship of these parts when in the receiver.

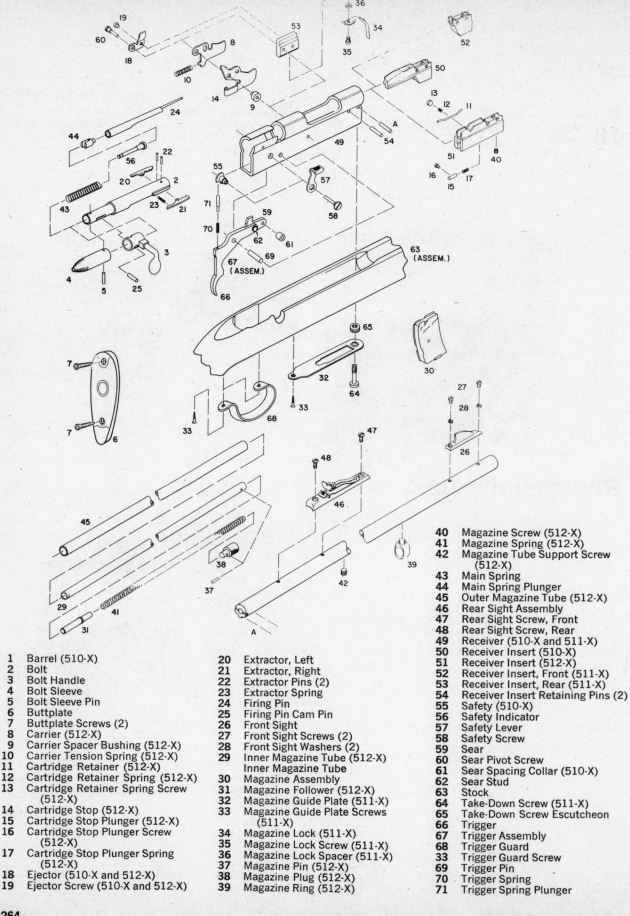

1	Barrel (510-X)	20	Extractor, Left
2	Bolt	21	Extractor, Right
3	Bolt Handle	22	Extractor Pins (2)
4	Bolt Sleeve	23	Extractor Spring
5	Bolt Sleeve Pin	24	Firing Pin
6	Buttplate	25	Firing Pin Cam Pin
7	Buttplate Screws (2)	26	Front Sight
8	Carrier (512-X)	27	Front Sight Screws (2)
9	Carrier Spacer Bushing (512-X)	28	Front Sight Washers (2)
10	Carrier Tension Spring (512-X)	29	Inner Magazine Tube (512-X)
11	Cartridge Retainer (512-X)		Inner Magazine Tube
12	Cartridge Retainer Spring (512-X)	30	Magazine Assembly
13	Cartridge Retainer Spring Screw (512-X)	31	Magazine Follower (512-X)
		32	Magazine Guide Plate (511-X)
14	Cartridge Stop (512-X)	33	Magazine Guide Plate Screws (511-X)
15	Cartridge Stop Plunger (512-X)		
16	Cartridge Stop Plunger Screw (512-X)	34	Magazine Lock (511-X)
17	Cartridge Stop Plunger Spring (512-X)	35	Magazine Lock Screw (511-X)
		36	Magazine Lock Spacer (511-X)
18	Ejector (510-X and 512-X)	37	Magazine Pin (512-X)
19	Ejector Screw (510-X and 512-X)	38	Magazine Plug (512-X)
		39	Magazine Ring (512-X)

40	Magazine Screw (512-X)
41	Magazine Spring (512-X)
42	Magazine Tube Support Screw (512-X)
43	Main Spring
44	Main Spring Plunger
45	Outer Magazine Tube (512-X)
46	Rear Sight Assembly
47	Rear Sight Screw, Front
48	Rear Sight Screw, Rear
49	Receiver (510-X and 511-X)
50	Receiver Insert (510-X)
51	Receiver Insert (512-X)
52	Receiver Insert, Front (511-X)
53	Receiver Insert, Rear (511-X)
54	Receiver Insert Retaining Pins (2)
55	Safety (510-X)
56	Safety Indicator
57	Safety Lever
58	Safety Screw
59	Sear
60	Sear Pivot Screw
61	Sear Spacing Collar (510-X)
62	Sear Stud
63	Stock
64	Take-Down Screw (511-X)
65	Take-Down Screw Escutcheon
66	Trigger
67	Trigger Assembly
68	Trigger Guard
33	Trigger Guard Screw
69	Trigger Pin
70	Trigger Spring
71	Trigger Spring Plunger

STEVENS FAVORITE

Data:	Stevens Favorite
Origin:	United States
Manufacturer:	J. Stevens Arms & Tool Company Chicopee Falls, Massachusetts
Cartridge:	22 Long Rifle
Over-all length:	36½ inches
Barrel length:	22 inches
Weight:	4 pounds

The little Stevens Favorite was certainly well-named. After its introduction in 1889, it became the most popular "boy's rifle" of all time, and lasted through 46 years of production. The gun was simple and reliable, a single shot with a lever-actuated falling block. In 1915 it was redesigned, the most notable internal changes being in the ejector and hammer spring. These differences will be noted in the instructions. The gun covered here is the early model, made prior to 1915.

Disassembly:

1. Back out the barrel retaining screw, located just forward of the lever on the underside of the gun. On guns made after 1915, the head of the screw will be a knurled piece, rather than a ring.

2. Remove the barrel and fore-end assembly forward.

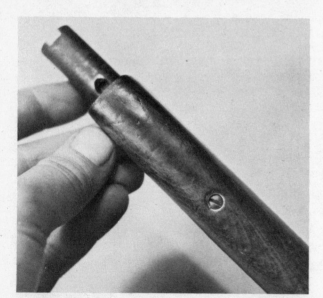

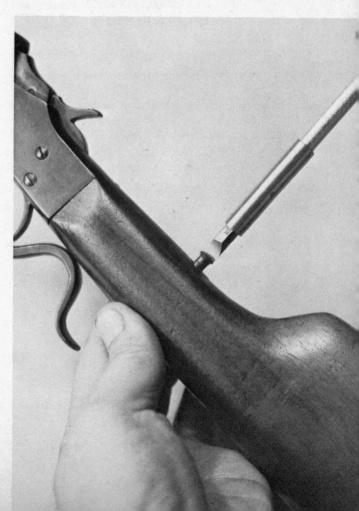

3. The fore-end is held on the underside of the barrel by a single screw.

4. Remove the screws at the rear tip of the upper and lower receiver tangs to release the stock for removal. Remove the stock toward the rear. If the stock is very tightly fitted, it may be necessary to bump the front of the comb with the heel of the hand or with a soft rubber hammer.

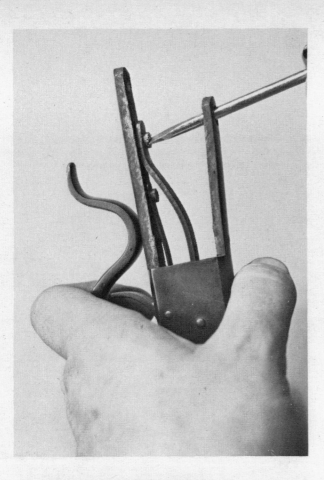

5. The screw that retains the hammer spring can be reached through the stock screw hole in the upper tang. Remove the hammer spring screw, and take out the spring toward the rear. On the post-1915 guns, the hammer spring will be a heavy coil, with an internal hammer strut and a base sleeve at the rear which bears on a groove in the head of a large screw in the lower tang. On these guns, grip the sleeve firmly with pliers and move it forward, then upward to clear the base screw. After the hammer spring is removed, in both models, the screw which retains the trigger spring will be accessible. For this screw, use either an offset screwdriver, or a screwdriver with the tip cut to an angle.

6. Taking out the hammer and trigger pivot screws will release the hammer for removal upward, and the trigger for removal downward.

7. Remove the lever pivot screw, located at the lower edge of the receiver.

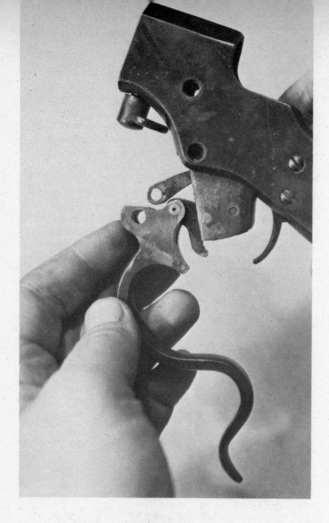

8. Remove the breechblock pivot screw.

9. Remove the lever and breechblock assembly downward. The ejector, which is retained by the lever pivot screw, will also come out at this time.

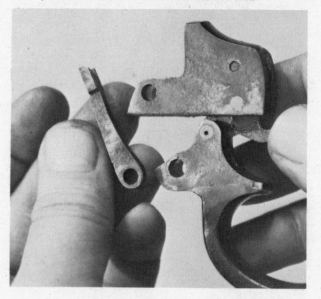

10. The ejector on the later model guns is different from the one shown. On the post-1915 guns, it has a front lobe which contains a plunger and spring, the plunger bearing on the breechblock pivot. The plunger is staked in place, and removal in routine disassembly is not advisable. Drifting out the upper cross-pin in the breechblock will release the firing pin for removal toward the rear. The lower cross-pin holds the link to the breechblock, and the pin at the top of the lever retains the lever on the link.

Reassembly Tips:

1. When replacing the lever and breechblock assembly in the receiver, be sure the ejector is in the position shown, with its cartridge rim recess and firing pin groove toward the rear. Also, be sure the link is in the position shown, with its hooked beak downward and pointing toward the rear.

When replacing the lever and breechblock assembly in the receiver, the forward arms of the breechblock should be inserted into the bottom of the receiver first, then the breechblock tipped into position.

On both models, insert the breechblock pivot screw first, then insert the lever pivot screw, being sure it passes through the lower loop of the ejector. On the later guns, it will be necessary to use a small tool to center the ejector loop while inserting the screw, holding it against the tension of its plunger and spring.

Savage
Model 71
Stevens Favorite
Single-Shot Rifles

1	Hammer	17	Breech Block Plunger
2	Hammer Spring	17A	Breech Block Plunger Spring
3	Firing Pin	17B	Breech Block Plunger Retaining
4	Firing Pin Spring		Screw
5	Firing Pin Retaining Pin	18	Link
6	Breech Block	19	Link Pin
7	Barrel	20	Fore-end
8	Rear Sight Step	21	Fore-end Screw
9	Rear Sight	22	Lever
10	Front Sight Assembly	23	Extractor
11	Frame	24	Buttplate Screw
12	Trigger Spring	25	Buttplate
13	Trigger	26	Stock
14	Hammer Block	27	Stock Bolt
15	Hammer Block Pin	28	Stock Bolt Washer
16	Hammer Pins (2)	29	Stock Bolt Lock Washer

SAKO FORESTER

Data:	Sako Forester
Origin:	Finland
Manufacturer:	Oy Sako, A. B., Riihimaki
Cartridges:	22-250, 243, 308
Magazine capacity:	5 rounds
Over-all length:	42 inches
Barrel length:	23 inches
Weight:	6½ pounds

A redesign of the original L-57 Forester of 1958 was done in 1960. It was designated the Model L-579, and was still called the Forester. In two varmint chamberings and one for medium game, it became very popular in its time, and is still treasured for the smoothness of its action. One of the reasons for this feature is a full-length guide on the bolt, mounted on a pivot-ring in the style of the old Mauser extractor. All Sako rifles are of outstanding quality in both materials and workmanship.

Disassembly:

1. Open the bolt and move it toward the rear, while pushing in the bolt stop, located at the left rear of the receiver. Remove the bolt from the rear of the receiver.

2. Grip the underlug of the cocking piece firmly in a vise, and pull the bolt body forward to clear the lug from the bolt sleeve. Turn the bolt until the lug on the bolt sleeve is aligned with the exit track on the bolt body, and separate the body from the sleeve and striker assembly.

3. Back out the striker shaft lock screw, located on the underside of the cocking piece at the rear.

4. With a firm grip on the bolt sleeve and the striker spring, use a screwdriver to turn the screw-slotted rear tip of the striker shaft clockwise (rear view) until the striker is free from the cocking piece. The spring is under tension, so keep it under control.

5. Remove the cocking piece, bolt sleeve, and spring from the striker shaft toward the rear.

6. Remove the cocking piece from the bolt sleeve.

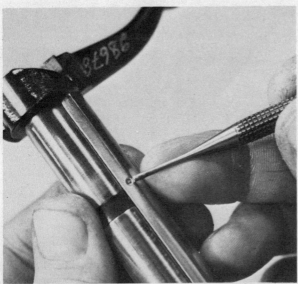

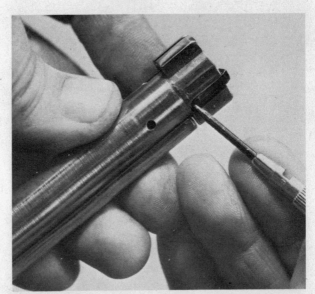

7. A small cross-pin retains the bolt guide on the side of the bolt. The mounting ring is not removed in normal takedown. If the guide is removed, take care not to lose the guide rib stop and spring, mounted inside the rib at the front.

8. Insert a small screwdriver between the extractor and its plunger, and depress the plunger toward the rear, lifting the extractor out of its recess. **Caution:** *The spring is compressed, and can send the plunger quite a distance, so control the plunger and ease it out.*

9. Release the magazine floorplate latch, located in the front of the trigger guard, and open the floorplate. Flex the magazine spring away from the plate at the rear, and slide it rearward and out of its mounting slots. The magazine follower can be taken off the spring in the same manner.

10. Close and latch the floorplate, and remove the large vertical screws at the front of the magazine housing and at the rear of the trigger guard. Lift the action out of the stock.

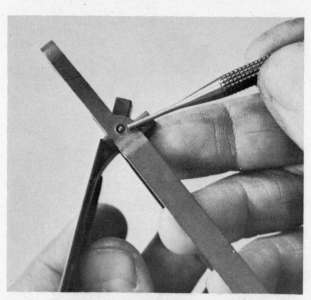

11. The trigger guard/magazine housing can now be removed downward. When this unit is removed, take care not to lose the steel spacer plates at the front and rear, inside the stock.

12. The magazine floorplate can be removed by drifting out its hinge cross-pin.

13. A small cross-pin at the front of the trigger guard retains the magazine floorplate latch and its spring. **Caution:** *The spring is very strong. Restrain the latch, and ease it off.*

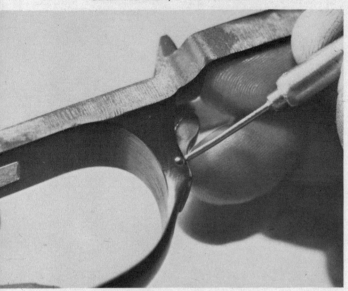

14. The magazine box is easily detached from its recess on the underside of the receiver.

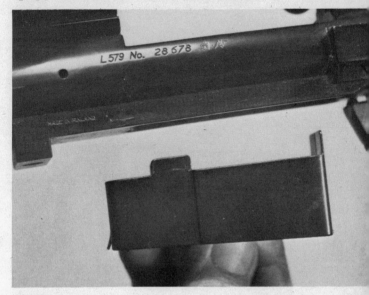

15. The bolt stop is retained by two screws on the left rear of the receiver, and is removed toward the left, along with its torsion spring. The bolt stop is also the ejector, and is pivoted inside its housing by a vertical pin. Drifting out the pin upward will free the stop/ejector and spring for removal.

16. Drift out the cross-pin at the upper front of the trigger housing.

17. Remove the trigger housing downward. Removal of this assembly will not disturb the trigger adjustment settings. Backing out the two screws on the right side of the housing will allow removal of the safety lever toward the right. **Caution:** *Removal of the safety will release the positioning ball and spring.* See the next step.

18. The safety ball and spring are mounted across the unit, and backing out this small headless screw on the left side will allow separate removal of the ball and spring.

19. After the safety is removed, driving out this cross-pin will allow the sear to be taken out upward.

20. Drifting out the trigger cross-pin, and the small stop pin behind it, will allow the trigger to be taken out downward. Unless the process of adjustment is known, the trigger adjustment nuts and screws should not be disturbed.

Reassembly Tips:

21. The safety cross-bolt is retained by a C-clip on the left side, and after its removal the safety bolt is taken out toward the right.

1. Note that the sides of the striker shaft at the rear have deep grooves lengthwise in the screw threads, and one of these must be aligned with the lock screw.

2. The degree of protrusion of the firing pin point from the breech face is governed by the level to which the striker shaft is turned on its threads during reassembly. Generally speaking, the rear tip of the striker shaft should be level with the rear of the cocking piece. To be more precise, the protrusion of the firing pin point at the front should be .055 inches, if you have a means of measuring this.

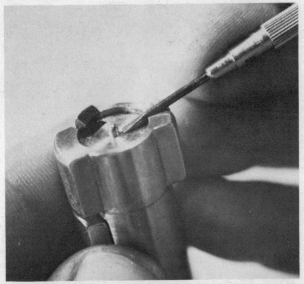

3. To properly check the protrusion, the bolt sleeve/striker assembly must be installed in the bolt. The photo shows an adjustment that has *far too much protrusion*. Adjustment can be made with the bolt fully assembled. After adjustment, be sure to tighten the lock screw securely. Note that the striker must be re-cocked before the bolt is put back in the gun.

Sako Rifle

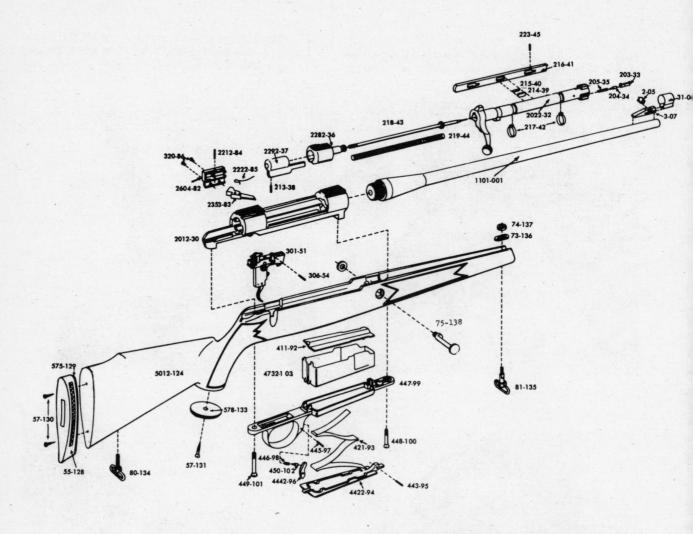

1101-001	Barrel	2212-84	Bolt Stop Pin
2-05	Front Sight Bead	2222-85	Bolt Stop Spring
31-06	Front Sight Hood	320-86	Bolt Stop Screws (2)
3-07	Front Sight Ramp	411-92	Magazine Follower
2012-30	Receiver	421-93	Magazine Spring
2022-32	Bolt Body	4422-94	Floorplate Cover
203-33	Extractor	443-95	Floorplate Hinge Pin
204-34	Extractor Plunger	4442-96	Floorplate Cover Catch
205-35	Extractor Spring	445-97	Catch Pin
2282-36	Bolt Sleeve	446-98	Floorplate Catch Spring
2292-37	Cocking Piece	447-99	Trigger Guard
213-38	Firing Pin Locking Screw	448-100	Front Guard Screw
214-39	Bolt Guide Stop Plate	449-101	Rear Guard Screw
215-40	Bolt Guide Stop Plate Spring	450-102	Floorplate Catch Plunger
216-41	Bolt Guide Strip	4732-103	Magazine Body
217-42	Bolt Guide Strip Ring	5012-124	Stock
218-43	Firing Pin	55-128	Recoil Pad
219-44	Firing Pin Spring	575-129	Buttplate Spacer
223-45	Bolt Guide Strip Ring Pin	57-130	Buttplate Screws (2)
301-51	Trigger Safety Mechanism	57-131	Pistol Grip Cap Screw
306-54	Trigger Housing Mounting Pin	578-132	Pistol Grip Cap
		80-134	Rear Stock Swivel
2604-82	Bolt Stop Body	81-135	Upper Swivel
2353-83	Bolt Stop Release and Ejector	73-136	Upper Swivel Bottom Plate
		74-137	Upper Swivel Nut
		75-138	Crossbolt (Recoil Lug)

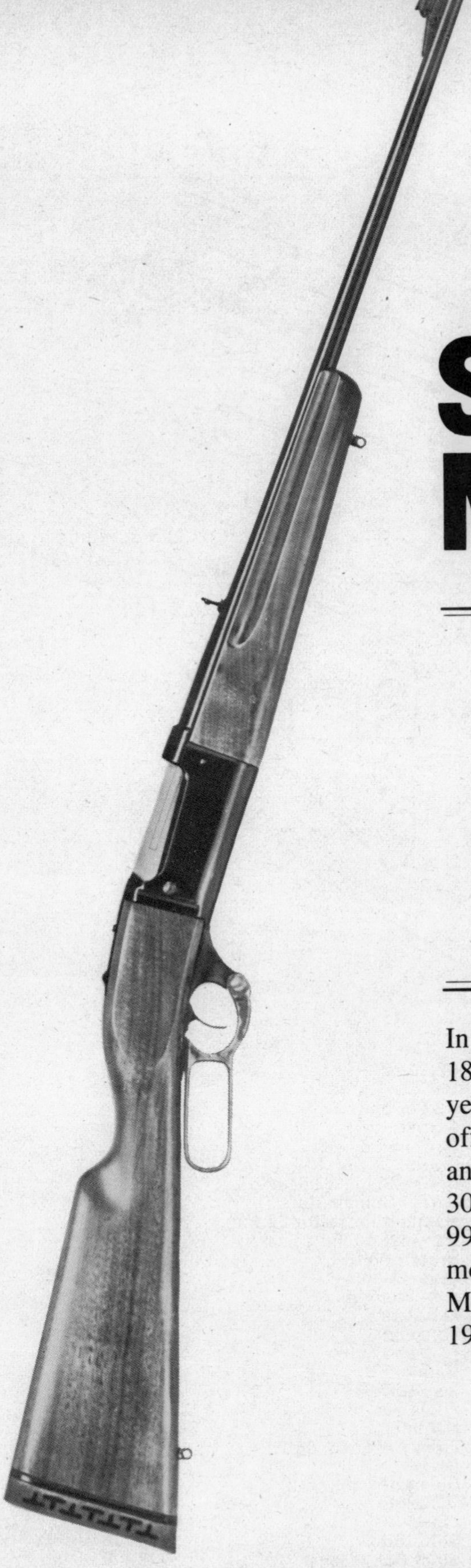

SAVAGE MODEL 99

Data:	Savage Model 99
Origin:	United States
Manufacturer:	Savage Arms Company
	Westfield, Massachusetts
Cartridges:	22-250, 243, 250 Savage, 300 Savage,
	308 Winchester
Magazine capacity:	5 rounds
Over-all length:	39¾ to 41¾ inches
Barrel length:	22 and 24 inches
Weight:	6¾ to 7 pounds

In 1899, Arthur W. Savage modified his original design of 1895, and the Model 99 rifle was born. Today, some 80 years later, this gun is still in production. It has been offered in a number of versions or sub-models in the past, and at the present time five are available. Two calibers, the 303 Savage and 30-30, are no longer made. The Model 99C has a detachable box magazine, but the other current models have the unique Savage rotary magazine. The Model 99A, which replaced the original Model 99 in 1922, is the example shown here.

Savage
Model 99A Lever-Action Rifle

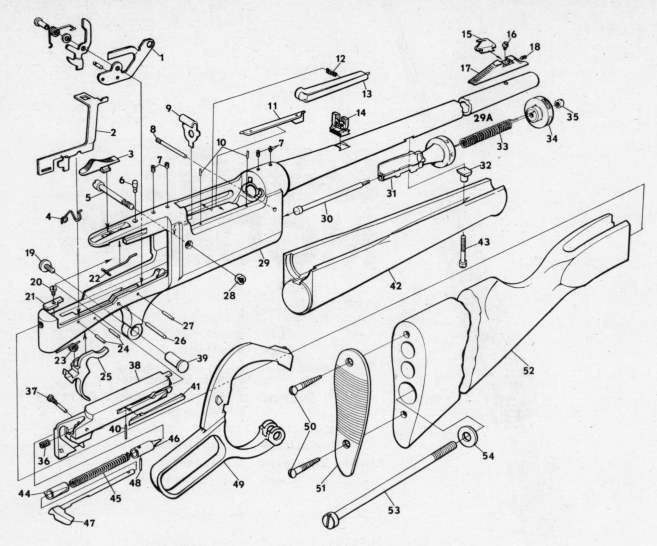

1	Sear Bracket Assembly	29	Receiver
2	Safety Slide	29A	Barrel
3	Safety Button	30	Carrier Spindle
4	Safety Slide Spring	31	Carrier
5	Sear Screw	32	Barrel Stud
6	Hammer Indicator	33	Carrier Spring
7	Dummy Screws (4)	34	Carrier Spindle Head
8	Carrier Spindle Head Screw	35	Carrier Spindle Nut
9	Carrier Spindle Support	36	Hammer Retractor Spring
10	Cartridge Guide Pins (2)	37	Hammer Bushing Screw
11	Cartridge Guide	38	Breech Bolt
12	Automatic Cut Off Spring	39	Lever Bushing
13	Automatic Cut Off	40	Extractor Pin
14	Rear Sight	41	Extractor
15	Front Sight	42	Fore-end
16	Front Sight Screw	43	Fore-end Screw
17	Front Sight Base	44	Hammer Bushing
18	Front Sight Adjusting Screw	45	Mainspring
19	Lever Bushing Screw	46	Firing Pin
20	Breech Bolt Stop Screw	47	Hammer
21	Breech Bolt Stop	48	Firing Pin Securing Pin
22	Hammer Indicator Spring	49	Lever
23	Trigger Spring	50	Buttplate Screws (2)
24	Safety Slide Spring and Stop Pins	51	Buttplate
25	Trigger	52	Stock
26	Trigger Pin	53	Stock Bolt
27	Sear Bracket Pin	54	Stock Bolt Washer
28	Sear Screw Nut		

Disassembly:

1. Remove the buttplate to give access to the stock mounting bolt. Use a long screwdriver to remove the stock bolt, and take off the stock toward the rear. If the stock is tight, bump the front of the comb with the heel of the hand to start it.

2. Remove the vertical screw at the left rear of the lower receiver extension, and take off the bolt stop.

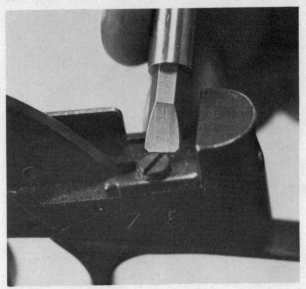

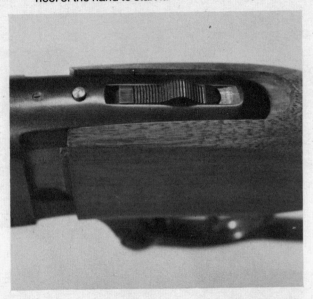

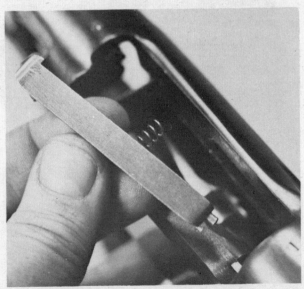

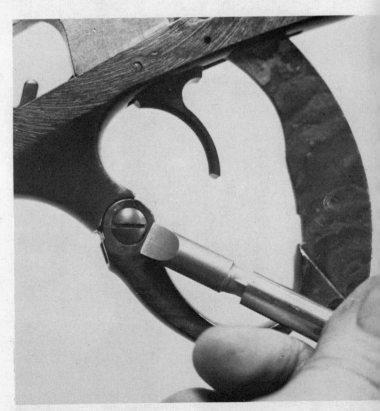

3. Open the action slowly, and restrain the cartridge cutoff, which will be released toward the right as the bolt clears it. Remove the cutoff and its spring toward the right.

4. Remove the cap screw from the lever pivot.

5. Remove the lever pivot toward the right

6. Remove the front of the lever from its pivot loop and turn the rear arch slightly to clear its inner lug from the bolt. Remove the lever downward.

7. Move the bolt all the way to the rear, and pull the trigger to release the sear. Tip the sear to clear the bolt, and remove the bolt toward the left rear. Turn the lower rear of the breech-block (bolt) out toward the left to clear the receiver as the bolt is removed.

8. Remove the hammer and bushing screw from the left side of the bolt at the rear. Note that the screw is usually staked in place, and may require some effort in removal.

9. Remove the hammer and striker assembly toward the rear. Take care not to lose the hammer rebound spring, which will be released as the assembly is moved out to the rear.

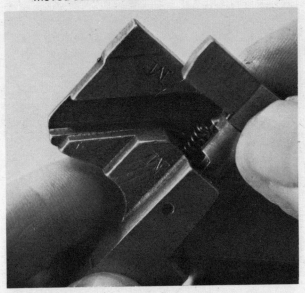

10. A vertical pin in the rear of the firing pin retains it on the front of the hammer shaft. Drifting out the pin will release the firing pin, hammer spring, and hammer bushing for removal toward the front. The pin is contoured at its ends to match the outside surface of the firing pin, and removal should be done only for repair purposes, not in normal takedown. If this unit is disassembled, proceed with caution, as the powerful hammer spring will be released.

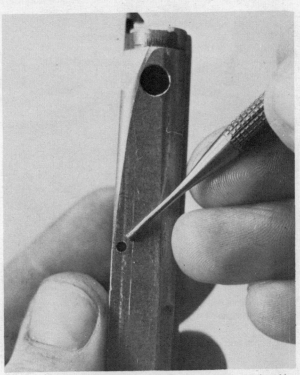

11. The extractor is its own spring, and is retained by a vertical pin on the right side of the bolt. The pin is driven out upward, and the extractor is taken off toward the right.

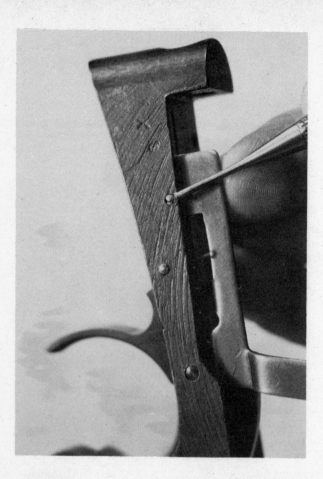

12. A small cross-pin at the rear of the lower receiver extension retains the safety slide. There is an access hole on the left side which allows the pin to be drifted out toward the right.

13. Move the saftey slide all the way to the rear, and tip it downward at the front and upward at the rear for removal.

14. Move the safety button all the way to the rear, and remove it from the top of the receiver.

15. The safety positioning spring is retained by a short cross-pin, and there is an access hole on the left side of the receiver which allows the pin to be drifted out toward the right. Remove the spring upward.

16. Drift out the trigger cross-pin, and remove the trigger downward and toward the rear. **Caution:** *The trigger spring is under tension, so control it and ease it out.*

17. Drift out the short pin at the lower rear of the sear bracket. There is no access hole for this pin, so it is necessary to angle a drift punch to start the pin out, then remove it toward the right.

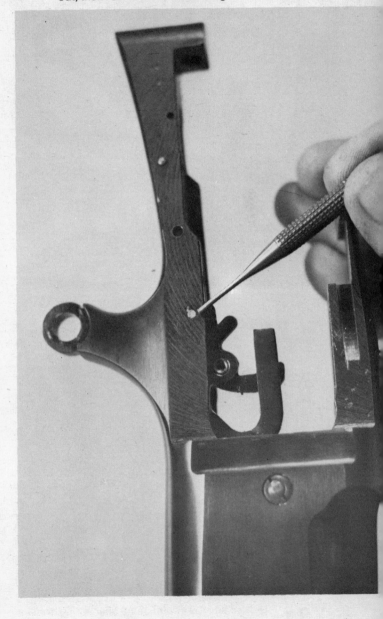

18. Removal of the sear bracket cross-screw and nut will require a special twin-pointed tool, easily made by cutting away the center of a screwdriver tip. If the screw is tight, it will be necessary to stabilize the slotted screw-head on the opposite side with a regular screwdriver as the nut is removed.

19. After the nut is removed, the screw must be unscrewed from the receiver and taken out toward the left.

20. Move the sear bracket assembly upward, out of its slot in the receiver, then remove it toward the rear.

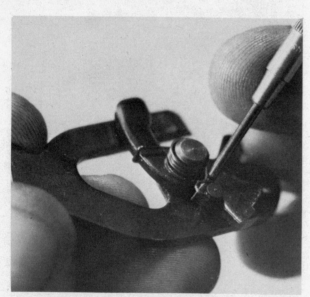

21. Unhook the lower arm of the sear spring from its groove on the stop stud, and allow it to swing around to the rear, relieving its tension. Remove the spring from the sear post.

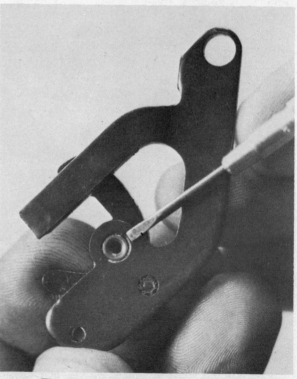

22. The sear is factory-riveted to the sear bracket, and should not be removed except for repair.

23. The hammer indicator can be removed from the top of the receiver by using a very small tool to lift the rear "T" of the indicator spring from its recess. Take out the spring toward the rear, and remove the indicator upward.

24. The fore-end is retained by a single vertical screw on its underside, and is taken off toward the front and downward.

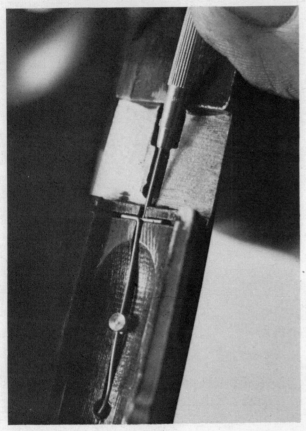

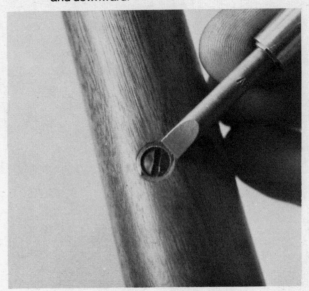

25. The same twin-pointed tool used to remove the sear bracket nut can also be used to take off the carrier spindle nut. **Caution:** *Disassembly of the magazine system of the Model 99 is not recommended unless this is necessary for repair, as reassembly is difficult for those not familiar with it.* If disassembly is unavoidable, begin by removing the spindle nut.

26. The carrier spindle head screw is located on the left side of the receiver near the front edge. Restrain the carrier spindle head against rotation, and remove the screw toward the left. Slowly release the tension of the carrier spring, allowing the head to rotate. The spindle head, carrier, and spring can now be removed toward the front, and the carrier spindle and spindle bracket are taken out toward the rear.

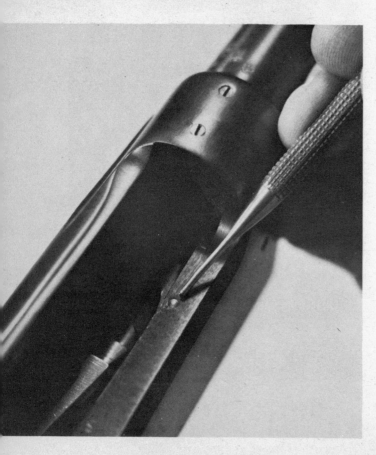

Reassembly Tips:

1. When replacing the safety slide, be sure the tip of the positioning spring engages its recess on the underside of the safety slide.

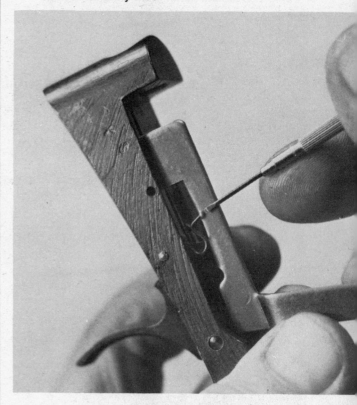

27. The cartridge guide is retained by two vertical pins in the lower edge of the ejection port, and is not removed in normal takedown. If necessary, the pins are driven downward and retrieved from inside the receiver, and the guide is taken off toward the left and upward.

2. When replacing the hammer and striker assembly in the bolt, remember to insert the rebound spring below the assembly just before pushing it into place for insertion of the retaining screw.

3. When replacing the lever pivot, note that there is a lug beneath its head on the left side that must be oriented to engage a recess in the lever loop on the receiver.

If the magazine has been dismantled, the carrier spring must be re-tensioned during reassembly by turning the spindle head before re-insertion of the cross-screw. The number of turns required depends on the strength of the spring, so this can't be specified here.

SAVAGE MODEL 110

Data:	Savage Model 110
Origin:	United States
Manufacturer:	Savage Arms Company
	Westfield, Massachusetts
Cartridges:	243, 22-250, 270, 308, 30-06,
	300 Magnum, 7mm Remington Magnum
Magazine capacity:	4 rounds (3 in magnums)
Over-all length:	43 inches
Barrel length:	22 inches
Weight:	7 to 8⅝ pounds

Since its introduction in 1958, the Model 110 has been offered in a wide variety of sub-models, and several of these are still in production. This is one of the few rifles that is also available in a left-handed action, and the moderate price of the Model 110 has made it very popular. Recent additions to the line include a version with a detachable magazine, and a gun specially designed for metallic silhouette shooting. The instructions can be applied to all of the sub-models.

Disassembly:

1. Open the bolt, pull the trigger, and push down the sear lever on the right side of the receiver. Hold it down, and remove the bolt toward the rear.

2. With a coin or a large screwdriver, unscrew the large knob at the rear of the bolt. Once it is started, its knurled edge will allow it to be turned by hand. Remove the knob toward the rear.

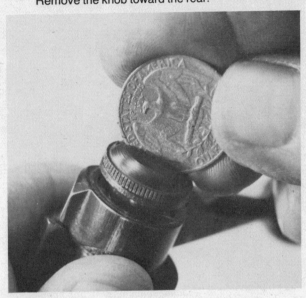

3. The attached cocking piece sleeve will come out with the knob as it is removed.

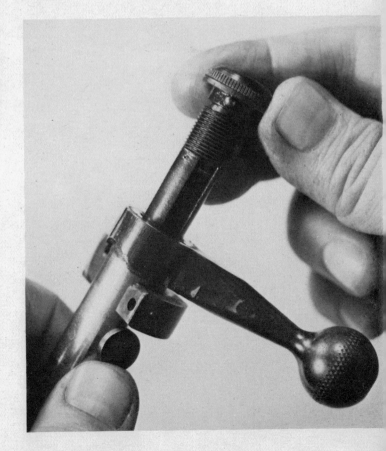

4. Remove the bolt handle toward the rear.

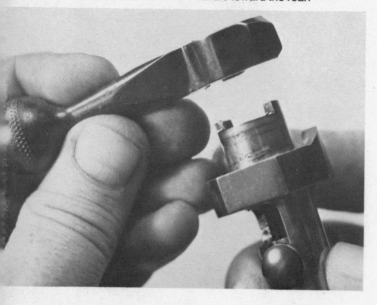

5. Remove the rear baffle piece toward the rear. If necessary, the two detent balls and spring can be removed from the baffle by pushing the inner ball outward until it aligns with the hole at the bottom of the baffle. The spring will then force both balls out. In normal disassembly, these parts are best left in place.

6. Remove the cocking piece pin from its hole in the side of the striker assembly.

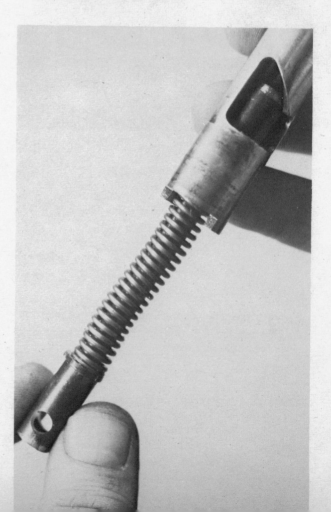

7. Remove the striker assembly from the rear of the bolt.

8. Grip the front of the striker firmly in a vise, insert a drift punch through the hole in the cocking piece, and unscrew the cocking piece from the rear tip of the striker shaft. **Caution:** *The striker spring is partially compressed, so control the parts and ease the tension slowly.* Take care not to disturb the striker stop nut at the front, as it controls the protrusion of the firing pin point at the bolt face. If the striker system does not need repair, it's best not to disassemble it.

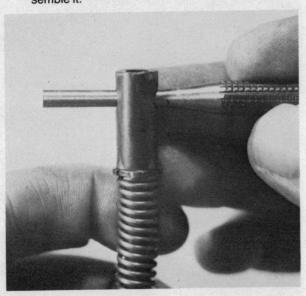

9. Drift out the bolt head retaining pin.

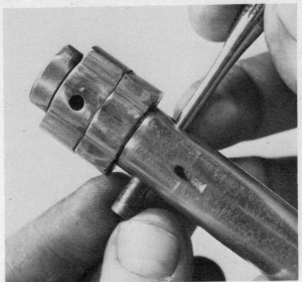

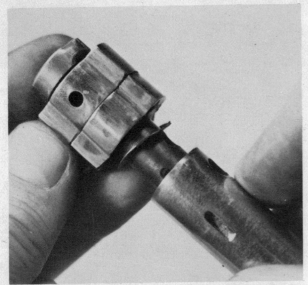

10. Remove the bolt head, baffle, and friction washer toward the front. The front baffle is easily taken off the bolt head toward the rear.

11. Insert a small screwdriver under the end of the extractor nearest the ejector slot, and twist the screwdriver toward the left, levering the extractor out of its groove and toward the front of the bolt.

12. Remove the large vertical screw on the underside at the front of the magazine floorplate. Remove the large vertical screw at the front of the trigger guard, in the rear tip of the magazine floorplate. Remove the floorplate and magazine insert downward, and take out the magazine spring and follower. Separate the action from the stock.

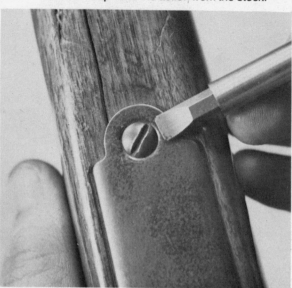

13. Depress the combination magazine latch and ejector housing upward, tip its lower end away from the magazine box, and remove the latch/housing, spring, and ejector downward.

14. The magazine box can now be moved toward the rear, tipped down at the front, and removed forward and downward.

15. While restraining the sear spring, push out the sear pin toward the left.

16. Remove the sear downward and toward the front, along with its spring and bushing. Take care that the small bushing isn't lost.

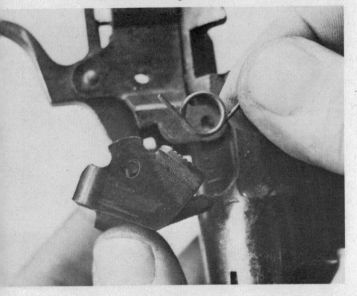

17. Tip the trigger housing down at the front, and unhook its rear lip from the underside of the receiver. Remove the trigger housing downward. After the housing is taken off, the small spring-steel trigger pull screw cover can be slid to the rear of its slot at the rear of the receiver, and removed. Remove the safety bearing pin from the housing.

19. The trigger adjustment screws in the safety block need not be disturbed. The one at top center retains the trigger spring and its plunger, and can be taken out to allow removal of the spring and plunger upward.

18. Lift the safety block from the top of the trigger housing.

20. Drifting out the trigger cross-pin will allow removal of the trigger from the housing. Note that this pin is held at center by a ball and spring in the front of the trigger, retained by a screw at the front. This screw should not be disturbed.

21. The barrel is retained in the receiver by a large grooved nut which also holds the recoil lug on the front of the receiver. In normal takedown, the barrel is best left in place.

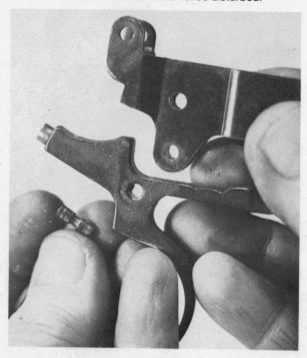

Reassembly Tips:

1. When replacing the sear system, insert the sear cross-pin from the left, and stop it short of crossing the spring recess. Insert the spring from the rear, and insert a drift punch into the spring bushing from the right to lever the bushing and spring into position for the cross-pin to be pushed through to the right.

2. When replacing the bolt head assembly, note that there is a recess in the rear tail of the bolt head and a depression and inside welt on the inside of the bolt body, and these must be aligned.

3. When replacing the bolt head retaining cross-pin, note that there is a hole at its center for passage of the firing pin, and this hole must be properly oriented as the cross-pin is installed.

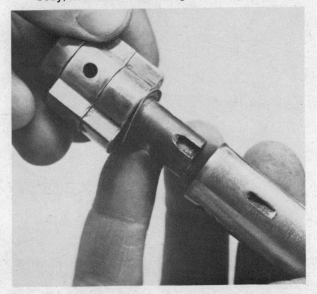

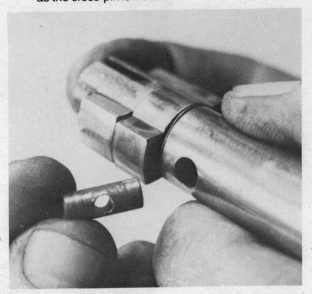

5. It is possible to install the rear baffle in reversed position. This photo shows its proper relationship with the bolt handle ring.

4. When replacing the bolt takedown screw, set the cocking piece pin in the cocked position, as shown. This will make tightening the screw a bit stiffer, but will leave the action cocked for re-insertion of the bolt into the receiver.

Savage
Models 110C, D and E, Series K
Bolt Action Rifles

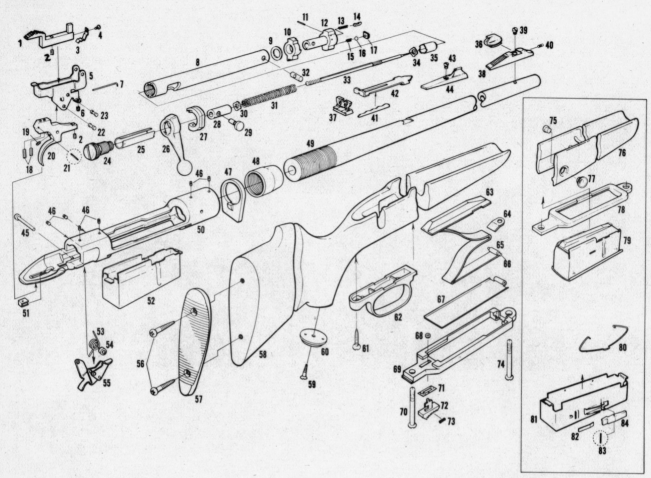

1	Safety	**30**	Cocking Piece Link Washer	**63** Magazine Follower Assembly
2	Trigger Pull Adjusting Screws (2)	**31**	Mainspring	**64** Hinge Plate Spring
3	Safety Detent Spring	**32**	Bolt Head Retaining Pin	**65** Magazine Spring
4	Safety Detent Spring Screw	**33**	Firing Pin	**66** Hinge Pin
5	Trigger Bracket	**34**	Firing Pin Stop Nut Washer	**67** Hinge Plate
6	Trigger Pull Adjusting Screw	**35**	Firing Pin Stop Nut	**68** Magazine Latch Retaining Ring
7	Trigger Pull Adjusting Spring	**36**	Front Sight	**69** Floorplate
8	Bolt Body	**37**	Rear Sight	**70** Floorplate Screw (Rear)
9	Front Baffle Friction Washer	**38**	Front Sight Base	**71** Magazine Latch Spacer
10	Front Baffle	**39**	Front Sight Screw	**72** Magazine Latch
11	Ejector Retaining Pin	**40**	Front Sight Adjusting Screw	**73** Magazine Latch Spring
12	Bolt Head Assembly	**45**	Sear Pin	**74** Floorplate Screw (Front)
13	Ejector Spring	**46**	Dummy Screws (6)	
14	Ejector	**47**	Recoil Lug	**Parts for Model 110E Series K Only**
15	Extractor Spring	**48**	Barrel Lock Nut	**41** Rear Sight Step
16	Extractor Detent Ball	**49**	Barrel	**42** Rear Sight
17	Extractor	**50**	Receiver	**43** Front Sight Screw
18	Trigger Travel Adjusting Screws (2)	**51**	Trigger Adjusting Screw Cover	**44** Front Sight Assembly
19	Trigger Pin Retaining Screw	**52**	Magazine Box	
20	Trigger	**53**	Sear Spring	**Parts for Model 110C Series K Only**
21	Trigger Spring Pin	**54**	Sear Bushing	**75** Magazine Latch Button
22	Trigger Pin	**55**	Sear	**77** Escutcheon
23	Safety Bearing Pin	**56**	Buttplate Screws (2)	**78** Floorplate
24	Bolt Assembly Screw	**57**	Buttplate	**79** Magazine Assembly
25	Cocking Piece Sleeve	**58**	Stock	**80** Magazine Ejector Spring
26	Bolt Handle	**59**	Pistol Grip Cap Screw	**81** Magazine Guide
27	Rear Baffle	**60**	Pistol Grip Cap	**82** Magazine Latch Spring
28	Cocking Piece	**61**	Trigger Guard Screw	**83** Magazine Latch Pin
29	Cocking Piece Pin	**62**	Trigger Guard	**84** Magazine Latch

SAVAGE MODEL 340

Data:	Savage Model 340
Origin:	United States
Manufacturer:	Savage Arms Company Westfield, Massachusetts
Cartridges:	22 Hornet, 222, 30-30
Magazine capacity:	4 rounds (3 in 30-30)
Over-all length:	40 and 42 inches
Barrel length:	22 and 24 inches
Weight:	6½ pounds

The model 340 was intended to be an in-between gun, a low-priced bolt action repeater chambered for two varmint cartridges and one medium-game round. In this category it has gained wide acceptance since 1950, and it is still in production. For a short time, a carbine version was made in 30-30 only, with an 18½-inch barrel. The basic Model 340 design has been marketed as the Savage Model 342, the Stevens Model 322 and 325, and the Springfield Model 840. They are essentially the same.

Savage
Models 340, B, C, D, V
Bolt Action Rifles

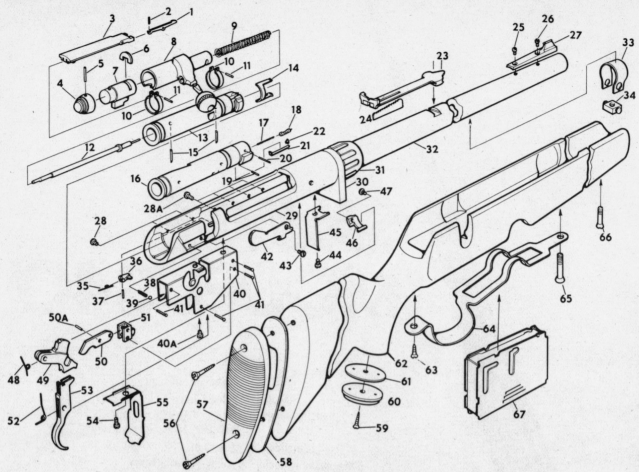

1	Gas Shield Key	43	Safety Screw
2	Gas Shield Key Spring	44	Magazine Retainer Screw
3	Gas Shield	45	Magazine Retainer Spring (Front)
4	Cocking Piece Cap	48	Sear Spring
5	Cocking Piece Cap Pin	49	Sear
6	Cocking Piece Key	50	Sear Lever
7	Cocking Piece	50A	Sear Cam Pin
8	Bolt Body and Handle	51	Magazine Stop
9	Mainspring	52	Trigger Spring
10	Gas Shield Clips (2)	53	Trigger
11	Gas Shield Clip Pins (2)	54	Trigger Bracket Screw
12	Firing Pin	55	Magazine Retainer Spring (Rear)
13	Bolt Head	56	Buttplate Screws (2)
14	Extractor	57	Buttplate
15	Bolt Head Retaining Pins (2)	58	Buttplate Spacer
23	Rear Sight	59	Pistol Grip Cap Screw
24	Rear Sight Step	60	Pistol Grip Cap
25	Front Sight Screw (Short)	61	Pistol Grip Cap Spacer
26	Front Sight Screw (Long)	62	Stock
27	Front Sight	63	Trigger Guard Screw (Rear)
28	Dummy Screws (2)	64	Trigger Guard
28A	Dummy Screws (4)	65	Recoil Lug Screw
29	Receiver	66	Barrel Band Screw
30	Barrel Lug	67	Magazine Assembly
31	Barrel Lock Nut		
32	Barrel		

Parts Common To 222 and 225 Cal.

33	Barrel Band	17	Ejector Spring
34	Barrel Band Nut	18	Ejector
35	Ejector Spring	19	Extractor Spring Pin
36	Ejector	20	Ejector Pin
37	Ejector Pin	46	Baffle Block
38	Safety Spring	47	Baffle Block Screw
39	Safety Plunger Ball		

Parts for 222 Caliber Only

40	Trigger Bracket	16	Bolt Head
40A	Trigger Bracket Screw (Short)	21	Extractor Spring
41	Sear Pins (4)	22	Extractor
42	Safety		

Disassembly:

1. Remove the magazine. Pull the trigger all the way to the rear, beyond its normal let-off position, and hold it there. Open the bolt, and remove it toward the rear.

2. With a small brass hammer, tap the cocking lug out of its detent notch at the rear of the bolt, allowing the striker to go forward to the fired position, as shown.

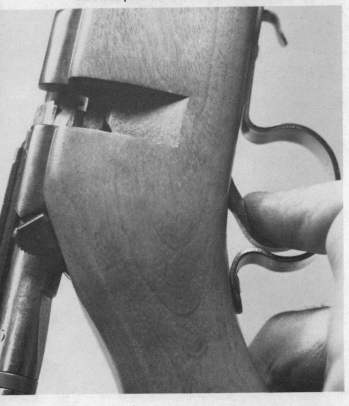

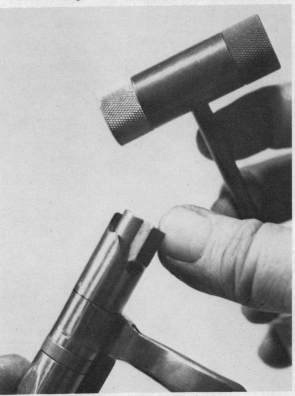

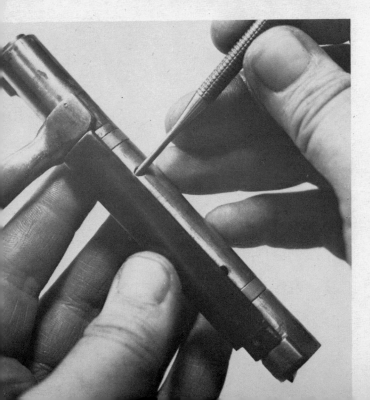

3. Drift out the cross-pin that retains the bolt head.

4. Remove the bolt handle and striker assembly toward the rear. If the assembly is tight, use a plastic hammer to tap it gently off.

5. Grip the front portion of the striker firmly in a vise, and push the bolt handle sleeve toward the front until the cocking piece is exposed. Remove the semi-circular key from the top of the cocking piece, and unscrew the cocking piece from the rear of the striker shaft. **Caution:** *Keep a firm grip on the bolt handle, as the striker spring is compressed.*

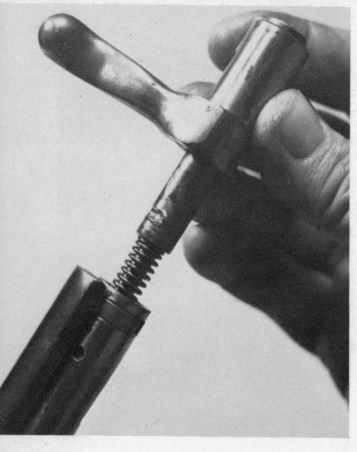

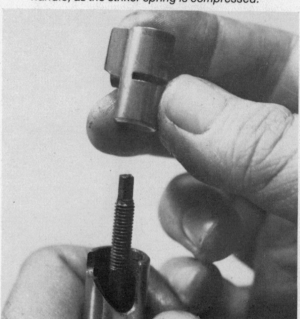

6. Slowly ease off the tension of the striker spring, and remove the striker and spring from the front of the bolt handle unit.

7. Some models of the 340 design have a clip-on extractor unit, and others, such as the one shown, have a hook-in type with a spring and plunger at the rear. To remove this type, restrain the plunger and spring, and pivot the extractor out toward the right and take it off. The clip-on type unit is simply pried out of its recess for removal.

8. The gas shield is retained on top of the bolt by two cross-pins, and mounted on twin rings which encircle the bolt. The cross-pins are usually staked in place, so if removal is necessary, be sure the shield is well-supported while driving out the pins.

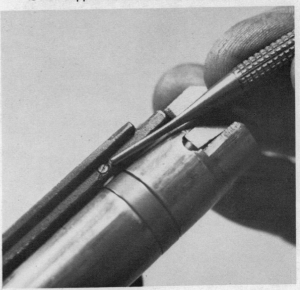

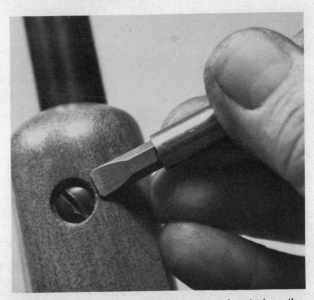

9. When the front gas shield cross-pin is drifted out, the gas shield key and its spring will be released along with the shield.

10. Remove the barrel band screw, located on the underside near the front of the stock.

11. Remove the main stock mounting screw, located on the underside in the front tip of the magazine plate. Separate the action from the stock.

12. To remove the barrel band, push the band nut toward the barrel, and disengage its side studs from the holes in the band. The band can then be taken off upward.

13. The magazine guide is retained on the underside of the receiver by a single screw, and the screw and guide are removed downward.

14. In the 22 Hornet version, the front magazine guide also contains a small cartridge ramp and a torsion spring for the ramp. Drifting out the cross-pin will release the ramp and spring for removal, but in normal takedown they are best left in place.

15. The cross-pins in the trigger housing that retain the trigger and sear mechanism have large heads on the right side and are semi-riveted on the left. It is not advisable to remove them in normal take-down. If necessary for repair, or if the trigger housing must be removed, the internal parts must be taken out, as the two vertical retaining screws for the housing are obscured by the parts. Drifting out the pin shown will release the trigger and its spring for removal toward the rear and downward.

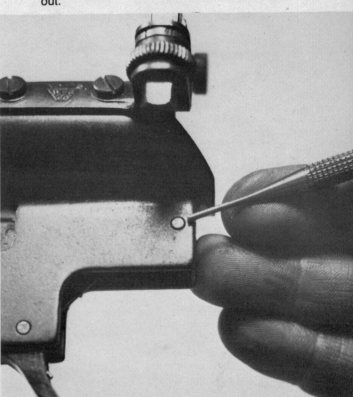

16. Drifting out the cross-pin at the upper rear of the trigger housing will release the sear and its spring for removal downward and toward the rear. The spring is under tension, so control it and ease it out.

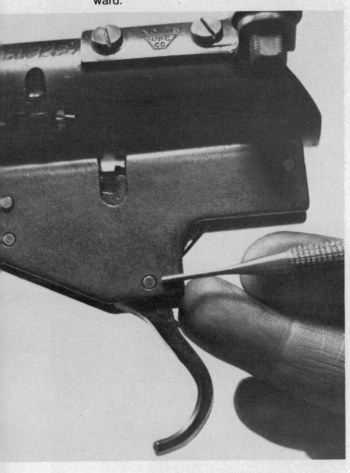

17. Drifting out the lower cross-pin at the front of the trigger housing will release the sear lever for removal downward. The upper pin holds the combination sear lever bracket and magazine stop in place, and its removal is not necessary.

18. Remove the safety lever screw, and take off the safety toward the right.

19. When the safety lever is removed, take care not to lose the small safety positioning ball and spring. If they do not come out freely, there is an access hole on the inside of the bolt tunnel in the receiver for insertion of a tool to nudge them out. Removal of the screw on the right side of the housing will allow the main safety block to be taken off toward the right.

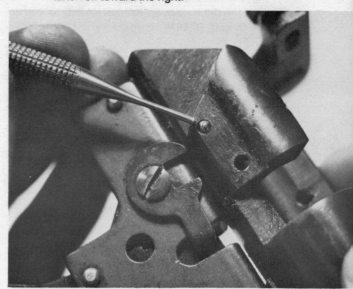

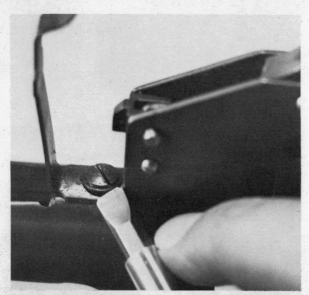

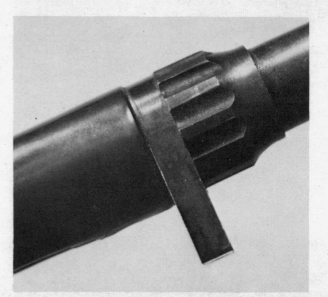

20. After the other parts are removed from the trigger housing, the vertical screws at the front and center will be accessible, and the trigger housing can be removed downward. The magazine catch screw can also be removed, and the catch taken off downward.

21. The barrel is retained in the receiver by a deeply grooved lock nut, requiring a special wrench which is not routinely available. It can be loosened or retightened by using a hammer and non-marring punch in one of the grooves, working in an area normally covered by the stock. Removal of the nut will allow the barrel to be taken out toward the front, and the recoil lug will also be freed for removal. In normal takedown, this system should be left in place.

22. Insert a screwdriver beneath the upper collar of the ejector pivot pin, and pry it out upward and toward the left. The ejector and its spring will be released for removal from their slot in the side of the receiver.

Reassembly Tips:

1. When replacing the cocking piece on the rear of the striker shaft, note that the degree of advancement on the threads controls the protrusion of the firing pin point from the bolt face. Check this by inserting the rear portion of the bolt, with the striker in the fired position, into the front portion of the bolt. If the protrusion is more than the amount shown, turn the cocking piece for adjustment.

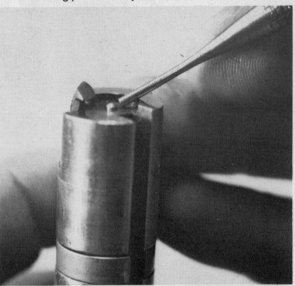

2. Before the reassembled bolt can be put back into the receiver, the gas shield must be aligned with the forward lug of the bolt and the bolt handle base, and the striker must be cocked. When the striker is in the position shown, the bolt can be re-inserted.

WEATHERBY MARK XXII

Data:	Weatherby Mark XXII
Origin:	United States
Manufacturer:	Weatherby's South Gate, California (Made under contract in Japan)
Cartridge:	22 Long Rifle
Magazine capacity:	5 and 10 rounds in box magazines, 15 rounds in tubular magazine model
Over-all length:	42¼ inches
Barrel length:	24 inches
Weight:	6 pounds

The Mark XXII has the classic Weatherby look, and in addition to its fine fit and finish, it has several unique features. One is a selector lever which allows the gun to be used as a single shot, the bolt remaining open after firing until released by the lever. With the lever in its other position, the gun functions as a normal semi-automatic. There are two separate versions of the Mark XXII, the only difference being in the magazine systems—one has a tubular magazine, and the other, shown here, has a detachable box type.

Disassembly:

1. Remove the main stock mounting screw, located on the underside, forward of the magazine well. Remove the screw at the rear of the trigger guard on the underside, and lift the action straight up out of the stock. It should be noted that it is possible to take off the barrel and receiver unit alone by pushing out the large takedown pin at the rear of the receiver toward the left, and moving the barrel/receiver unit forward and upward, but this will leave the trigger group sub-frame in the stock. After the two screws are taken out, the trigger guard unit can be taken off downward.

2. Push out the cross-pin at the rear of the receiver toward the left, and remove it.

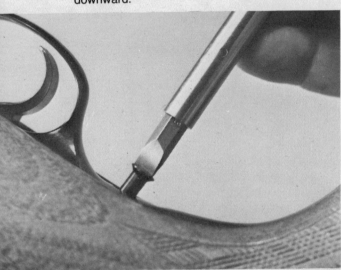

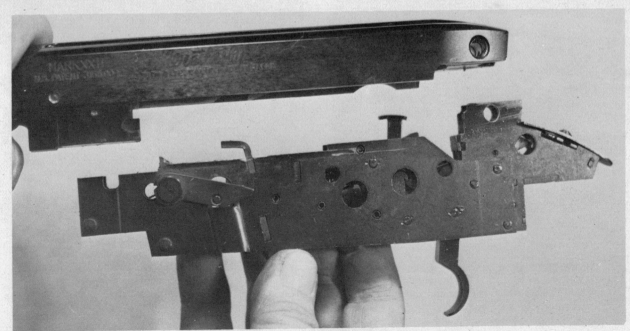

3. Move the trigger group about one-eighth of an inch toward the rear, then remove it downward.

4. Before any disassembly of the trigger group, hold the hammer against its spring tension, pull the trigger, and ease the hammer down to the fired position. The selector lever on the right side of the group is retained by a large C-shaped spring clip. Carefully slide the clip off downward, and remove the selector lever toward the right.

5. The pivot and mounting stud for the single-shot bolt-catch is retained inside the group by a C-clip. Use a small screwdriver to slide the clip off upward, and take care that it isn't lost. There is an access hole on the left side through which the clip can be reached. The bolt-catch piece is then removed toward the right, along with its pivot-post, unhooking its spring at the front. The torsion spring is held in the group by a roll cross-pin.

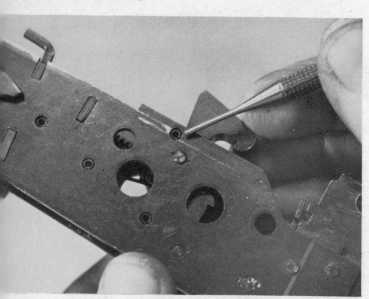

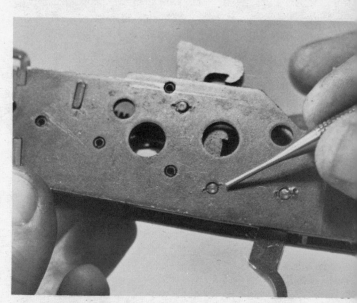

6. Set the hammer on its first step, and drift out the roll cross-pin just forward of the hammer at the top edge of the group. Restrain the hammer, pull the trigger to release it, and let it go forward beyond its normal down position, relieving the tension of the hammer spring. Drifting out the solid pin just below the roll pin, the hammer pivot, will allow removal of the hammer and its spring and guide upward.

7. The sear is retained by a solid pin near the lower edge of the receiver. Drifting out this pin will allow removal of the sear and its spring downward.

8. The trigger is retained by a cross-pin just to the rear of the sear pin. The trigger and its attached sear bar and spring are removed downward. The coil trigger spring will be released as it clears its plate at the rear of the trigger, so restrain it and take care that it isn't lost.

9. Drifting out a small roll pin at the rear of the trigger group will allow removal of the safety bar toward the front. **Caution:** *The safety bar plunger and spring will be released upward as the bar is moved out, so restrain them against loss.* The rear portion of the safety, the button and indicator plate, are not easily removable, as this would require taking off the staked tang-plate. This is not advisable in normal takedown.

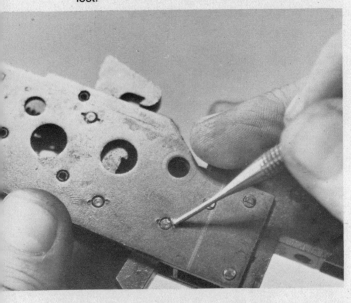

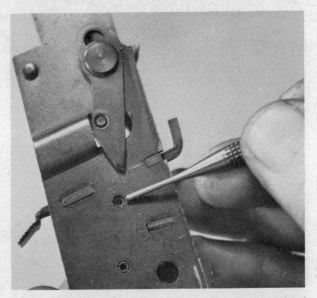

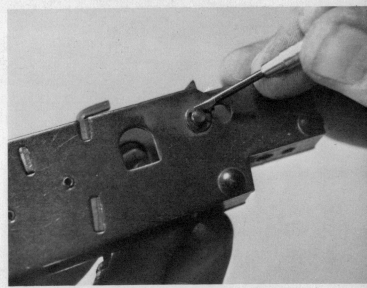

10. The magazine catch and its spring are retained by a roll cross-pin. Note the relationship of the spring and the catch before removal, to aid re-assembly. The catch and spring are removed downward. The ejector is staked in place between the riveted sideplates of the trigger group and is not removable in normal takedown.

11. The bolt hold-open device is retained by a C-clip on the right side of the group, the clip gripping the end of its cross-shaft. Note that there is also a small washer under the C-clip, and take care that it isn't lost. The hold-open is removed toward the left.

12. Firmly grasp the bolt handle and pull it straight out toward the right.

13. Invert the gun, and move the bolt slightly toward the rear. Lift the front of the bolt enough to clear the receiver, and ease the bolt out forward, slowly relieving the tension of the bolt spring. **Caution:** *Control the compressed spring.* Remove the spring and its guide from the rear of the bolt.

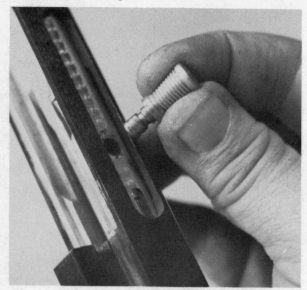

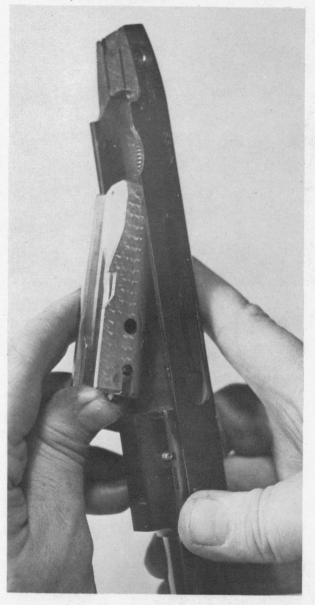

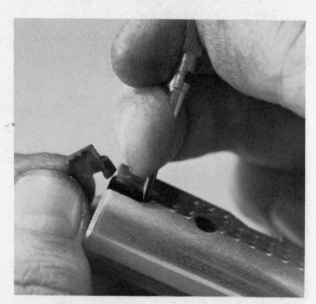

14. Use a small screwdriver to depress the extractor spring plunger, and lift the extractor out of its recess at the right front of the bolt. **Caution:** *Do not allow the screwdriver to slip, as the small plunger and spring will travel quite a distance if suddenly released.*

15. The firing pin is retained by a vertical roll pin located at the left rear of the bolt, and the firing pin and its return spring are removed toward the rear.

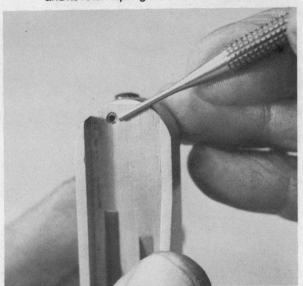

Reassembly Tips:

1. When replacing the single-shot bolt-catch on the right side of the trigger group, remember to hook the torsion spring under its forward end. The spring may be installed first, then its end moved out, downward, and up to hook it under the part.

When replacing the large takedown cross-pin at the rear of the receiver, be sure it is inserted from left to right. Otherwise, the stock will block its removal when the rifle is fully reassembled.

Weatherby
Mark XXII Auto Rifle
Tubular Feed

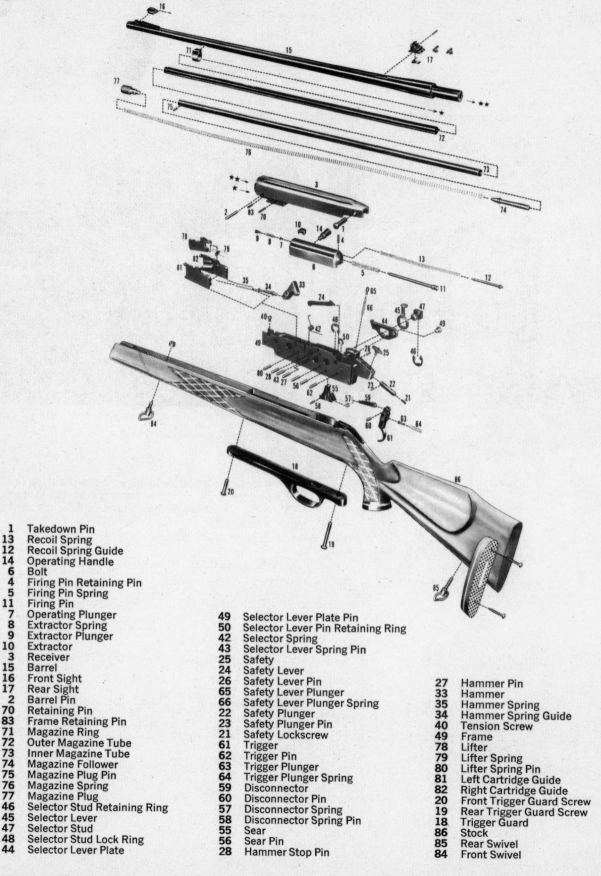

1	Takedown Pin	
13	Recoil Spring	
12	Recoil Spring Guide	
14	Operating Handle	
6	Bolt	
4	Firing Pin Retaining Pin	
5	Firing Pin Spring	
11	Firing Pin	
7	Operating Plunger	
8	Extractor Spring	
9	Extractor Plunger	
10	Extractor	
3	Receiver	
15	Barrel	
16	Front Sight	
17	Rear Sight	
2	Barrel Pin	
70	Retaining Pin	
83	Frame Retaining Pin	
71	Magazine Ring	
72	Outer Magazine Tube	
73	Inner Magazine Tube	
74	Magazine Follower	
75	Magazine Plug Pin	
76	Magazine Spring	
77	Magazine Plug	
46	Selector Stud Retaining Ring	
45	Selector Lever	
47	Selector Stud	
48	Selector Stud Lock Ring	
44	Selector Lever Plate	
49	Selector Lever Plate Pin	
50	Selector Lever Pin Retaining Ring	
42	Selector Spring	
43	Selector Lever Spring Pin	
25	Safety	
24	Safety Lever	
26	Safety Lever Pin	**27** Hammer Pin
65	Safety Lever Plunger	**33** Hammer
66	Safety Lever Plunger Spring	**35** Hammer Spring
22	Safety Plunger	**34** Hammer Spring Guide
23	Safety Plunger Pin	**40** Tension Screw
21	Safety Lockscrew	**49** Frame
61	Trigger	**78** Lifter
62	Trigger Pin	**79** Lifter Spring
63	Trigger Plunger	**80** Lifter Spring Pin
64	Trigger Plunger Spring	**81** Left Cartridge Guide
59	Disconnector	**82** Right Cartridge Guide
60	Disconnector Pin	**20** Front Trigger Guard Screw
57	Disconnector Spring	**19** Rear Trigger Guard Screw
58	Disconnector Spring Pin	**18** Trigger Guard
55	Sear	**86** Stock
56	Sear Pin	**85** Rear Swivel
28	Hammer Stop Pin	**84** Front Swivel

MARLIN MODEL 99

Data: Marlin Model 99
Origin: United States
Manufacturer: Marlin Firearms
North Haven, Connecticut
Cartridge: 22 Long Rifle
Magazine capacity: 18 rounds in rifle, 9 in carbine
Over-all length: Rifle—42 inches, Carbine—37 inches
Barrel length: Rifle—22 inches, Carbine—18 inches
Weight: Rifle—5½ pounds, Carbine—4½ pounds

The original Model 99 semi-auto was introduced in 1959, and was soon followed by several sub-models—the 99DL, 99C, and 99M1, the carbine shown here. The same basic action was later used in the Model 49 and its sub-models, the 989, and the current 990 and 995 rifles. There have been several minor modifications along the way, but the instructions can be applied generally to all of these. The gun is available in both tubular and box magazine types. The gun in the photos is the 99M1 tubular version.

Disassembly:

1. Remove the barrel band retaining screw, located on the right side of the barrel band, and take off the band toward the front. Remove the inner magazine tube.

2. Remove the two screws at the top rear of the handguard, and take off the handguard piece.

3. Remove the screw on the underside at the rear of the trigger guard, the screw nearest the guard. Remove the main stock mounting screw, located on the underside just forward of the trigger guard, and lift the action out of the stock.

4. Removal of the screws at each end of the trigger guard will allow the guard to be taken off downward. The rear screw is a wood screw, and the front screw has a flat internal nut-plate which may have to be stabilized during removal. The trigger and its spring are retained in the guard unit by a cross-pin. Note the position of the spring before removal of the pin, to aid reassembly.

5. Remove the cap screw and screw-slotted post at the rear of the sub-frame below the receiver. If this assembly is very tight, it may require two opposed screwdrivers, to immobilize the post while the screw is taken out.

6. Remove the two opposed screws at the front of the sub-frame below the receiver.

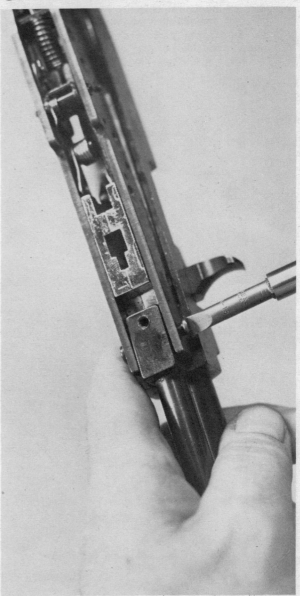

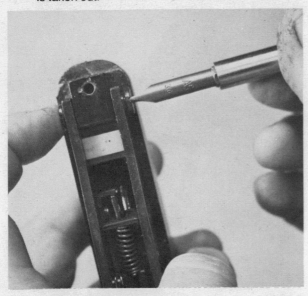

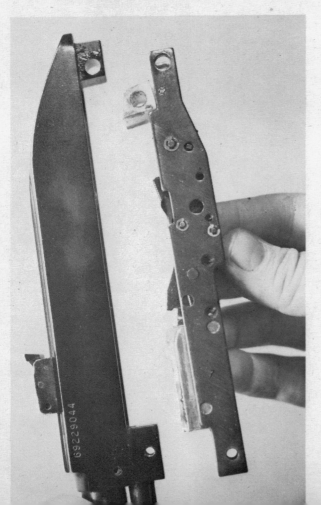

7. Remove the sub-frame downward.

8. Before disassembling the sub-frame, note the relationship of all parts and springs, to aid reassembly. Lower the hammer to the fired position, easing it down. Unhook the right arm of the carrier spring from its resting place on the carrier, and ease it downward, relieving its tension. Remove the C-clips from the tips of the hammer/carrier pivot and the sear pivot on the **right** side only, taking care that the small clips are not lost. Depending on its tightness, it may also be necessary to remove the cross-pin at the rear of the sub-frame which retains the recoil buffer. Remove the right sideplate of the sub-frame toward the right. This will allow disassembly of all the internal mechanism parts except the disconnector, which is mounted on the left sideplate on a post retained by a C-clip on the left side.

9. Invert the gun, and retract the bolt far enough that a finger or tool can be inserted in front of it. Lift the front of the bolt away from the inside top of the receiver, and remove the bolt handle from the ejection port. Continue to lift the bolt, until its front will clear the underside of the receiver, and take out the bolt, bolt spring, and follower. **Caution:** *The spring will be compressed. Control it, and ease its tension slowly.*

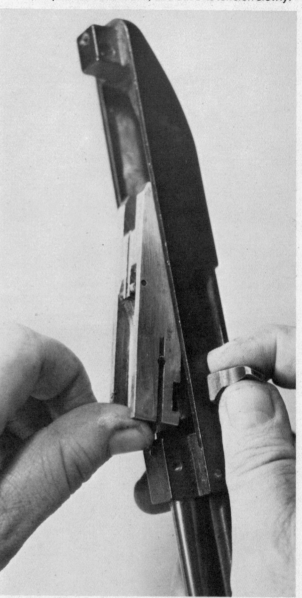

10. The firing pin is retained in the bolt by a cross-pin at the lower edge of the bolt. Note that there is also a small roller on the cross-pin (arrow), on the right side of the bolt, and take care that this roller isn't lost. When the pin is out, the firing pin can be removed toward the rear.

11. The extractors are retained by vertical pins on each side of the bolt, and these are driven out toward the top. The extractors and their small coil springs are then removed toward each side. **Note:** Keep each spring with its extractor, because the springs are not of equal tension. The stronger spring must be put back on the right side.

12. Drifting out the small cross-pin in the magazine tube hanger will allow removal of the outer magazine tube toward the front. The hanger can then be driven out of its dovetail cut toward the right. The front sight is retained by a single Allen screw in its top, just to the rear of the sight blade. After the screw is backed out, the sight is removed toward the front. After its large positioning screw on the right side is loosened, the rear sight can be slid off the scope rail in either direction.

Reassembly Tips:

When replacing the sub-frame in the receiver, be sure the hammer is cocked. There will be some tension from the carrier spring as the sub-frame is pushed into place. Insert the rear screw-post first, then start the two front screws. Do not tighten the screws until all three are in position and started.

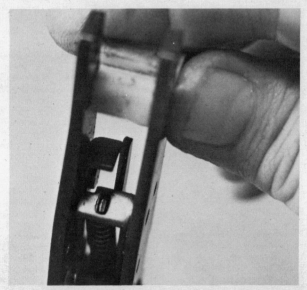

1. When replacing the hammer spring base plate in the sub-frame, note that there is a notch in one corner of the plate. This must go on the left side at the top, to clear the rear portion of the disconnector.

MARLIN
MODEL 99M1

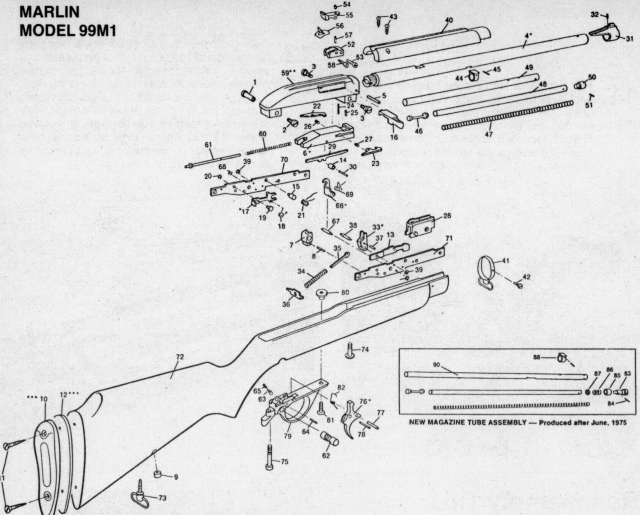

NEW MAGAZINE TUBE ASSEMBLY — Produced after June, 1975

1	Assembly Post	**32**	Front Sight Binding Screw	**65**	Safety Plunger Spring
2	Assembly Post Screw	**33**	Hammer	**66**	Sear
3	Assembly Screw, Front (2)	**34**	Hammer Spring	**67**	Sear Pin
4	Barrel	**35**	Hammer Strut	**68**	Sear Pin Ring (2)
5	Barrel Retaining Pin	**36**	Hammer Strut Bridge	**69**	Sear Spring
6	Breech Bolt	**37**	Hammer Strut Pin	**70**	Sideplate, Left Hand
7	Buffer	**38**	Hammer/Lifter Pin	**71**	Sideplate, Right Hand
8	Buffer Pin	**39**	Hammer/Lifter Pin Ring (2)	**72**	Stock
9	Bullseye	**40**	Hand Guard	**73**	Swivel, Rear
10	Buttplate	**41**	Hand Guard Band w/Swivel	**74**	Takedown Screw, Front
11	Buttplate Screw (2)	**42**	Hand Guard Band Screw	**75**	Takedown Screw, Rear
12	Buttplate Spacer	**43**	Hand Guard Screw (2)	**76**	Trigger
13	Cartridge Lifter	**44**	Magazine Tube Band	**77**	Trigger Pin
14	Cartridge Lifter Roller	**45**	Magazine Tube Binding Pin	**78**	Trigger Stop Pin
15	Cartridge Lifter Spring Stud	**46**	Magazine Tube Follower	**79**	Trigger Guard Only
16	Charging Handle	**47**	Magazine Tube Spring	**80**	Trigger Guard Nut, Front
17	Disconnector	**48**	Magazine Tube Inside Only	**81**	Trigger Guard Screw, Front
18	Disconnector Spring	**49**	Magazine Tube Outside	**82**	Trigger Spring
19	Disconnector Stud	**50**	Magazine Tube Plug	**83**	Magazine Tube Plug
20	Disconnector Stud Ring	**51**	Magazine Tube Plug Pin	**84**	Magazine Tube Plug Pin
21	Ejector/Lifter Spring	**52**	Rear Sight Base	**85**	Magazine Tube Plug Cap
22	Extractor, Left Hand	**53**	Rear Sight Binding Screw	**86**	Magazine Tube Plug Spring
23	Extractor, Right Hand	**54**	Rear Sight Elevator Screw	**87**	Magazine Tube Plug Bushing
24	Extractor Pin, Left Hand	**55**	Rear Sight Leaf	**88**	Magazine Tube Band
25	Extractor Pin, Right Hand	**56**	Rear Sight Leaf Spring	**89**	Magazine Tube Outside
26	Extractor Spring, Left Hand	**57**	Rear Sight Pin		
27	Extractor Spring, Right Hand	**58**	Rear Sight Windage Screw		
28	Feedthroat	**59**	Receiver		
29	Firing Pin	**60**	Recoil Spring		
30	Firing Pin Retaining Pin	**61**	Recoil Spring Guide		
31	Front Sight Complete	**62**	Safety		
		63	Safety Plunger		
		64	Safety Plunger Pin		